D0805979

# A BOOK
# OF
# JEWISH WOMEN'S
# PRAYERS

# A BOOK
# OF
# JEWISH WOMEN'S
# PRAYERS

## Translations from the
## Yiddish

selected and with commentary
by
NORMAN TARNOR

JASON ARONSON INC.
*Northvale, New Jersey*
*London*

This book was set in 11 pt. Berkeley Oldstyle by Alpha Graphics, Pittsfield, New Hampshire, and printed by Haddon Craftsmen in Scranton, Pennsylvania.

**Library of Congress Cataloging-in-Publication Data**

A book of Jewish women's prayers: translations from the Yiddish / selected and with commentary by Norman Tarnor.
    p.  cm.
    Includes bibliographical references.
    ISBN 1-56821-298-4
    1. Techinnot–Translations into English.   2. Jewish women–Prayer-books and devotions–English   3. Judaism–Prayer-books and devotions–English   I. Tarnor, Norman.
BM675.T4Z556   1995
296.7'2–dc20                       94-28363

Manufactured in the United States of America. Jason Aronson Inc. offers books and cassettes. For information and catalog write to Jason Aronson Inc., 230 Livingston Street, Northvale, New Jersey 07647.

# CONTENTS

Contents

On a bus in Tel Aviv, a mother was talking animatedly, in Yiddish, to her little boy—who kept answering her in Hebrew. And each time the mother said, "No, no, talk Yiddish!" An impatient Israeli, overhearing this, exclaimed, "Lady, why do you insist the boy talk Yiddish instead of Hebrew?"

Replied the mother, "I don't want him to forget he's a Jew."

Leo Rosten, *The Joys of Yiddish*

# INTRODUCTION

Interesting circumstances have given rise to the phenomenon of prayer in Yiddish. While it is currently true that a Jew may pray in any language he understands if he does not understand Hebrew, this wasn't always so. The Hebraic tradition carefully guarded its linguistic prerogative of Hebrew for the Hebrews. On the other hand, how are we to reckon with the Talmud passage in *Berachot* 13a that states that the Jew may recite the *Shema* in any language he understands (שמע–בכל לשון שאתה שומע)? The specific prayer referred to in the *Berachot* passage is the *Shema*. No other prayer is mentioned or permitted. In *Sotah*, chapter 7 (the first *mishnah*, later expanded in the *Gemara*), we find in addition to the *Shema* that the "Prayer" is also mentioned; that is, the *Amidah* or *Shmoneh Esray* (Eighteen Benedictions). The "Prayer" may also be recited in any language. The rabbis permitted these two prayers to be said in whatever language one understands, plus a few others; not all the prayers in the *siddur* may be recited in any language. In the talmudic period Aramaic was the generally spoken language, not

Hebrew—hence the limited leniency for prayer in Aramaic. Yet the historical record shows that, from the time of the Second Commonwealth to the period when Yiddish began to flourish and prayers began to appear in Yiddish, more than just the *Shema* and the *Amidah* came to be read in the vernacular.

Israel Zinberg, in the first volume of his monumental twelve-volume *History of Jewish Literature* (originally written in Yiddish and subsequently translated into Hebrew and English), emphasized two points that distinguished Jews and their literature from other peoples in both the ancient and modern worlds. These were, first, the fact of the separation of ancient Israel from its land and, second, a bifurcation of the language. Among other peoples in the ancient world, the branches of their cultural activity developed in the same language: from an old, primitive, oral vernacular into a modern, unified, cohesive medium. This was not so with the Jews. Many contacts with foreign cultures beyond the boundaries of their homeland compelled adjustment and adaptation to a variety of environments, each of which left indelible imprints on Judaism—whether Aramaic, Spanish, French, German, Arabic, or any of the Slavic tongues.

A gap existed between the popular, common vernacular and the intellectual, sophisticated, written medium that manifested itself in the national creative literature cultivated by the spiritual leaders and preservers of the most important parts of the group's culture. Isaac bar Sheshet, a Spanish rabbi of the fourteenth century, in one of his responsa, lamented the fact that "the majority of common people could not read the prayers and it was therefore necessary to be content with having the *chazzan* . . . chant them, with the congregation repeating them after him." To which Zinberg added: "One must also take into consideration in this connection that even in the fourteenth century a significant percentage of the Spanish Jews were common laborers—peasants and artisans" (*ZHJL*, vol. 7, p. 7).

This situation continued for Jews during the last four to five hundred years when, in the course of their migrations through France into the Rhineland communities in the medieval period, they came in contact with the German language. "From the sixteenth to the nineteenth century, there developed in Germany an extensive Judeo-German literature consisting of storybooks, ethical treatises, songs, dictionaries, translations of the daily and holiday prayer books, and manuals of private devotion." These "manuals of private devotion,"[1] as they were called, were material for the first extensive article on the subject in English. It was written by Solomon Freehof.[2]

Freehof regretted that little had been written on the Judeo-German *techinnot* and, indeed, except for Zinberg's remarkable *History* published years later, there is little else available. Freehof speculated on what, for Zinberg, later became hypothesis: perhaps "this neglect is due to the fact that these prayer books are in the humbler vernacular and not in the more dignified Hebrew, or perhaps to the fact that most of these books were anonymous, the work of unknown writers, and thus lacked the prestige of famous authorship, or perhaps also because being written primarily for women, they dealt with the humble needs of everyday life rather than with the great philosophical problems of faith."

Despite the fact that a century ago almost every Jewish home had collections of such Yiddish prayers, these once popular books have gradually disappeared and today are almost nonexistent.[3] Originally written for the masses of humble Jewish men and women, these books were for what we would today call grassroots consumption. They reflected conditions of Jewish life in central and eastern Europe for centuries.

In some prayers, we find the concern of a worried wife who expresses anxiety for her husband, who has to travel on business and is often on the road. She prays for his protection from violent men, from imprisonment, from death. Incidental passages reflect social and economic problems, the tribulations of raising children, illnesses, and a hundred other details of daily life.

The *techinnot* are also a vital source, in Freehof's words, of "the theology of the masses of the people." They are definitely not books of theology because, according to him:

The masses of the people are not primarily concerned with what the world thinks of their idea of God or immortality. With them religion is a life rather than a science. . . . [W]hen the individual is alone with God he speaks to Him in terms in which he actually conceives Him, he prays for things that he believes God will grant, and expresses hopes which really move his heart.[4]

The Jew prays to a compassionate God; he readily accepts the yoke of the kingdom of heaven and is aware of His omnipotence. More than a systematic theology, the relatively small selection of *techinnot* presented here reveals religious values by which the Jew lived and for which he prayed, tried to emulate, and sought to achieve in his daily life: study of Torah, prayer with *kavono*; maintenance of the home as the primary human environment for the cultivation of other values, the religious education of children, the quality of life, Sabbath (*Shabbos*) and *yom tov, klal Yisroel,* communal worship, *tikkun olom, teshuvo,* and so on.

The relationship with God is also typical. The Jew is close to Him, speaks directly to Him. He is always approachable. He is not a stereotyped God of the Old Testament, a jealous and vengeful deity. He is frequently addressed as "Compassionate Father" and "Merciful One," always available, always hearing prayers, abundant in goodness, truth, and mercy.

The idea of sex, for example, was dealt with in a simple, straightforward manner. No blushing, stammering, or embarrassment is found in these texts. Traditional, so-called old-time Jews were always regarded as sexual prudes, something of a counterpart to the colonial Puritans; but we would never find the typical Puritan speaking to God in the following manner: "May the discomfort of [sexual] separation from our husbands atone for those times when we conducted ourselves improperly in [the marriage] bed" (*"Techinno* for Forgiveness," #75).

"Children" referred mainly to sons, but Jews were not "anti women libbers." Such an idea was unknown. Sons simply carried on the tradition of fulfillment of more *mitzvot* than daughters did because so many of the *mitzvot* are related to and depend upon a time element for their performance. Women were occupied with running the house and raising children. It was more a division of responsibilities and functions than an innate inequality between the sexes. In the "Prayer for Good Children" a mother hopes and prays she will be able to pay the children's (the sons') tuition because it was they who received the formal *cheder* education. The daughters' no less important education was obtained in an informal home environment.

The idea of the male child as a "golden ornament" must therefore be viewed in this light; it is he, in this patrilineal society, upon whom rested the ultimate responsibility for receiving, preserving, and transmitting a major portion of the religious tradition. It was not the intention to exclude or prevent the daughters of Israel from living within the tradition; rather, it was a practical and intelligent division of responsibilities.

One of the commentators, the author of the *Sha'aray Tzion* (Gates of Zion), introduced a remarkably revolutionary idea for the study of the Pentateuch by children: it should be studied in its proper sequence, in contrast to the old prevailing practice of following the weekly Sabbath portions, which the child could never completely cover because of his tender age. On the other hand, it was not such a progressive pedagogy as would seem at first glance. It failed to take into account passages inappropriate for young minds. The practice was: the whole text and nothing but the text—whether understood or not.

One incidental and delightful discovery in the course of these translations was the absence of an historical sense as we know it today. King David, for example, rarely "said" in his psalms. He mostly "says." The Sages of the Talmud almost always "speak" to us; they rarely "spoke" in the sense that they were dead and gone. They live and speak today; in every generation their wisdom and relevance are known, appreciated, understood, and remembered.

In bygone days, simple Jews were known as *Tillim Yiddn—* psalms Jews. If they were not learned, could not study Talmud for whatever reason, they could and did recite psalms. An outstanding example of this pervasive psalmic influence is found in "Embarking on an Ocean Voyage," in which the author brilliantly

blends selected sea passages from the psalms into a verbal sym-
phony conveying the sense of awe and grandeur of all nature under
God's control.

There is a general structure to the collections of *techinnot* that
evolved over the centuries. According to Freehof, the *techinnot*
developed in three areas:

1. *techinnot* "intended to be inserted into the regular daily service;
as the worshiper goes through the regular service he intersperses
additional prayers from the book of *techinnot*;
2. "special prayers for each important day of the religious year;
3. "various petitions to be said for the various needs of the life of
the individual as prayers in time of sickness, prosperity and so
forth."[5]

Freehof was mainly concerned with *techinnot* written in Judeo-
German. There are differences that distinguish Judeo-German from
eastern European Yiddish. The latter reflects more of what may
be called *Mamma-loshen*—"mother's language." *Mamma-loshen* is
an intimate, warm, earthy medium lacking the formality found in
the Judeo-German that Freehof translated into pseudo-Victorian
prose. His translations are stilted today, however intimate and
sincere the petitioner seems to have been. I tried to avoid this in
my own translations but must confess to a certain discontent. The
idiom, the spice and fragrance of the Yiddish, is infrequently preserved in translation however much one tries. A delicate element
of the spirit is too often lost.

Another consideration complicates the problems involved in
translating from Yiddish to English. Emanuel S. Goldsmith pointed
out that "something of a nation's soul is always revealed in its
language."[6] There is more than a merely formal relationship
between a language and the nation that speaks, reads, and writes
it. In distinguishing between one language and another, one has
to be aware of the difference of internal structure. And, while the
primacy of language became the foundation of modern national-

ism for many peoples, it could never serve as such for the Jewish people. Put another way, the translator directs his efforts

> toward the discovery of relationships in a text . . . the relationships between the word and its philological and etymological background, relationships between the word and its cultural ambiance, relationships between one word and its historical tradition, relationships between the word and its context within a text.[7]

What has this to do with *techinnah* Yiddish? First, *techinnah* Yiddish was a religious Yiddish, distinct from the secular Yiddish that came to full flower at the First Yiddish Language Conference in Czernowitz, Bukovina, in 1908. Secular Yiddish was conceptualized and formulated in response to the flourishing Hebrew culture movement that had staked out its claim to "national significance in the life of the Jewish people."[8] In so doing, Yiddish secularists were competing with Hebrew in an intellectual struggle destined to fail because of a number of historical factors as yet unborn, the *Shoah* among them. Besides, there was manifest in Hebrew a "religious Torah culture and its halakhic regimen. Scripture and liturgy continuously reinforced the idea that all Jews were the heirs of the Patriarchs and that they were all brothers responsible for one another. The laws and ideas of Judaism . . . were considered primary in the scale of Jewish values and central to daily existence."[9] Additionally, *techinnah* Yiddish did not arise in response to modern nationalism. Its premodern origins filled the religious needs of Jews who, for various reasons, were unable to gain entry into the hallowed corridors of Hebrew. As will be shown, this Johnny-come-lately Yiddish of roughly half a millennium in age absorbed much from the ages-old religious Hebrew tradition.

Determining the historical evolution of the word or term, the idea or concept, is part of the job, but by far the more difficult part is to decide whether it can be rendered into a contemporary terminology that will satisfy discriminating readers. This is the crux of the matter. Nine times out of ten, the translator's results, despite his best efforts, fall short. What happens on the tenth try? Despairing, he translates word for word, hoping the intelligent reader will

catch something of the original flavor. He tries to get by with the
"sin of omission." Here is an example.

Two Hebrew words (three in English) that appear often in the
*techinnah* literature are *keesay ha-kavode*, or "Throne of Glory." They
refer to God's throne upon which, as it were, He sits. The words
appear denotatively on the following selected pages, each accompanied in the text by a parenthetical connotation within the translation:

1. Pages 6, 76—a prayer that the soul may return to its place
from which it had originally been taken when transferred to
life in this material world at birth.
2. Pages 8, 46, 91—prayers that, with the assistance of angelic messengers, are brought to the Throne of Glory.
3. Pages 34, 54—the soul after death reposes beneath the
Throne of Glory.
4. Page 83—the soul stands in judgment before the Throne
of Glory.
5. Pages 100, 189—God made a hole beneath His Throne of
Glory to receive King Manasseh's prayer despite angelic opposition.
6. Page 107—the period during the *Olaynu* prayer on High
Holy Days is a time of grace before the Throne of Glory.
7. Page 109—petitioner's tears arrive at the Throne of Glory.

What is the Throne of Glory? Since the idea of God is symbolically rendered as a kind, beneficent, wise, and loving monarch, it
is understandable that He would sit on a throne, but we must also
bear in mind what G. Scholem has pointed out, that the "earliest
Jewish mysticism is throne-mysticism."[10] Throne, or *Merkavah*
(Chariot), mysticism is a central theme for Jewish esoteric literature, penetrating many Jewish areas of thought. Throne of Glory
mysticism has also appeared often in *techinnah* literature.

In a passage in *Midrash on Proverbs* Rabbi Nehemiah states that
the Throne of Glory was one of seven items created before the
universe.[11] In an imagined, but inspired, conversation between
God and a recently expired righteous and learned soul, God

informs the soul that of all the subjects it has studied (Torah, *Mishnah*, etc.), Chariot mysticism is the most important.[12]

Having established the throne's significance, the *Midrash* inquires how various elements of the throne function—the first leg, the second leg, and so on. This is followed by a partial insight into the nature of the throne: Righteousness and justice are at the base of Your throne (Ps. 89:15). God's sovereignty and, by extension, His throne are rooted in Judaism's ethical attributes.

The *Midrash Tanhuma* attempts to understand "Great is the Lord, and highly to be praised" (Ps. 145:3) in light of the Genesis narrative relating to the nature of God. It does this by comparing a king of flesh and blood to the Holy One, blessed be He, and highlighting the difference. When a king of flesh and blood sits upon his elevated (i.e., raised) throne, his feet do not reach the footstool. By contrast, the Lord declares that "the heaven is My throne,/ And the earth is My footstool" (Isa. 66:1). God's dimensions, as it were, and His influence extend far beyond those of a mere flesh-and-blood monarch and his throne. Indeed, we cannot grasp the implications of His dimensions. Thus the nature of the throne on which He sits, even trying to envision it, is beyond the scope of finite human minds.

Notwithstanding the foregoing doubts, we now have obtained some insight into the abstract, nonphysical nature of the throne, but we still must ask: What is meant by "glory"? Scholem, quoting Saadiah, regards *kavode* (glory) as "the great radiance called *Shechinah*." It is also identified with

> *ruach ha-kodesh*, the "holy spirit," out of whom there speaks the voice and word of God. It is the primeval light of divine glory . . . later revealed to the prophets and mystics in various forms and modifications. . . .[13]

Dictionaries at this point are less than helpful. The Hebrew *kavode* is usually translated as honor, as in the Decalogue, where one is enjoined to honor one's parents. But translators have generally persisted in translating the term as "glory."

The term appears infrequently in the *Tanach* (Cf. Jer. 14:21,

OJPS: the throne of glory; NJPS reveals its perplexity by convert-
ing the noun *glory* into an adjective: ". . . Your glorious throne").
We fare little better in postbiblical literature:

1. In *Chagigah* 15a, the Throne of Glory was created before
the world was created; this distinction is shared with the Torah,
which is also precreation.
2. *Shabbat* states the view that righteous and scholarly souls
repose beneath it.

The above are a few of many references in rabbinic literature
concerning the Throne of Glory. We have some idea, however
small, of what the throne is, when it was created, and have identified a few of its functions, but we still don't know what is meant
by the word *kavode*. There are several direct and indirect references to the term in the *siddur*, but they are no more enlightening
than what we have hitherto uncovered:

1. In a Sabbath morning prayer, God is the King who sits
upon a "high and lofty *throne*" (Birnbaum *Siddur*, 339-340,
based on Isa. 6:1); perhaps "Throne of Glory" is understood
here.
2. In the *El Adon* prayer (Birnbaum, *DPB*, 339-340), "Purity
and justice stand before his *throne*;/Kindness and mercy are in
his *glorious* presence (*k'vodo*)." Taking the last word in each half
of the verse, we could have *keesay k'vodo*–His Throne of Glory.
3. Immediately following the *El Adon*, in the prayer beginning with the words *La-el asher shavaht*, "To the God who rested"
after the labors of creation and "ascended to sit upon his throne
of glory."

The plethora of so-called explanations continues to perplex. As
translators, we are still unable to convey the core idea, the quin-
tessence of the term. We are forced to yield to the inevitable and
translate *keesay ha-kavode* as "Throne of Glory," retreating into
what was referred to earlier as the sin of omission.

Consider now the practice of blending biblical and/or talmudic phrases and passages into *techinnot*. These phrases or passages are bracketed and sources indicated for the reader's information. Such source citations are absent in the original, which shows how great a grasp the anonymous authors and (most likely) readers had of their literary-religious tradition, acquired through a lifetime of daily use. In the Yiddish text, quotations or phrases are used in Hebrew (and sometimes Aramaic) without the source given. They flow with, and blend, into the text. These quotations or phrases were once common, everyday usages by and on the Yiddish tongue and did not grate on the Yiddish ear. It would never have occurred to the man or woman reading or hearing them that these passages were out of context, out of time or place, so perfectly assimilated into Yiddish had they become. We must not regard them as artificial grafts however much they seem to us at first but, rather, as normal cultural and linguistic accretions. This "blending" technique has precedents, not the least of which is found in the *piyyutim*, medieval liturgical poems that also used "skillful allusions to biblical and midrashic phrases."[14] It is a part of the literary-religious tradition extending far back into Jewish history.

The warmth and intimacy of eastern European Yiddish seem absent from Judeo-German. In reading the *techinnot* in *Stunden der Andacht* (Hours of Devotion),[15] one finds a formality reminiscent of a small Protestant country church. And when *techinnot* are read in Hebrew (for an example of which, see the Zinberg *ZHJL* in Hebrew, vol. 4, chap. 9), Hebrew's formal diction predominates.

This is also why I fault my own translations. They lack the quality of the informal, intimate conversation I first heard when my mother spoke softly to her Father in heaven as I sat on the floor, a preschool child, playing silently with a rubber ball and jacks. One is nourished throughout life by such early memories of a time when words have barely formed in the mouth. A child thrives on the images and sounds he absorbs. Perhaps this early memory, as much as anything, motivated my interest in this aspect of Jewish literature many years later.

While my childhood interest was subjective, if anything, something else was at work within me over the years of a more objective nature. As an undergraduate studying the "new" Hebrew literature in Lachower's *History of the New Hebrew Literature* (Tel Aviv: Dvir, 1951), I pestered the instructor frequently for information about the wives of literary figures we were studying. What was known about them? Why weren't they included in the biographical essays on their husbands? Other than Rachel, weren't there any other women poets, storytellers, or essayists worthy of mention? All I got were silent, polite shrugs and, it seemed to me, a weak smile.

Later, I realized a similar fate had been destined for women in English literature. Although dimly aware of the condition, my disease was gently rationalized away. There were, after all, Fanny Burney, Jane Austen, the Brontë sisters, and Virginia Woolf. Was this enough, or simply the merest of nods in the ladies' direction?

Elaine Showalter's accusation of an exclusivist patriarchal tendency at work was further confirmed by Michael Gluzman's insights into the Hebrew literary scene. Showalter and Gluzman held "that the exclusion of women from many accounts of literary history is too systematic to be considered accidental."[16] Individuals were appearing on the intellectual horizon who were seriously concerned about feminine literary disenfranchisement. Finally, along comes a *techinnah* sampler that, for the most part, is anonymous. What a delicious irony!

Certain words and phrases appear over and over again in this text. They have a flavor, a scent, an intimacy; they conjure sights and sounds: my mother baking *challo* on Friday mornings, the kitchen warmth of a preholiday graced with the preparation of special dishes; continuity and rootedness in something vibrant and alive. *Ribono shel olom* (Lord of the universe), *yirahs shomyim* (fear of heaven), *Moshe Rabenu* (Moses our teacher), and countless other terms that ought to be transliterated rather than translated (*mitzvo, klal Yisroel, teshuvo, rachmonus, Tatenyu, yom tov,* etc.), all convey a wealth of connotations immediately recognizable by a Yiddish speaker and/or reader. Steven T. Katz (*Jewish Ideas and Concepts,* p. xi) succinctly presented this problem concerning the "contextual nature of language" by pointing out that "concepts have to be closely scrutinized in their contexts." This has been the goal basically throughout this work, however little stated or repeated. It is appropriate at this point to mention it as one of the underlying points for my literary approach.

Ashkenazic spelling and pronunciation have been deliberately retained to contrast with the Sephardic one currently in vogue in the State of Israel because it is what eastern European Jewry spoke and read. There is also a difference in accentuation. Israelis generally accent the final, ultimate syllable in words, whereas eastern European Ashkenazic Jews generally accent the penultimate one. The differences do not stop here; even Hebrew vowels assume regional characteristics of their own. To keep matters simple, these elements have rarely been highlighted in my transliterations, since these were calculated to be anything but "scientific" and were generally meant to emphasize the milieu's commonly used words, expressions, values, and ideas connotatively. Whether the writer was a Galician, Romanian, Hungarian, Lithuanian, or Russian Jew has been deemphasized. I have followed this route despite excellent contributions by YIVO, the admirable *Encyclopaedia Judaica* and the *U.S. Government Printing Office Style Manual* (1973) to the advancement of a systematic transliteration for Jewish studies. The U.S. Library of Congress has also recently issued an attempt to standardize transliteration, but I have not yet seen it. Finally, the Protestant-sounding *Amen* has been deliberately abandoned in favor of *O-mayn*.

There is an interesting peculiarity found in the *techinnot* as one continues to read them. The anomalous nature of the peculiarity grows as one's attention is drawn to it, partly because it is not necessarily a common feature in the mental makeup of twentieth-century citizens. I refer to the lachrymose quality found in the *techinnot* as authors sought to establish the Jewish woman's or Jewish man's spiritual connections with their Creator. Indeed, such spontaneous emotional outpouring is rarely found in contemporary western literatures. Twentieth-century men and women tend more toward objective, calm expressions, sometimes ironic, at other times deliberately understated, rarely given to tearful emoting. We tend to regard crying as unmanly, often unwomanly, an embarrassing revelation of intimate emotions and desires. One doesn't behave like that. The accepted norm is to keep a stiff upper lip—except, of course, when citizens lobby political representatives, strike against employers for better wages and working conditions, or shout favorite slogans and expletives in the highest vocal decibels possible at what they regard as unfair penalties against their favorite team in the intensely physical arena of sports.

Salo Wittmayer Baron wrote somewhere in his magisterial *A Social and Religious History of the Jews* (or once remarked in a lecture) that the purpose of his work was to present an alternative to the usual lachrymose Jewish histories earlier historians had written. Current generations are no longer attuned to spontaneous outpourings (genuine or otherwise) of teary emotions.

A particular scene stands out in my boyhood memories, a last gasp, as it were, of a fading religious custom. The funeral procession proceeds slowly along Lucerne Street on its way to one of the nearby synagogues on Woodrow Avenue in Dorchester, Massachusetts. The deceased must have been an important communal leader in his day. Immediately following the hearse were several women weeping, wailing, crying loudly, beating their breasts, raising their hands to heaven, publicly mourning the deceased. They were professional mourners. Behind them also on foot were immediate family members and a long line of relatives and friends. I never saw such a scene again and it did not particularly impress me, except to make me feel that it seemed strange and out of place. As a boy, I was unaware of this being a carryover from Europe, one of many exotica that first-generation public school–educated Jews would drop from their cultural baggage. Jewish funerals these days are sedate, sober affairs. Emotional outpourings are restrained and tears flow silently among the non-Orthodox. I write this as neither praise nor condemnation. It is simply a fact.

The expressive and mournful shedding of tears is not rooted in medieval ignorance or in the spiritual darkness of gloomy superstition. It is a well-established metaphor found in the *Tanach*. When Jeremiah mourns the slain of the daughter of his people, he wishes his head were filled with water and his eyes a source for (unlimited) tears (Jer. 8:23). David, that most human of biblical figures, troubled and beset by enemies, finds himself emotionally at his weakest in his bed at night. His suffering overwhelms him and prevents his sleeping; he is weary with groaning. Figuratively speaking, he melts his bed with an abundance of tears (Ps. 6:7).

In a little-known poem ("The Cup") Russian-Jewish poet Shimon Frug (1860-1916) used a legend about tears to create a sensitive scene concerning a child who inquired of his mother whether what his grandfather had told him was true. Was there any truth in the story that there was a cup in heaven into which God's tears flowed as He looked upon Israel's suffering in exile and that, when the cup would someday be filled, redemption would come?

King David prays to God that He collect the tears he, David, has shed and place them in a skin bottle to preserve them so that they will serve as a reminder of what is recorded in God's Book of Remembrance (Ps. 56:9).

Tears can stimulate sad recollections of Jewish dispersions and sufferings; they can be deep expressions of mourning; they can serve as a partial instrument for Israel's redemption; they can be used to remind God to save His faithful servants; they can serve as a conduit to God's heart in an attempt to bestir His compassion for His faithful ones; finally, they can draw His attention to their prayers and compel Him to come to His children's aid, as we find often in the *techinnot*.

These are a few of the many examples of how tears served Jews in their historic march through the centuries toward collective redemption. The outpouring of tears throughout the *techinnot* is a somewhat unique phenomenon in the history of Jewish liturgy, perhaps even in the history of religions. Beyond this, one hesitates to draw unwarranted conclusions. There is need for further extensive investigation.

This selection of *techinnot* was initially made from two readily available editions: one published in Vilna (now Vilnius)[17] and the other in New York.[18] The Vilna edition, despite a later publication date (which simply means it went through many printings), is the older of the two. The New York edition is generally derivative, as a cursory examination of both reveals. The Vilna edition is by far the more interesting and includes much material deleted by the other.

Even the reverse side of the title page sometimes makes for interesting copy. Among other things, the author informs us that the *techinnot* were

> for pouring out the heart before our compassionate Father in heaven with warm words on sad and happy occasions, that He may have mercy upon us and send help in all our 248 limbs.
>
> These holy *techinnos* flow from the divinely inspired sources of our holy ancestors, from the holy prophets and *Tannaim* and *Amoraim*, the *Geonim* and *tzaddikim*, also from righteous women, may their merit be a shield for us.
>
> Collected by Dr. [*sic*] Ben Tzion, son of the great and righteous Rabbi Jeremiah Akiva, may his memory be for a blessing, Alfes, who was found worthy of praying at the Western Wall in Jerusalem.

A worthy goal for an anthology collected by a worthy gentleman dedicated to combating the secular inroads and depredations of European Enlightenment among young Jews.[19]

Introductory remarks to selections have been removed to the notes section at the end of the book. They set the stage, as it were, for a fuller appreciation of the text during second and subsequent readings. Elsewhere, remarks found in the notes illuminate the text just read. Notes generally are brief, but occasionally they are extended to reveal the nature or background of some aspect of the *techinnah*. The *techinnot* can, and probably should, be read first by themselves without recourse to the notes to gain a sense of their continuity and cyclical quality. Second and subsequent readings with the aid of the notes will be both enlightening and profitable. After all, the study of Torah in the broadest sense (of *Tanach*, *Mishnah*, *Halachah*, *Aggadah*, *Midrash*, etc.) has always been a major component of Judaism. Optimally, it is religious discourse of the highest caliber with the Divine.

The following points must therefore be kept in mind: (1) brackets indicate a Hebrew or Aramaic passage, often followed by the author's explanation or interpretation in Yiddish; (2) parenthetical material has sometimes been added by the author of the *techinnah* to ensure a smooth flow of thought; (3) paragraph division and punctuation are nonexistent in the originals; (4) a crude transliteration system has been deliberately adopted to reflect the dominant Ashkenazic pronunciation in use throughout pre-twentieth-century eastern European Jewish communities rather than today's scientific transliterations.

In view of my "crude" transliteration system, the following must also be borne in mind: (1) while in Hebrew and Yiddish there are no capital letters as in English, I have capitalized names of prayers, *piyyutim*, proper names, holidays, synonyms for God, the Jewish months, names of books, and commentaries; (2) in some cases, generally accepted usage as indicated in *Merriam Webster's International Dictionary* has been followed; (3) the careful reader may note a difference between what appears in the unscientifically transliterated text and what I use when making my own remarks; my spelling will often reflect contemporary Sephardic pronunciation and accentuation. Pity the poor reader looking for consistency. He is doomed to be disappointed.

Because it seemed a sensible approach to material in the Vilna and New York editions, I have basically followed the cycle of the Jewish religious year, exceptions being made for *techinnot* devoted to special occasions.[20]

After completion of the early translations from the Vilna and New York editions, I had the pleasure of visiting accessible Judaica collections in the United States and Israel. (Recognition and acknowledgments are found in the notes section.) The results were nothing less than astounding. With the simile of the iceberg as a gauge, I realized I'd examined but a fraction of the iceberg visible above the water line and next to nothing of what was hidden below. An explorer's excitement has spurred me on ever since. Some of the fruits of these delightful discoveries have been incorporated into this anthology, which originally had been conceived on a more modest level. Both the original sources and the special collections in which they were found are recorded in the notes section. My indebtedness to the various institutions for their generous assistance in supplying my needs is boundless. I am deeply grateful to them all and thank both them and their talented, devoted personnel for their enthusiastic cooperation in helping to make this volume possible.

May this labor of love stand as partial testimony to a once vibrant Yiddish civilization decimated by the European Holocaust. Regardless of whether that Yiddish civilization will survive in the future as a dynamic phenomenon or be relegated to the annals of history, it will remain a prime example of the religious zeal beating in the collective breast of Jewish men and women. May their memory be for a blessing.

Encino, California

# ABBREVIATIONS

| | |
|---|---|
| *ADPB* | *Authorised Daily Prayer Book* |
| CCAR | Central Conference of American Rabbis, Cincinnati |
| C.E. | Common Era |
| *DPB* | *Daily Prayer Book* |
| *EJ* | *Encyclopaedia Judaica* |
| *HHPB* | *High Holyday Prayer Book* |
| HPC | Hebrew Publishing Company, New York |
| *ICC* | *International Critical Commentary* |
| JNUL | Jewish National and University Library, Ramat Gan Campus, Jerusalem |
| JPSA | Jewish Publication Society of America, Philadelphia |
| JTSAL | Jewish Theological Seminary of America Library, New York |

NJPS    New translation by the Jewish Publication Society of America: *The Torah*, 1962; *The Prophets*, 1978; *The Writings*, 1982

OJPS    Old translation by the Jewish Publication Society of America: *The Holy Scriptures*, 1917

PB       *The Prayer Book: Weekday, Sabbath and Festival*

WHJL    *A History of Jewish Literature*

YIVO    Institute for Jewish Research, New York

ZHJL    *A History of Jewish Literature*

Note: Abbreviations of the books of the Bible follow standardized procedure of the *Encyclopaedia Judaica*, index volume (vol. 1), p. 79 ff.

# A BOOK
# OF
# JEWISH WOMEN'S
# PRAYERS

# 1. To Our Esteemed Women[1]

You, noble women, are the mothers of our children and our entire people. [There follows an enumeration of women's contributions in Israel's history: they saved the lives of the newborn in Egypt[2] and ultimately were the main cause of Israel's successful Exodus; at the construction of the Tabernacle in the wilderness [Exod. 25:8–... let them make me a sanctuary ... ], they were the first to contribute generously and participated through their handcraft of spinning in its construction [Exod. 35:25–And all the skilled women spun with their own hands ... ]; they contributed their copper mirrors for the copper laver [Exod. 38:8–And he made the laver of brass, from the mirrors of the serving women that did service at the door of the tent of meeting].[3]

There are many beautiful stories for which our nation is grateful to you, such as the story about Deborah, Hannah the mother of Samuel, Queen Esther and the miracle of Purim, Judith and the miracle of Chanuko,[4] and many more beautiful stories in the *Tanach*, *Gemoro* and *Midrashim*. Even now, there are among you many righteous women who possess many good qualities inherited from their mothers.

## MORE UNDERSTANDING IN WOMEN

When the Creator of the world wished to appear on Mount Sinai to give us the beloved holy Torah, He honored you women when

He told *Moshe Rabenu* [Moses our teacher] to speak to you first
[ . . . Thus shall you say to the *house of Jacob* . . .–Exod. 19:3],
concerning which Rashi writes: ". . . this refers to the women,
then to the men [ . . . and tell the *children of Israel* . . .–Exod.
19:3].
    Already in Genesis, He made much of you. When He created
Mother Eve, the Torah phrased it thus: [Gen. 2:22–And the Lord
God fashioned the rib . . . ]. That is, He made her into a sensible
being; He gave her *bino* [understanding], more than He gave Adam.
(This is why a girl matures at twelve and a boy at thirteen.) Now,
since the Torah has honored you, it is obvious that you should be
prized and conversation held with you on an intelligent level.

## PREPARE YOURSELF IN THE VESTIBULE

The *Tanna* Rabbi Jacob says [*Ethics of the Fathers* 4:21] that this
world is like a vestibule to the other world; prepare yourself in
the vestibule to enter the hall[5] [to enjoy heavenly pleasures there].
Everyone understands that the nine months a child is in the womb
do not constitute the ultimate purpose in life. The womb is like a
small vestibule in which to prepare [the child] for entry into the
world-chamber. So it is that this world is a vestibule in relation to
the world to come, in which one is wrapped with the entire spiritual strength implanted in his soul. As our Sages write, we teach
him the entire Torah in preparation for his departure from this
world. This is the teaching he must activate through study of holy
books that instruct him in God's way and he performs each *mitzvo*
when opportunity comes his way. . . . By means of the [perfor-
mance of] 248 positive *mitzvos* and the 365 prohibitions[6] (which
he strives to avoid despite the Evil Inclination's attempt to mislead him), the 248 spiritual limbs and the 365 spiritual veins of
his soul are wrapped. When his appointed time comes, he leaves
the vestibule, this dark world, to enter the world of light easily, as
with a divine kiss.
    When, however, man is not wrapped here [with the *mitzvos*] in
the vestibule, because of his evil choice he closes his ears to that
which the Torah, his parents, and good people seek to teach him

and he scorns the *mitzvo*; a defect appears on the spiritual body of the soul . . . as, for example, he desecrates the *Shabbos*, which is at the heart of Judaism, this becomes a blemish on the soul and the shame and the pain in the great hall [the world to come] are unimaginable. . . .

## 2.  Upon Arising in the Morning

Dear God [in whose hand] I place my soul upon going to sleep and upon awakening,[1] I pray You deal kindly and mercifully with me. Bless me today and every day. May my conduct find favor with my husband and children. May the cleanliness and neatness of my home be such that no illness [heaven forbid!] can enter. Although, *Ribono shel olom* [Lord of the universe], You are our Protector and have written in the holy Torah that one should not rely upon miracles but take care of one's self, I seek Your help as well. As is well known, many contagious diseases come from unhygienic conditions. Grant me the strength and wisdom to know how to keep my house clean. Enable me to take care of my health and strength as well as that of my husband and children and of the entire household with healthy and tasty foods; may each meal be on time so that we have the strength to serve our Creator for, as it is written in the *Perek*: [If there is no flour (bread, food) there is no Torah—*Ethics of the Fathers* 3:21].[2]

The *Rambam* [Maimonides] says that in a healthy body the mind is more sound and less prone to err than in a weak one, especially in these times when [because of our many transgressions] the [burden of making a living] is so hard, and we must be resolute.

The thing is to be happy with one's portion and not [envy] a neighbor because she has good food or expensive clothes or jewelry. May I be diligent only in the pursuit of good Jewish behavior, happy with whatever the Lord bestows. May my home be a happy one, knowing no misfortune. . . . May my husband and children be happy upon entering our home; may I be able to please them with agreeable and sensible conversation in order that the blessing of abundant livelihood and success dwell in my house, thereby enabling me to give *tzedoko* [charity] with a happy heart and pray with pure thoughts. May You grant all our prayers for good. *Omayn.*

## 3. A *Techinno* for Evening and Morning

*Author's note: This* techinno *should be said evenings and mornings before prayers.*

*Ribono shel olom* [Lord of the universe], You know that we are flesh and blood. You, Lord of the entire world, are an almighty God and know full well that we are merely blood and flesh and have no strength with which to direct or combine the holy names and *kavonos* [intentions] found in each prayer and blessing. Even if we knew the combinations and names of the blessings we would still be unable to tell of Your fame and wonder for we are merely human, blood and flesh, and we lack the intelligence with which to understand greatness and holiness. Therefore, may it be Your will, God, that my Morning Service, or Musaf Service, or Evening Service shall be reckoned [accordingly]. May my every prayer be regarded . . . [as having been correctly said] and ascend [heavenward] to join with all Israel's prayers and become a crown for You. . . .

## 4. Before Going to Sleep[1]

*Ribono shel olom* [Lord of the universe], the soul that You have given me goes now to Your Throne of Glory. Take it unto You and return it to me early in the morning. Accept and guard faithfully the deposit we leave [in Your safekeeping], the soul that You have created and that You return to us each morning. We praise and give thanks to the Creator of all times. Your servant, *Avigayil* [Abigail] *Bas Tovim*.[2]

## 5. A Little with *Kavono*[1]

Every woman should read her *techinno* with great *kavono* [intention], namely, with a warm heart and attentively because it contains the collected wisdom of prophets and righteous men and women whose holy words penetrate the heavens and go straight to the Throne of Glory. For the woman who has time to read many *techinnos* daily, all well and good—they ease the state of mind, warm the heart, and incline it favorably to God.

## 6. Strong as a Lion

The holy Rabbi Jacob [Ben Asher, author of *Ba'al Ha-turim*, d. 1340] writes that one should be as strong as a lion upon arising to perform the service of the Creator. . . .[1] before the *yetzer ho-ro* [Evil Inclination] is able to strengthen its hold on him with false arguments. In the winter, he argues: "How can you rise so early when it is cold?" In the summer: "It's still early and you haven't had enough sleep." Thus he leads one into sloth. Accordingly, one should be "strong as a lion" to overcome the enemy, the *yetzer horo* [the Evil Inclination], and immediately upon awakening recite the prayer [*Modeh ani*] "I give thanks, etc."

## 7. *Techinno Modeh Ani*[1]

Almighty God, I place my soul in Your hand while I yet live and my mind is clear. May You and all the Torah scrolls in the *ohron ha-kodesh* [Holy Ark] bear witness to the fact that I acknowledge

You are One and there is no other. May my soul expire when I am over a hundred [years] with the words *Shema Yisroel* [Hear, O Israel: the Lord our God, the Lord is One]. May my soul be able to return to the place from which it was taken.

I ask now from this day on, should Satan come to persuade me to do evil, that his words be rendered as powerless and valueless as a shard. I pray that my soul come to that place which I desire, to be with Sarah, Rebecca, Rachel, and Leah. Should Satan, *chas ve-choleelo* [heaven forbid!] come and try to mislead me into transgressing a *mitzvo* that You have enjoined in Your Holy Torah, or to deny Your holy Name—reprove him and chase him away.

I believe in the living God, blessed be He, and in His beloved holy Name. He is truth and His Torah is truth and *Moshe Rabenu* is truth and God, blessed be He, is One and there is no other. He has been, is, and will be forever King over the entire world. *Omayn, kayn yehhe rohtzone* [so may it be Your will].

*Ahv ho-rahchamim* [Compassionate Father], I beg of You that You create a new heart for me with which to serve You. Allow my evil acts that I have committed from childhood on to drop away. May I become today as [pure as] a newborn child without transgression. You know full well that what I sinned against You was not in order to anger You. My [immature] foolishness brought it about. Would that I had considered how venerable You are, that You created the world and surrounded it with a great ocean [i.e., the atmosphere] that has no foundation and no end, all of which compared to the heavens is like [the proverbial] drop of water in the ocean.

You created seven heavens, each of which is separated by a distance of five hundred years. That is *olom ho-ahseeyo* [the world of doing, making]. Above it is *olom ha-yehtzeero'* [the world of formation]; above it is *olom ha-b'ree'o* [the world of creation]; above it is *olom ho-ahtzeelus* [the world of emanation].[2] All these worlds are as nothing compared to Your *keesay ha-kovode* [Throne of Glory], and it in turn is without value compared to Your beauty, reverence, awesomeness, and power. It is impossible to praise You adequately.

However foolish I have been, I shall no longer rebel against You. What I did was without understanding. Today, at long last, I have confidence in Your loving-kindness and compassion, for You open Your hand to receive the *teshuvo* [repentance, return] of those who do so wholeheartedly. As You have said through Your prophets: "Return, backsliding children, I will heal your backsliding" [Jer. 3:22]; do *teshuvo*, my children, and I shall heal your waywardness.[3]

Accept my prayer and the tears I shed before You today. Grant me an honorable *parnoso* [livelihood] so that I shall be able to serve You joyfully and merit life in *olom ha-bo* [the world to come] among righteous men and women who bask in the radiance of the *Shecheeno* [Divine Presence]. Enable me to participate in *techiyas ha-maysim* [resurrection of the dead] for all Your people Israel. May it be quickly and in our time. *Omayn.*

## 8. A New Jerusalem *Techinno*

*Author's note: This precious* techinno *was composed by a woman of great piety in Jerusalem. It should be said daily before and after prayers.*[1]

[In the name of the Lord God of Israel who dwells among the cherubim] I beg of You, God of my ancestors, with my entire heart, have mercy upon me [As a father has compassion for his children . . .—Ps. 103:13], hear my prayer and guard me from all evil, lead me in the right way and accept my prayer that I offer up wholeheartedly each day; do not turn me away empty-handed. Permit me, my husband, and children to live in holy service to You. [Compassionate King,] have compassion for me and mine, do not deal with us strictly according to justice but mercifully; turn away Your wrath from us, hear our prayer when we call upon You. Help us in all our troubles. . . . Fill our requests that we ask of Your holy Name. Help us as You helped our ancestors and delivered them from their great suffering in Egypt.

Grant me good and religious children who will be righteous, pious, and learned. Enable me to raise them in Your holy service. May they find grace and favor in Your eyes and in the eyes of others. Enable us to live out our years in happiness and see our children honorably married. . . . Cause me to rejoice as You caused our Mother Channo, may she rest in peace, to rejoice with that which she sought of Your holy Name.[2] [Compassionate Father], King of the world, I entreat You day and night not to abandon us; grant our livelihood and supply our needs with Your holy, reliable, and relief-giving hand and not [heaven forbid!] through any human agency. Grant our needs in happiness, not in sorrow. Permit me to merit a long life[3] and live to see my husband and children at my table. May we also have good advocates on our behalf for the world to come. . . . Shield me, my husband, and children from a [strange (i.e., unnatural) death]. Remember us at all times and inscribe us for good years and long life. I hope only for Your help, as do all who live throughout the world. Remember us always [for good and for blessing[4]] and hear our prayers. . . . Do not let us leave Your presence empty-handed. . . . *Omayn.*

## 9. Upon Arrival at Synagogue for Morning Services[1]

God of hosts, send soon to the beloved *shul* [synagogue] those holy angels appointed over man's prayers to You. May they bring all my prayers before Your Throne of Glory [*keesay ha-kavode*]. Accept my prayer as You did the beautiful singing of the Levites, which they sang to You when the *bays ha-mikdosh* [Holy Temple] yet stood.

Permit us, dear God, to enjoy the *z'chus* [merit] of our Mothers Sarah, Rebecca, Rachel, and Leah. Remember that from them came forth the entire polity of Your precious people Israel, who render unto You [their declaration of] *Shema Yisroel* . . . [Hear, O Israel, the Lord our God, the Lord is One].

Remember that we are Your people Israel. You accepted us as

Your children and we, in turn, acted as a child will toward its father: we received from You the Ten Commandments at Mount Sinai.

As You once accepted the prayer of the High Priest in the Holy of Holies, as You accepted the prayer of our ancestors, accept now our prayer to You in the beloved *shul* and forgive us at once. Accept our tearful prayer. We no longer have a Holy Temple, nor an altar, nor someone to forgive our sins [in Your Name].

When the *bays ha-mikdosh* stood and one prayed to You, the accuser had no power to wield over our prayer. But, today, the beloved *shul* has replaced the *bays ha-mikdosh* [of necessity]. May the prayers I am about to utter [in *shul*] nullify all that which is evil. *Omayn*.

## 10. *Techinno* to Be Recited after *Mah Tovu* (Version 1)

*Ribono shel olom* [Lord of the universe], Master of the entire world, I know full well that I am a poor sinner unworthy of standing in prayer before Your great and venerable Name. One cannot speak of Your greatness and power. You alone are the all-compassionate One desiring prayer from those who call upon You wholeheartedly and do not put their prayers to shame; for which reason I permit myself to plead, merciful Father, with humble heart and soft speech. I regret all sins that I have committed from my youth to this day. Send those angels who are appointed over the prayers of Israel in order that our prayers be accepted. *Omayn*.

## 11. *Techinno* to Be Recited after *Mah Tovu* (Version 2)

*Ribono shel olom* [Lord of the universe], in Your holy Torah after "How goodly are thy tents, O Jacob, etc." it is written: [As streams stretched out . . .–Num. 24:6]. This means that synagogues and houses of study where Jewish children study and pray are like flowing streams that purify a person who has been made impure through sin. The synagogue and house of study are the stream passing through him as he pours out his heart while he prays. When he studies Torah, his eyes are enlightened to see the importance of a *mitzvo* and the baseness of transgression. When he sees how base he has made himself through evil conduct, repents and resolves firmly to improve his actions, then is he purified of sin.

When we think more deeply on Your holy teaching, we realize the wisdom contained in it. Thus, when one stands in a stream that covers him entirely except for his head, he cannot be cleansed of his impurity. This is as though someone were in the synagogue or house of study [with his body] but his head, his mind, is elsewhere. He forgets he's in the synagogue. He imagines he's in the market place and permits himself to speak idly; especially during the cantor's repetition [of the *Amido*] or during the Torah reading, he gives vent to gossip and contentious speech. The synagogue's sanctity cannot purify him. . . . A person must be in the synagogue both in body and mind. He must be aware of where he is. Our Father Jacob said [How awesome is this place!—Gen. 28:17], "How awesome is this holy place!" [This is none other than the house of God—Gen. 28:17]; in other words, this is a divine house, a miniature sanctuary. Only then will his prayers work on him to soften his heart and pour over it love and fear [of God] so that whether at home or at work he will remember he is a descendant of our Father Abraham, conduct himself honorably, and do good to others.

Since we women habitually commit the great sin of speaking in the synagogue, especially during [the cantor's repetition of] the *Amido* and during the [Torah] reading, I beg You to help me absorb Your sacred teaching and to beware of this terrible transgression; help me set an example for the other women, that they learn from me to sit [respectfully] and with [humility] in synagogue. [By virtue of such merit] of which I may be deemed worthy, listen to my prayers, grant me an easy frame of mind and [*naches fun kinder*] pleasure from [my] children. *Omayn.*

## 12. Acceptance of the Yoke
## of the Kingdom of Heaven[1]

Almighty God, Master of all worlds, King of kings in whose hand are the souls of all creatures, the world is full of Your glory, but the human is unable to comprehend Your greatness and Your deeds.

The heavens, the rivers and the fish in them, the mountains and valleys, the deserts with their animal life, the minutest worm on and in the earth, each tree and blade of grass—all praise Your beloved Name daily and testify to Your glory over the world.

You formed man from the dust of the earth and breathed into him the breath of life. His role is to declare in all his deeds Your divinity over everything. Man must, as King David says in his psalm, keep God before him always. In all You have done I behold Your divinity and imagine You standing beside me and seeing all I do.

The Jew always remembers that his total life is judged; not only his religious devotion, but also those acts calculated to make him a more humane person; whether he maintains according to our holy Torah that which is due God or that which is due his fellow man. One ought not to conduct oneself on the animal level. Each act should be carried out intelligently and with considered forethought.

Upon us women lies the responsibility to manage the home and raise the children. As mistresses of our homes, we must carefully consider each step to take. Each thing must be done with wisdom. As the beginning of wisdom is the fear of the Lord [Ps. 111:10], so do I take upon myself with trepidation the yoke of the kingdom of heaven.[2] [I am ever mindful of the Lord's presence, He is at my right hand . . .—Ps. 16:8]; may He strengthen me, give me the understanding I need to conduct the affairs of my home and raise my children to be God-fearing and humane.

May my conduct be regarded as [sound understanding—Ps. 111:10b] in the eyes of God and man; this is the correct goal for every woman, and through the merit thereof may I be found worthy of possessing both worlds in joy [naches] and riches, in health and strength, in raising good children. May I not be found worthy [heaven forbid!] of punishment in the next world; may I always find grace and have the good fortune to grow old along with my husband. *Omayn.*

## 13. . . . Who Has Not Made Me a Heathen[1]

Thank You, my God and God of my ancestors, for not having created me a gentile, for having granted my portion among the holy people of Israel who are descended from such magnificent men as Abraham, Isaac, and Jacob, whom the entire world to this day honor and esteem. Your Providence [*hashgohcho*] has clung to them [my ancestors] from time immemorial. In olden times You performed miracles for them that the entire world beheld: You brought them out of the house of bondage with great wonders, fed them forty years in the wilderness with manna from heaven and water from a stone. You appeared in Your great glory on Mount Sinai and instructed them in Your holy Torah, which guided them in the way of life. To this very day, You perform hidden miracles, leading them through a wilderness of savages (anti-Semites and hooligans) who seek to devour them. You shelter them under Your protecting wings, as do those righteous rulers who prevent the hooligans from killing Jews. For all these things do I give thanks.

I pray for Your compassionate help. Enable me to live as a pure Jewish daughter, to love my people and fellow man. Enable me to implant in my children love for their people and all mankind henceforth and forever more. *Omayn.*

## 14. . . . Who Created Me According to His Will[1]

Beloved Father, when I hear of the great importance of our Torah, so highly esteemed by the wise men of the world who regard it as a world-famous diamond, a gold medallion with precious stones, which the King of the world by His own hand presented to the descendants of Abraham—then do I regret not being a man who has the opportunity to study it diligently and understand the deep wisdom and nobility contained in it. But, as I believe that You know better what is good for one and have created me a woman—this too is good. Therefore, I thank You for having created me according to Your will. Enable me to educate my children in Your Torah and grant me the ability to understand what I read in Your holy books so that I may enjoy some of the sweetness of Your beloved Torah. *Omayn.*

## 15. . . . Who Clothes the Naked

I do not understand how a stalk of flax grows out of a kernel of linseed and from it people make linen with which to clothe themselves. Nor can I fathom how You have given the sheep hair from which we make wool fabrics. You created the silkworm that spins out of itself the silk fiber from which beautiful dresses are made. How great are Your wonders! When we consider all this, we must humbly acknowledge Your greatness. And the more I deck myself out in beautiful dresses, the more humble I should be.

Grant me a good heart in order to practice Your precepts. As You clothed the naked (Adam and Eve), so may I with compassion cover the nakedness of the poor and thereby also cover my soul with a cloak of *tzedoko* [charity] and garments of salvation. *Omayn.*

## 16. You Favor Men with Knowledge[1]

*Melech malchay ha-m'lohchim* [King of kings], the entire world is filled with Your *kovode* [glory]. The human mind is completely unable to understand Your greatness and deeds. Your great wis-

dom shows itself in everything, from the smallest blade of grass
to the largest tree, from the tiniest worm to the biggest body, from
a granule of sand to the sun and moon, both of which are thousands of times bigger than the earth's globe.

Your greatness shows itself in the human mind upon which You
have bestowed the ability to think and understand so much that it
can absorb bookcases full of books. Similarly, the great scholars
who know by heart the entire *Tanach*, the entire Babylonian Talmud [*Shas Bavli*], the Jerusalem Talmud [*Shas Yerushalmi*], Alfes,[2]
*Rambam*, *Midrashim*, and much else—how can all this enter a brain
about the size of a clenched hand? Wonder of wonders!

Therefore, I thank and praise Your holy Name for the gift of
understanding that You have implanted in me and pray that You
in Your compassion not take away this good gift of understanding. How unfortunate is he whose understanding is disturbed, who
runs about aimlessly like an animal, who is fortunate only when
admitted to an asylum. Ah, how dark is his world and that of his
family!

Grant me the wisdom and understanding as *akeres habyis* [mis-
tress of the house (cf. Ps. 113:9)] to conduct my affairs properly
and raise my children in fear of God and love of man so that my
house shall be as the Sages say: [Let your house be open wide
. . .—*Ethics* 1:5]. May my house be as open as our Father Abraham's so that the oppressed and sad find comfort and courage in
it. And, for this, may I quickly earn the merit to see pleasure [*naches*]
from my children. *Omayn*.


# 17. Take Good Care[1]


Compassionate Father! Imperfect woman that I am, poor in good
deeds and rich in sins, a fragment, a withered flower, with contrite heart and warm tears do I come to pray before You, great
and holy God. Grant me a pure heart and firm, courageous spirit
with which to resolve firmly to shun wicked persons who avoid

Your Torah and tread in dark ways where their lusts draw them [The way of the wicked is in (sic) darkness—Prov. 4:19][2] and they drown their soul. As King David, may he rest in peace, says: Happy is the man [who has not walked in the counsel] of the wicked— Ps. 1:1] who avoids the advice of the wicked (ones who urge others to follow their practice), [and in the way of the sinners has not stood—Ps. 1:1], and in the place of the sinners has not stood [and has not sat in the seat of the mockers—Ps. 1:1], and has not sat in the company of scorners and card players, nor associated with idle chatterers [but his delight is in God's Torah—Ps. 1:2a]. May I desire only to go in the right way of Your Torah.

Help me so that when I have some time (having completed my household and shopping chores), especially on *Shabbos* and *yom tov*, that I not sit down and while away time with idle talk. May I read only books of wisdom that warm the heart with holy feelings, to love Your holy Name and to love those who know Your Torah and do good, and study to know all the laws a Jewish daughter should know, whether law or *derech eretz* [upright conduct].[3]

By virtue of this, may it be realized for me that which King David says further on [And he shall be like a tree planted . . .—Ps. 1:3]. May I be like a tree planted by a spring of water, which gives its fruit in season and the branch that one takes from it (to plant elsewhere) is blessed with great success. Likewise, may I merit good generations (of children) with whom both God and people will be happy. *Omayn.*

## 18. Remember Three Things[1]

*Atto zocher* [You remember] everything, Lord, having created the power of memory. Strengthen my memory so that I may never forget these three things: that I am created from a stinking drop [of semen]; that I am destined for the grave, a place of dust, worms, and maggots; that I must give an account and reckoning before You, King of kings.[2] Remembering these three things, I shall not sin, but serve You wholeheartedly. Your maidservant, the daughter of Your servant Jacob.

## 19. A Pregnant Woman's Prayer[1]

I pray unto You, Lord God of Israel, that You consider my prayer as You did that of Mother Channo, the prophetess who prayed for a son, the prophet Shmuel.[2] May her *z'chus* [merit] stand me in good stead. May I, Your maidservant, who am with child (Your creation!), carry full term and give birth to a healthy child who will become a pious Jew and serve You heart and soul; one who will love Torah and be God-fearing according to Your holy will, a beautiful plant in the Jewish vineyard for the beauty of Israel [*tiferes Yisroel*].[3] *Omayn.*

## 20. On Behalf of a Pregnant Woman[1]

Compassionate and gracious God, have pity on the woman [A, daughter of B; here mention name of the one about to give birth and the name of her mother], that she give birth without complications. May the *z'chus* [merit] of our holy Matriarchs Sarah, Rebecca, Rachel, and Leah, together with the merit of our prophetesses Miriam, Deborah, Hannah, Huldah,[2] and the merit of Yael,[3] stand her in good stead during this dangerous time so that she shall have an easy delivery. May the newborn be a pure soul dedicated to Your service, a *tzaddik* [righteous person] who will busy himself with [the study of] Torah and [the performance of] *mitzvos*. Should it be a girl child, may she grow into a modest woman, God-fearing, blessed with *mazel* [good fortune]. May mother and child be well and may the newborn enter into a world of salvation and consolation for *klal Yisroel* [all Israel]. In that time, may all Jews be fortunate enough to merit a true and lasting redemption. *Omayn.*

## 21. To Synagogue the First Time after Rising from Childbed

Great King, when we were deserving of it and dwelled in our land and You dwelt among us in Your holy palace (the Holy Temple), a woman after giving birth was obliged to bring an offering [korbon] of two doves, one a sin offering [korbon chattos] and the second a burnt offering [korbon oloh][1] for the kindnesses rendered her during pregnancy and delivery, that she survived the danger. But now, since we no longer have our Holy Temple and cannot bring a sacrifice, the prophet says [. . . we will render for bullocks the offering of our lips—Hos. 14:3]. You accept the songs and praises we utter as though we actually offered sacrifices. Therefore, I have come into Your small sanctuary [mikdosh me'aht] to praise and give thanks for the kindnesses done me.

Beloved are You, holy God, King of the universe. You do good to the sinner and have saved me from the great danger and blessed me with the fruit of my womb, a child, may he live long. [In the abundance of Your mercy shall I come into Your House, I shall bow down in Your Holy Temple in awe of You—Ps. 5:8][2]

I pray for Your compassion. Turn not Your mercy from me. Enable my husband and me to raise our child without sorrow in the Jewish faith and with fear of heaven [yirahs shomyim]. May it be Your will that the Holy Temple be rebuilt in our time so that we can bring once more the offerings [korbonos] ordained in Your holy Torah. Omayn.

## 22. The First Tooth[1]

Your wonders and hashgohcho [Providence] over all creatures are so great and numerous they cannot be recounted. When a child begins to be weaned, You give him teeth with which to chew food.

For the precious gift, for the little pearl I have found in my child's mouth, I thank You and praise Your beloved Name. May the remainder of his teeth cut through easily so that he will be able to do Your will, to eat and gather strength with which to go to *cheder* and study Your holy Torah.

Strengthen him in his resolve and help us guard him so that with these teeth he will not eat forbidden foods. May he become a good and pious person, enabling both You and men to rejoice in him. *Omayn.*

## 23. Your Mouth Is Lovely[1]

Merciful God, You have created in Your world millions of living things of all sizes and shapes. On none have You bestowed the gift of speech except man in order that he recognize his significant place in the scheme of things, that he preserve and use this gift for such important things as study of Your holy Torah, making peace between men, [and] comforting sad hearts. . . .

So that he not forget his position and speak foolishly, You surrounded the speech mechanism (the tongue) with two walls, one of bone (the teeth) and one of flesh (the lips) to remind him that the tongue is a valuable instrument signifying man's supremacy over all creation. God has entrusted in his hands all of nature. With the intelligent use of speech, he can ennoble nature; with a foolish word, he can debase it. As King Solomon says: [Death and life are in the power of the tongue—Prov. 18:21].[2]

As You have found me worthy of the pleasure of hearing his little voice as he says "Mama, Papa," please find me worthy of hearing him able to speak well and recite the holy words of "Moses has commanded us the Torah,"[3] to recite a blessing and give thanks for the food You created for nourishment.

Enable me to bring him to *cheder* and hear him learn the precious words of Your holy Torah. Help us guard his little mouth from obscenities, not to curse or lie. May he speak only words of Torah and wisdom, pleasing to God and men. *Omayn.*

## 24. A *Techinno* for Good Children

*Author's note: To be said at the end of the* Amido *after the* Y'heyu
*l'rohtzon—May the words of my mouth and the meditations of my
heart be acceptable unto Thee. . . .*

Merciful Father and King, our heart is open before You. You know
how we seek to serve You faithfully, but a man is mortal and the
time will come when our light is extinguished. Thus You have ordained that we should marry, have children, raise them to know
Torah and fear of heaven [*yirahs shomyim*], that they be faithful
servants to You. When one leaves good children behind him, one
is not regarded as having died;[1] in [the children's knowledge of]
Torah and their good deeds, parents have a large portion.

However, in these times when evil winds blow from every direction and seize them with evil thoughts to lead them astray from
the Jewish way [of life] into dark and muddied paths, it is very
hard to cultivate them in Torah and fear of heaven [*yirahs shoma-
yim*]. I pour out my prayer before Your holy throne and beg You
to guard them from evil companions. Enable them to associate
with those who desire to study Torah and perform good deeds so
as to learn from them. Open their heart to understand Your holy
Torah thoroughly and strengthen them in this. Guard them from
an evil eye, and from all weaknesses. Bless them with length of
days and years. May I be able to pay their tuition so that I and my
husband can hear them expound Torah at their *bar mitzvo* and,
in due time, lead them to the wedding canopy [*chuppo*], ultimately,
to witness good generations flowing from them together with long
life. *Omayn.*

## 25. To Ward Off the Evil Eye

Dear God, You have created the great world as well as the little
world (that is man). You created him with 248 joints [limbs], equal

to the 248 positive *mitzvos* in Your Torah; also, with 365 veins [sinews], equal to the 365 negative *mitzvos* of the Torah. One of man's organs is the eye. You require one to look upon all favorably with a good eye and not to begrudge or envy anyone for what God has given him.

The Sages asked [*Ethics* 2:13]: Which is the good way to which a man should cleave? [Rabbi Eliezer said:] a good eye.[1] Since, however, man is sinful, many have an evil eye with which to envy others. [In such an eye there] dwells a venom that can harm even unintentionally. Therefore, I implore You to protect my child from the evil eye [*ahyin ho-ro*]. As *Moshe Rabenu* [Moses our teacher] says: [For He will command his angels to guard you in all your ways–Ps. 91:11][2] so that no evil eye will befall him.

I invoke all evil eyes that harm Jews and non-Jews not to have control over [name of the person] nor to harm him/her. . . .[3] [May all these owners of the different kinds of evil eyes] have no sway over him/her. May the eternal eyes of those [guardian angels] who neither slumber nor sleep always protect the God-fearing. As King David, may he rest in peace, says [Behold, the eye of the Lord is on those who fear Him–Ps. 33:18]: the Lord of the world protects His devoted ones who fear Him so that nothing harmful may befall them. Depart, you evil eyes, from [name of the person], from his/her room, from his/her entire house, have no power over him/her neither by day nor by night, neither when awake nor asleep! May he/she be protected from all evil eyes, as the Creator protected the Jews in the wilderness from the evil eye of Balaam the wicked one. [I call you to curse my enemies and, behold, you have blessed them . . .–Num. 24:10]. [I hope for Your salvation, O Lord.–Gen. 49:18.][4] *Omayn.*

# 26. A *Techinno* for Sick Children[1]

*Author's note: To be recited when a child suffers, heaven forbid, from an illness or blisters.[2] The woman should also contribute charity.[3]*

*Ribono shel olom* [Lord of the universe], how I suffer with worry and anxiety about my little children who have been visited with illness! May it quickly be identified not as blisters, heaven forbid! I pray that the plague be quickly removed.

*Ribono shel olom*, what have the little children done? The poor things have not sinned. Dear God, remember them and let them live to study Your precious Torah. Remember that because of their *z'chus* [merit] You split the sea. Therefore, dear God, let them escape [the illness]. Let them cross over [survive]. Remove from them every unfortunate decree, compassionate and righteous One, so that they will soon enjoy the [blessing of the] merit of small children who study Your Torah each day with their teacher. May they also enjoy the merit of Abraham, who would willingly have sacrificed his son had You not sent an angel to save him. Likewise, send many good angels to save all the little children.

*Ribono shel olom*, remember the little children who refused to abandon Mordecai when Haman sought to kill the Jews. They prayed mightily with Mordecai and their prayers saved all Israel.[4]

Permit me also to benefit from the merit of the seven children who were slaughtered in their mother's arms.[5]

Dear God, let my children benefit from the merit of the deaths of those children who were cast into the Nile by Pharaoh, so that no evil or suffering will befall them.

Deal with them mercifully and don't let the accuser have any power over them, the poor little lambs, now and forever.

*Ribono shel olom*, grant them the strength and courage to study Your Torah.

Dear God, allow them to live to serve You in old age and observe Your beloved Law.

*Ribono shel olom*, You are our Father and the Father of our little children who have in no way sinned. Protect them from every ill wind. Silence every evil decree against them. Don't punish them with the sickness of blisters . . . they are innocent of sin.

Dear God, may the merit of children who died before their time serve as a guarantee that Israel will continue to learn Torah and act righteously. Remove Your anger from our beloved children and treat them with compassion.

Accept the entreaties and prayers of many tearful persons on behalf of the little children so that they will no longer know of blisters and sorrows. Enable them to live with their fathers and mothers so that we may be able to bring them to Torah, to the *chuppo* [bridal canopy], and to good deeds. May we also live to have many children, and children from them as well, in honor and in dignity. *Omayn*.

## 27. To *Cheder* the First Time (Version 1)

Dear God, thank You for the precious gift You bestowed upon me—my dear son; I am grateful I have been found worthy to bring him to *cheder* on this happy day to learn Your holy Torah. How fortunate I am to be able to appreciate this golden ornament beset with precious stones that the great King by His own hand granted us!

You gave us our Torah on Mount Sinai with great ceremony. Its light has and continues to illuminate the lives of all. And I have been found worthy to have my child begin his study of it today! This is the highest merit for me as a woman. Our Sages write in the holy Talmud: "By what do women merit?" That is, by what merit are women able to conquer the great "blood enemy" [the Evil Desire] who seeks to mislead people in both worlds [in this world and in the world to come] since they are free from [the *mitzvo* of] the study of Torah? There is no other antidote against the Evil Desire except Torah. Our Sages write that the Name, blessed be He, says "I created the Evil Desire[1] but I also created the Torah which is [*sahm chayim, Yoma* 72b], an elixir of life, a curative against it [the Evil Desire]." How may we women conquer the Evil Desire? The holy Talmud responds: By bringing our children to *cheder* to learn Torah, we thereby merit [the blessings of] Torah. Therefore, my heart is most happy today and I am grateful to You for this.

I ask of You, compassionate Father, that by virtue of Your holy Torah his body be strengthened—the more to serve You with his study of Torah. Grant him intelligence and the capacity to understand and remember what his *rebbe* [teacher] will teach him. Give him a sound religious heart so that he will go quickly and willingly to *cheder* [to learn].

Grant us an abundant livelihood so that we may be able to afford excellent *melamdim* [religious teachers] to teach him Torah and fear of heaven [*yirahs shomyim*]. Finally, grant us peace of mind so that we shall be able to listen to him and follow his progress in his studies.[2] *Omayn.*

## 28. To *Cheder* the First Time (Version 2)

. . . protect my child from the Evil Eye so that nothing harms him. May the merit for his study of Torah and the merit of all *cheder* children whose mouths are pure and free from sin help us obtain health and an honorable livelihood. May I and my husband live to see him begin the study of *Chumosh* and, later, *Gemoro,*[1] to reach the age of *bar mitzvo* when we shall be able to hear him deliver a *derosho* [exposition of Scripture and/or Talmud] of substance that will please everyone. . . . *Omayn.*

## 29. At His *Bar Mitzvo*

Compassionate, merciful Father and King, we thank You for the joy You have given us this day in that we have been found worthy of enjoying our son's *bar mitzvo*. May he live a long and healthy life filled with peace and blessing. He has put the holy signs and reminders (the phylacteries) on his hand and head, which remind one to be a Jew with hand (i.e., deed) and head (i.e., learning), with Torah and good deeds.[1]

Today he has been found worthy of having a divine, heavenly light enter his soul, the *yetzer tov* [Good Inclination], to guide him

in the proper paths ordained in Your holy Torah, to study Torah
and perform *mitzvos* and good deeds.

*Ribono shel olom* [Lord of the universe], we pray that You help
our child with his Good Inclination to overcome his *yetzer ho-ro*
[Evil Inclination], that he be a good, pious Jew according to Your
holy will, that he find favor in Your eyes as well as in the eyes of
men. May we derive pleasure [*naches*] from him in this world and
through him be found worthy of the world to come [*olom ha-bo*].

*Ribono shel olom*, just as You have dealt kindly with us and
helped us raise our son until his *bar mitzvo*, please continue Your
kindnesses and allow us to raise him and all our other children
to Torah and *yirahs shomyim* [fear of heaven] in honor and dignity.
May our happiness never be marred and may we be able to lead
him to the *chuppo* [bridal canopy] when that happy time comes.
*Omayn.*

## 30. A Contribution to the Alms Box of Rabbi Meir *Ba'al Ha-ness*[1]

*Ribono shel olom*, I give alms (money or candles) in memory of
the *tzaddik*, the great *Tanna*, Rabbi Meir *Ba'al Ha-ness*, God of Meir,
answer me![2] (These words must be repeated three times.) As You
listened to his prayer and wrought miracles and wonders for him,[3]
hear my prayer with great compassion. Bring me out of the sorrow in which I find myself. Perform miracles and wonders for me
and Your entire people Israel for the sake of the merit of the holy
*Tanna* Rabbi Meir *Ba'al Ha-ness*. (At this point one may insert a
special personal prayer as needed; for example, when a child,
heaven forbid, is ill.)

Send a *refu'o shelaymo* [complete recovery] to my child, along
with all the sick and ailing in Israel. By virtue of these alms, bring
relief to *klal Yisroel* [all Israel] as it is Your nature to do. [You sow
righteousness and cause deliverance to flourish. . . .][4] May You
foresee the acts of righteousness and cause that help to sprout
which You will bring upon us and all Israel speedily. *Omayn.*

# 31. A Prayer at the Western Wall¹

*Author's note: This prayer at the Western Wall is to be said on Friday afternoon at the time of the* Mincho *Service.*

*Ribono shel olom* [Lord of the universe], You created the entire world. Before that, You created the sacred spot of the Holy Temple together with the Foundation Stone [*Even shehseeyo*],² from which all the earth of the world originated and spread out. This Temple spot is opposite the heavenly gate through which all of the world's prayers pass. It is Mount Moriah, to which our Father Abraham brought his son, Isaac, for the *ahkaydo* [binding] . . . to sacrifice him according to Your will. You sanctified this place upon which the Holy Temple was destined to be built. To it the sinner would bring a sacrifice, confess his sin, do *teshuvo* [repent, abandon his sin], and be forgiven by You.

Because of our many transgressions, the Holy Temple was destroyed and we are no longer able to bring a sacrifice. But, in Your greatness, You are forgiving and compassionate, accepting our prayers and *teshuvos* [repentances] as though they were sacrifices and incense. As King David prayed: [Let my prayer be set forth before You as incense–Ps. 141:12]³ like that which was offered up on the altar. Thus may my prayer be acceptable. . . . Answer my requests and those of all Israel, especially at this sacred place of the Western Wall; where the *Shecheeno* is, *teshuvo* [will also be found]. . . . May the Holy Temple be rebuilt through Your help. May there once again be rejoicing at this sacred place. May we again be able to serve You wholeheartedly and joyously in the Holy Temple. The entire world shall know that You are One and there is no other. Then will the entire world come and bow down before You in the Holy Temple. As King David, may he rest in peace, said: [All flesh shall come to bow down before You–Isa. 66:23].⁴

Lord of the universe, I have come at the time of the *Mincho* sacrifice, when the Afternoon Service takes place. This is a time of compassion and I welcome the coming *Shabbos*. Grant me the additional soul [that gives added spiritual pleasure] in honor of

the *Shabbos*. Hear my prayer and all the prayers of Israel, just as
You responded to Elijah the prophet, may he rest in peace. It is
written: [And it came to pass at the time of the *Mincho* offering (in
the Sanctuary)—1 Ki. 18:36]. [. . . Elijah the prophet approached—
v. 36] the altar which he had made and said: [. . . God of Abraham,
Isaac, and Jacob, let it be known this day—v. 36] to the Jews that
You are the One God. God answered him with fire from heaven.
All the Jews beheld [the miracle] and said: [The Lord, He is God;
the Lord, He is God.—1 Ki. 18:39] and there is none other.[5]

Implant within the hearts of kings and officials, in every place
where Jews dwell, the intention to deal with them kindly and
compassionately, especially with our brethren who dwell in the
Diaspora, and contribute funds that enable us to dwell in the Holy
Land and study Torah and worship [You]. Deal with them benefi-
cently and grant them honorable life and sustenance and, finally,
bless the world with peace. *Omayn*.


## 32. Untitled

I, (name of the person), hereby contribute this coin for the welfare
of the poor of the Holy Land. May the merit of our holy Patriarchs Abraham, Isaac, and Jacob and our holy Matriarchs Sarah,
Rebecca, Rachel, and Leah stand us in good stead so that my prayer
will be found acceptable by the Name, may He be blessed. May it
be Your will, our God and God of our ancestors, that their merit
stand by me and my husband, my children, and my home. Spread
over us abundant blessing, good life and peace, sustenance and
success in our endeavors, abundance and length of days and years.
Grant complete healing to ailing Jews everywhere. May I be worthy of having scholarly sons who will busy themselves with Torah
and *mitzvos* and who will be blessed with length of days and years.
May the blessing of Abraham, Isaac, and Jacob come upon us. And
may the *mitzvo* of lighting the *Shabbos* candles strengthen us and
be our salvation. *Omayn*.

# 33. Three Gates *Techinno* by Sarah *Bas Tovim* (Version 1)[1]

## INTRODUCTION TO THE "THREE GATES *TECHINNO*"

I, Sarah *Bas Tovim*, do this for the sake of beloved God, blessed be He and blessed be His Name, and compose another beautiful *techinno* in three gates in Yiddish [*oif Teitsch*] with great love, fear, and trepidation, with contrite limbs, prayerfully, and with reliance upon the merits of our Matriarchs (Sarah, Rebecca, Rachel, and Leah). May they entreat God on my behalf. May the fact that I have been a wanderer be atonement for my sins. And may the blessed Name forgive me for having chattered in *shul* [synagogue] in my youth at the time when the beloved Torah was being read.

Master of the whole world, heed my prayer as I am about to arrange my beautiful new *techinno* with complete *kavono* [concentration] and with all my heart. Protect us from pain and suffering. Be compassionate toward Your people as You were toward our Fathers and Mothers. Remember our Father Abraham as he grasped his son, Isaac, by the throat with his left hand, the slaughterer's knife in his right, prepared to sacrifice his son out of love for You, stifling his paternal compassion. In like manner, restrain Your anger. I beseech heaven and earth and all the holy angels to entreat on behalf of my two (*sic*) *techinnos*, that they be found acceptable to become a crown for His holy Name. *Omayn.*

## GATE ONE

### CHALLO

Women were commanded to fulfill three *mitzvos* (Sabbath bread, etc.). . . . [The first of your dough you shall set apart as a gift . . .–Num. 15:30]. The meaning [*teitsch*] of the verse is that you shall set aside a first portion of your [baking] dough for the purpose of observing the commandment of the Sabbath bread, hereafter, the *mitzvo* of *challo*, by merit of which God will fill your granaries,[2] meaning that, by virtue of observing the *mitzvo* of *challo*, God, blessed be He and blessed be His Name, will bless your granaries unfailingly so that they will be full.

In former times the priest used to accept the tithe on produce [*terumo*], also the Levite received the tithe [*ma'aser*] and the poor man the poor man's tithe [*ma'aser onee*]; finally, there was also for people the second tithe [*ma'aser sheni*] (consumed by the owner in Jerusalem). But nowadays, since the Holy Temple was destroyed because of our many sins, all has been nullified except for the *mitzvo* of *challo*. Therefore, *Ribono shel olom* [Lord of the universe], we ask that You accept the *mitzvo* of *challo* and send us great blessing in our wanderings and do not let our children become estranged [from our religious tradition]. Enable my husband and me to support them by ourselves throughout a long life. May the *mitzvo* of *challo* be acceptable to You as though we were fulfilling all 613 *mitzvos* [commandments].

NIDDO

[God accepts all the inward parts—Prov. 20:22.] This means [*teitsch*] that God, blessed be He, searches all the inner chambers of the [woman's] abdomen.[3] If you keep the commandment regarding the menstrual period, when a Jewish woman removes herself from physical contact with her husband (the *mitzvo* of *niddo*), He will protect your children from the fatal illnesses of diphtheria and dropsy [edema]. . . . The meaning is that if you take care to observe constantly the *mitzvo* of *niddo*, God, blessed be He, will take care of your children and spare them from fatal illnesses. [A garden shut up is my sister, my bride . . .—Songs 4:12], meaning my sister (i.e., wife) is as a locked garden.[4]

God is proud of women who separate themselves from their husbands earlier than is required (one *onah* prior to her menstruation).[5] If she is correct in her calculation regarding her period, she must not come in [physical] contact with her husband. This rule was established as a precautionary measure for women so that they would be able to avoid violating the actual prohibition. Since the average woman is unfamiliar with the laws of menstruation, many could stumble and be misled; for this reason, we have included the law here so that they will be alerted to it. As a reward for observing the law, they will have good, religious, and wise sons. They will also receive the reward of the world to come.

May the merit of our Mother Channo protect her daughters, that they may properly observe the commandments, especially the *mitzvo* of *niddo*. May they not esteem it lightly, so that when they give birth they will not be punished and their lying-in will be quick and of short duration.

## HADLOKAS NER

In honor of God, in honor of our commandment [that is,] in honor of the beloved, holy *Shabbos* that our Lord has given us, [I pray] that I shall be able to fulfill the commandment [of lighting the Sabbath candles] properly, and that it be regarded as equal in importance to the 613 *mitzvos* of Israel. *Omayn*.

Lord of the world, may my [performance of the] *mitzvo* of candle-lighting be as acceptable as the high priest's *mitzvo* when he kindled lights in the Holy Temple, as it is written: [Your word is a light (candle) for my feet and a light for my path—Ps. 119:105]. This means [*teitsch*]: May Your words [teachings] illuminate the way for my feet so that they will proceed along life's way [successfully]; may the *mitzvo* of my candlelighting be acceptable [to You] so that my children's eyes will be illuminated by the Torah.

I pray also that beloved God, blessed be He, will accept favorably my *mitzvo* of candlelighting as was the olive oil that burned continuously in the Holy Temple.

May the merit of the beloved *Shabbos* candles protect us as the beloved *Shabbos* protected Adam from a quick death.[6] May our merit of the candles that we have lit protect our children's candles [of life], that they may be illumined in the [study of] Torah. May their candles illuminate the heavens and may our performance of the commandments be as acceptable as the [performance by] our Forefathers and Mothers and the holy tribes [of Israel]. May we be as pure as a newborn child, fresh out of its mother's womb. *Omayn*.

## GATE TWO

PRAYER FOR THE NEW MONTH [*ROSH CHODESH BENSHEN*]

Look down upon Your holy congregation as they stand in prayer with contrite hearts wrapped in emotional and spiritual intensity. Heed their plea. Great is Your loving-kindness though our sins cover us like a cloud. Scatter them, strengthen and blend Your mercy with Your Thirteen Attributes. Cause them to shine brightly and accept our prayers together with those of our ancestors on the threshold of the New Month [*erev Rosh Chodesh*]. May they be as a crown for You, O King of kings, the Holy One, blessed be He.

Arise, our ancestors, from your graves and go to the Throne of Compassion to plead for us. Arise, stand up, Abraham, before God and say to Him: "Remember the covenant of the parts [*bris bayn ha-b'sorim*—Gen. 15:9-21], that my children would be as many as the stars in the sky [Gen. 15:5]. Dear God, have mercy upon the Children of Israel. When they have sinned and should be punished by fire,[7] remember that I willingly allowed myself to be cast into the fiery furnace[8] for the sake of Your holy Name, to die for *kiddush ha-Shaym* [Sanctification of the Name]."

Arise, stand up, Isaac, you who were bound upon the altar, and plead for us: "Remember that I would have allowed myself to be slaughtered upon the altar. May it be considered as a merit [*z'chus*] for my children [descendants] who deserve execution."

Arise, stand up, Jacob, and plead your case (on our behalf) before God and say: "I sacrificed myself for them.[9] If they sinned, remember my pain and sorrows. I had to leave my father's house and endure the heat of day and cold of night."

Arise, stand up *Moshe Rabenu* [Moses our teacher], and plead with God. They cannot bear [the suffering]. I beg of you, truthful prophet, who defended the Israelites in the wilderness. When they sinned, you averted God's burning wrath so that they would not be destroyed. Arise now and beg Him not to destroy your people whom you brought out of Egypt with many wonders before the

eyes of the nations and say: "Remember, dear God, that I went
ahead of them [to see to it that] no enemy strike and destroy them.
Behold them, God, and remember the vine You planted with Your
hands."

Arise, stand up, King Messiah, and cry out: "You have broken
their walls and allowed plunderers to destroy the [once strong]
state. The plunderers went unpunished and Your throne was cast
down to earth. Gladly would I suffer all to atone for Israel's sins.
Do not turn away from their wretchedness, and may Your rule
extend over all the world. . . .

"Man's life and death are in Your hands. . . . You, beloved
God, raise up man or cast him down when he fails to go in the
right path. You bring him pain and healing. In Your relationship
with man, guide Yourself by the Thirteen Attributes" [of mercy].[10]

May it be Thy will, O Lord our God and God of our Fathers, to
renew unto us this coming month for good and for blessing [*Yehhe
rohtzone milfonehcho*, etc.][11] and grant us long life, a life of peace,
of good, of blessing, of good sustenance with happiness [*naches*]
and without sorrow, of bodily health, that our bodies be strengthened, a life in which there is fear of Heaven and dread of sin, and
our children continue to believe in God, blessed be He, to walk
in His paths, a life free from shame and reproach so that I shall
not be shamed, neither in this world nor in the world-to-come
before the court on high. Grant us a life of prosperity and honor,
that we may be able to raise our children in the study of Torah, to
bring them under the *chuppo* [bridal canopy] and perform *ma'asim
tovim* [good deeds]. As King David, may he rest in peace, prayed
to the Lord of the universe: "Let me die with dignity and not as a
pauper." Grant us a life in which there will be love of Torah and
fear of Heaven, in which my children will believe in God, blessed
be He, as did Jacob's children.

As he lay on his deathbed, he wanted to reveal to them the final
redemption. The spirit of prophecy, however, left him and he was
greatly disturbed. He said: "Perhaps, heaven forbid, there is some
[moral] blemish among my children, or a wicked one. . . ." To
which they all responded: "Hear, O Israel: the Lord is our God,

the Lord is one!" [*Shema Yisroel*] Why did they call him Israel? His name was Jacob. Because he went in the ways of Torah and good deeds; therefore, he was called Israel. Grant us a life in which the desires of our heart shall be fulfilled for good. *Omayn selo.* *Ribono shel olom* [Lord of the entire world], I pray to You as Queen Esther did. Spread Your mercies over me as You have over the world You created.

In Paradise [*Gan Ayden*] there exist six chambers in which dwell thousands of righteous women who never endured the sufferings of Hell [*Gayhenom*]. There [in Paradise] is Bithia, daughter of Pharaoh. There, too, is a curtain ready to be used by her to reproduce a picture of *Moshe Rabenu* [Moses our teacher]. She bows and says: "How fortunate am I to have drawn such a luminary [as Moses] from the [Nile's] water, O beloved light!"

Serach, daughter of Asher,[12] is like a queen. Three times daily she calls out: "Behold, here comes the form of Joseph the Righteous One!" She bows and says: "How fortunate I am that I merited being able to tell my grandfather (Jacob) that my uncle (Joseph) still lives. In the uppermost chamber he studies [Torah]."

In a third chamber is our Mother Yocheved, mother of Moses our teacher, with many [women] praising God, blessed be He, thrice daily and [they] recite the Song of the Sea with great happiness. There is Miriam the prophetess with drum in hand, saying the verse alone. Many holy angels with her praise the Name, may He be blessed.

In a fourth chamber sits Deborah the prophetess with many thousands of women who praise the Name, may He be blessed, and sing the Song [*Shiro*, Moses' Song at the Red Sea]. The chambers of the Matriarchs are indescribable. No one is admitted. How great is the pleasure, dear women, when the souls are together in Paradise! What pleasure there is! Therefore do I urge you to praise God, blessed be He, with great *kavono* [concentration] and with prayer so that you will be found worthy to be in the presence of our Matriarchs.

Lord of the world, hear my outcry and answer me. Free us this year, for we are as a firstling groaning with pain, like fatherless orphans, like motherless infants. I hope unto the living God, blessed be He, that He will accept my prayer as He accepts all the prayers of those with a heavy and broken heart because of the merit of Abraham, Isaac, and Jacob. May those who died before their time intercede for us. May the merciful angels also plead for us. When You judge us, do so with compassion and not, heaven forbid, in anger. May my hope not be turned aside from the presence of the Lord of hosts. You see into all the chambers [of the heart] and examine the thoughts in all hearts. Open, O windows of heaven, allow the merciful angels to bring my prayers before the Name, may He be blessed. My merciful angel will surely be an advocate [*maylitz*] and bring me favor and mercy [*chayn v'chesed*] from the Name, may He be blessed. May the favor of the righteous Joseph and Queen Esther be granted me this day. How good for the one whose faith is in the Name, blessed be He, for He shames no one who trusts in Him.

*Ribono shel olom* [Lord of the universe], with the same hands with which You created the world, spread Your help over us. May the God who delivered Abraham from the furnace not cast evil upon our children. May He who saved Isaac from being sacrificed upon the altar bless our children fully. May He who saved Jacob from his brother and later from Laban enable us to bless our children with our own hands at the *chuppo* [bridal canopy].

In the time-to-come[13] the [Holy] Presence [*Shecheeno*] will return[14] to the gate from which She has departed. Standing on the Mount of Olives opposite that gate, we shall see that gate exactly as in the verse [And His feet shall stand in that day upon the Mount of Olives . . . –Zech. 14:4]. [ . . . eye to eye they shall see the Lord returning to Zion–Isa. 52:8] by way of that same gate. They will stand on that very same holy mountain and see with their own eyes as God returns to Zion and She [the *Shecheeno*] will become great. And Jerusalem will be faithful. The Messiah will come quickly, and soon. We shall see and hear miracles. We shall cry out to heaven for the Messiah to prepare himself. He will be crowned with the sacred crown. He will arise!

May I, Sarah, be permitted to behold the joy of the Patriarchs and Matriarchs when that precious time arrives. The holy *Zohar* writes that Redemption depends only upon repentance and prayer [teshuvo and tefillo] accompanied by tears that come from the heart. Therefore do I implore you [women] that you pray with great kavono [intention] and fear of Heaven [yirahs shomyim]. For prayer without kavono is like a body without neshomo [soul].

I pray to dear God that my soul return without fear to that place whence it came, beneath the Throne of Glory [keesay ha-kovode]. And may the Messiah come quickly in our time. Omayn, selo.

## GATE THREE

### Prayer on Yom Kippur

Ribono shel olom [Lord of the universe], on this day You judge the world with justice. Remember on this day that I have abandoned rebelliousness; incline the scales in my favor. You concern Yourself with the spilled blood of innocents. May it be granted me on this day to overcome the accuser and silence him with my tefillo [prayer].[15] Do not allow my light to be extinguished before its time. As You have written: You forgive sins during the Ten Days of Repentance (between Rosh Ha-shono and Yom Kippur). During this time, You are favorably inclined to our fervent tears and pleas, since You want to forgive the transgressions we have committed. At this time, you have much compassion for us. Therefore, we pray not to be equated with evil; remember not our misdeeds. Permit us to live happily in this world, for You do forgive one's waywardness.

On this day,[16] do not remember my headstrong youth.

On this day, when You judge me, may Your burning wrath be withheld.

On this day, accept my confession with which I beseech You tearfully and forgive me.

On this day, may I have several speakers on my behalf for life and health.

On this day, dear God, open for me the gate of forgiveness and mercy.

On this day, forgiveness is prepared for man.

On this day, the remission of sins is prepared.

On this day, may there be release from sins I have committed. On this day, beloved God, do I repent. May You act mercifully.

On this day, *Ribono shel olom* [Lord of the universe] accept the menses[17] that I have discharged as substitute for the blood and suet[18] sprinkled on the altar.

On this day, deal justly with me.

On this day, You examine every heart.

On this day, *Ribono shel olom*, may I find favor in Your eyes; I come with bitter heart because of the sins I have committed and beg forgiveness.

On this day, dear God, we afflict[19] ourselves until evening as You have commanded us. May my prayer not be locked out.[20]

On this day, *Ribono shel olom*, may the full account (of my deeds) be brought before You and may my upright intercessors [*melitzim*] rebut those misdeeds I committed during the year. Inscribe me in the Book of Life [*Sefer ha-chayim*] together with my husband and children.

On this day, may my husband's and children's (evil) decree [*g'zar din*] be torn up.

On this day, we cry out in anguish and great fear. Dear God, in ancient times the High Priest bore the sins we committed, but since then we no longer have a High Priest to whom we can speak.[21]

Dear God, remember that we are but flesh and blood, only what the Evil Inclination [*yetzer ho-ro*], in misleading, has made of us. I pray for Your mercy. Of what avail will my (shed) blood (my death) be to You? Do not remove me from this world before my time, so that I may be able to keep all Your *mitzvos* properly. Since we sorrow on this day, enable us to be happy the rest of the year.

On this day, do for me as You did for us in Balaam's time: his intended curse became a blessing.

On this day, grant us Your divine help. *Omayn, selo.*

# 34. The Three Gates *Techinno* (Version 2)[1]

Dr. Alfes: This *techinno* is based on the three *mitzvos* given specifically to women, the acronym of which is *channo*, and stands for *challo, niddo, hadloko.* Our Mother Channo besought God to grant her a son because of the merit of having observed the three *mitzvos* carefully as enjoined by the Torah.[2] The Name, blessed be He, heard her prayer and granted her a son, the prophet Samuel, who was as important as Moses and Aaron together. As King David says, [Moses and Aaron are among His priests, and Samuel among them who call upon His name . . . —Ps. 99:6].[3] May it be so for the woman who carefully observes the three *mitzvos.* God grant her good children and a pleasant disposition. *Omayn.*

Sarah: I do this for the sake of the living, eternal God, blessed be He, and compose this beautiful "Three Gates *Techinno*" with abounding friendship for our dear sisters, the children of Abraham, Isaac, and Jacob, of Sarah, Rebecca, Rachel, and Leah, and with great fear of the Name, blessed be He, along with a mighty plea that He soon take pity on me and all Israel [*klal Yisroel*], so that we shall not long need to endure our wanderings in *golus* [exile].

May He answer us soon, as He answered our Father Jacob who, because of his brother Esau's anger, had to leave the holy land and not see his parents for twenty-two years.

May He answer us for the sake of King David's *z'chus* [merit] who, from the time that the prophet Samuel anointed him until he ascended the throne (eighteen years later), wandered about in the wilderness, pursued by King Saul. He (David) was deathly afraid for, as they say, "When chased by a king, the world's a small thing."

May David's *z'chus* [merit] protect us so that, having wandered about in exile in deathly fear for eighteen hundred years, the Creator will return us quickly to our land and to our own rulers. *Omayn.*

Before we write the *techinno* on taking *challo,* we deem it necessary to consider what makes taking *challo* such an important *mitzvo* that all the holy books make a to-do about it.

The *midrash* tells us that the letter *bays* of the word *b'rayshis* really stands for [*beeshvil b'rayshis*], for three things that are called *rayshis* and for which God created the world. For example, the Torah is referred to as "the *beginning* of His way" [*rayshis darko—*

Prov. 8:22].[4] Jews are referred to as "The *first* fruits of His harvest" [*rayshis t'vu'ohso*—Jer. 2:3]; and the *mitzvo* of taking *challo* is referred to as "the *first* yield of your dough you shall set aside . . ." [*rayshis ahreesosaychem tohreemu*—Num. 15:20]. Thus, we see that the taking of *challo* is one of the three things for the sake of which God created the world. Still, what is so significant about it? Simply to recite a blessing over a bit of dough and throw it into a hot oven? In the explanation of it we shall also understand the importance of *niddo* and *hahdlohkas ha-ner*.

We mentioned that the prophet Jeremiah refers to Jews as [*rayshis t'vu'ohso*], the first and best of all the fruits in God's world (the prime, the best merchandise). Our ancestors recognized God as the Creator at a time when the world was still half wild. Our Father Abraham [*Avrohom Oveenu*] was the first who made known to all the existence of the Creator.

The *midrash* likens the story of Abraham to that of a traveler wandering about lost on a dark night. In the distance, he sees a light. Walking toward the light, he arrives at a house. He opens the door and enters into a bright light. It is a splendid house. The ceiling is painted dark blue and many little gas flames are set therein. In the middle of the ceiling are two large, bright flames. The windows are covered with curtains on the inside and there are shutters outside. The floors are covered with costly carpets and in the corners stand large vases. About the house on the outside are a garden, trees, a pond, and a large variety of birds and animals. The house is well stocked with various necessities and it is evident the owner is a rich person who has planned everything intelligently. The owner, however, is nowhere to be seen. The traveler sees only the children playing with dolls and puppets, calling the dolls "Mama" and the puppets "Papa."

He asks them where the master of the house is, but they are unable to answer. The traveler wonders where he is. Is it possible that such a splendid house is run without a master? A father certainly wouldn't abandon his children.

As he wanders about deep in thought, a noble-looking count appears suddenly and informs him: "I am master of all you behold. With my own hands have I built, planted and illuminated—all by myself. And these are my children whom I wish to keep forever happy, if only they will know how to conduct themselves [in life]."

The traveler is surprised at the count's ability to have carried out single-handedly such a project replete with all the conveniences. Then he realizes how upright and compassionate the count is and he is deeply impressed. Turning to the children, the traveler urges them to abandon their dolls and puppets and apply themselves to appreciation of their father's great wisdom. They ought diligently to apply themselves to follow his counsel, which is only for their own happiness. All their actions ought to reflect the fact that they are descended from a wise and noble parent.

The traveler is none other than our Father Abraham, who wandered about aimlessly when his father Terach was an idol worshiper at a time when idol worshiping predominated and Abraham at first did not find the right way. He considered the sun and then the moon as divinities. His sound mind, however, prevented him from believing in them. He labored long and hard to reach the truth about the creation of the world, as well as the little world that is man; man, who has within his grasp the forces of all nature. For what purpose had man been created? Is it possible he was destined to be animal-like, to eat and drink and live a daily existence; that these days are like calendar leaves we tear off once the day has passed without a moment's thought?

If this be so, he is more unfortunate than the domestic beast. The beast receives its food without effort on its part, gives birth, and raises its young without pain and suffering, without anxiety and concern for what tomorrow may bring.

It is the opposite with regard to man. These thoughts allowed Father Abraham no peace. He forgot to eat and drink, devoting all his energies to the search for the truth. God beheld his pure heart, his efforts in his search for the truth, and caused a ray of truth to enter him.

The more he thought, the more he began to appreciate the universal order and arrangement. He saw the two electric flames illuminating the world, the sun and the moon. He regarded the stars scattered about in the dark heavens of night. They and the night were a buffer of insulation against the great luminaries. The air was fragrant everywhere, the earth covered with all sorts of growing things. Many kinds of metals were in the ground. Every kind of creation had its natural intelligence with which to survive. The oceans abounded with creatures, and the clouds each had their exact weight and correct measure of rain.

Abraham was a great philosopher. How is it possible, he wondered, that such a world in which everything has been so artfully wrought, in such a world there can be no one who has arranged and run it? It is impossible to believe that. But mankind seems not to understand this. They busy themselves with dolls and puppets (with idolatry).

While Abraham was absorbed in such profound thoughts, God revealed Himself to him through prophecy, saying: "I am the Lord,[5] the creator and master of the world, and all men are my children whom I created with a great purpose in mind."

At that moment, Abraham recognized his Creator and knew happiness. Worldly pleasures are nothing compared to that moment when man sheds his physical garment, as it were, and clings to God. He experiences ecstasy. From that moment on, he [Abraham] began to divest himself as much as possible of the coarse materialism that places one on a par with domestic animals. He sought to imitate the ways of God, the ultimate source of righteousness [chesed], by acting rightly with all men until his name became synonymous with chesed [chesed l'Avrohom—Mic. 7:20],[6] not merely in the sense of chesed, not of being helpful to others materially and physically but, above all, helping them spiritually to acknowledge the Name of the Lord and Master, to acknowledge Him as the one who has built the splendid palace (the world).

The teachings that he gave to the world cost him good and plenty. Because they didn't appeal to Nimrod and his followers, he was severely persecuted and eventually thrown into the limekiln. Nevertheless, he held fast to his beliefs and never wearied in his wandering about the world to spread the noble ideal; God helped him illuminate a large part of the world and his enemies were overcome.

Jeremiah says in God's name: [I remember in your favor the *chesed*, the devotion of your youth—Jer. 2:2] when Judaism at the same time began to develop, your Father Abraham dealt with Me in *chesed*, in devotion, and made Me known in the world. I remember also your love as a bride [ . . . your love as a bride—Jer. 2:2], when Abraham's descendants concluded a covenant with God to cast off the abominations of Egypt and serve only the God of Abraham and receive the Torah on Mount Sinai [How you followed Me in the wilderness . . . —Jer. 2:3]. I remember also your faithfulness and your submission to Me, casting off such a fruitful land as Egypt [ . . . like the garden of the Lord, like the land of Egypt . . . —Gen. 13:10] and following Me in the wasteland [in an unsown land—Jer. 2:2]. [Israel is holy to the Lord . . .—Jer. 2:3]: Because of this [that you followed Him into the wilderness] you shall be as holy to Me as your Father Abraham, who had the first understanding of what true pleasure is, content to teach men the true way. So shall you (the entire nation of Israel) teach the nations the true way of life and earn the reputation of sanctity that began with your Father Abraham.

The three *mitzvos* of women must be understood in terms of this historical background. The woman is *ahkehress ha-byiss* [mistress of the Jewish home]. As the Talmud says: "I designated you the first [Israel was holiness unto the Lord, *first* fruits of his increase—Jer. 2:3]: wherefore I commanded you concerning the *first* [the first portion of the dough, which is *challo*—Num. 15:20]"[7] You are the crown of My world. By your deeds shall you illumine the world and instruct mankind. How is it possible for Jews to attain such a lofty status as teacher of the world and transform it into God's garden [ . . . the vineyard of the Lord of hosts . . . —Isa. 5:7]?[8] The daily struggle for bread occupies the major portion of one's time. As for the little remaining time, there's always the *yetzer ho-ro* [Evil Inclination] to reckon with. But who says we have to spend the little time left in theater-going and card-playing? With such behavior, how can we possibly be a light to the world?

This is why God set aside the tribe of Levi, which has no portion in the Land of Israel, and divided its portion among the remaining eleven tribes with the understanding that they would sustain the Levites, free them from material cares, and enable them to study Torah and engage in good deeds. In return for this, the Levite who has studied Torah all his life will teach the entire nation so that it will observe the Torah, elevate itself to the service of God, and avoid the vanities of the nations of the world.

We have been instructed to give the first of all our yields to the priest [kohayn].[9] When I am ready to pour the grain into the bin in the storeroom, I must give the first of it (the tithe on the produce) to the priest and Levite so that the priest's wife and Levite's wife will grind it and bake it for the young priests and Levites studying in the academies [yeshivos] . . . so that they may study Torah and perform good deeds undisturbed by mundane necessities, thereby enabling the entire people to become [a kingdom of priests and a holy nation—Exod. 19:6], that all the nations will be guided by their light to recognize the Creator, Lord of the world.

Since we and the priests are today [ritually] unclean and they [the priests] may not eat the challo, we take only an olive-sized portion and consign it to the flames in order that the mitzvo of taking challo be not forgotten among us. [We also do it to serve as a reminder] to fulfill the mitzvo through other means such as support of [the study of] Torah and strengthening the yeshivos. . . .

Now, dear sisters, consider how the mitzvo of taking challo imparts to the Jewish daughter loyalty to her religion. A small voice resonates gently in her ear as a reminder: Dear soul, consider how precious must that teacher be who instructs you in God's way, that you remember when kneading the dough to set aside the first piece for him and only then for yourself! This holy thought influences the Jewish woman so much that she is motivated constantly to cultivate the flavor of the beloved Torah in her children, to kindle in them the Torah's flame, which, in turn, is related to the mitzvo of candlelighting [licht-benshen].

Our Sages say: ["How do women earn merit?"][10] What is the

chief merit of women that they bring the brightness of the Torah
to their husbands and children?

That excellent philosopher, author of *Bechinas Olom*,[11] writes
that a man with Torah is a divine light in the world. The body is
the braided wick, the soul is the oil, and the Torah is the spark.
When the spark comes in contact with the lamp, the Jewish home
is suffused with illumination, hopefully both in this world and in
the world-to-come. Who alone is able to bring this about? Only
the woman who is truly the mistress of her house, a helpmate when
[her husband] returns home from work. She brings food, enables
him to rest a bit, and then offers him spiritual food, gently urg-
ing: "Take a book in hand, my dear husband, study a bit, listen to
what the children have learned in *cheder* today."

With kind words, the influence of a wife upon her husband is
limitless. As the wise man says [A capable woman is a crown for
her husband—Prov. 12:4, NJPS trans.]: A wise, God-fearing wife is
a crown for her husband. [Wisdom has built her house—Prov. 9:1.]
The wise wife builds up her house and kindles the divine light.
This is the *Shabbos* light that symbolizes eternity [*yom shehkulo
Shabbos*], a day that is completely *Shabbos*.[12] Whoever is familiar
with our history knows how much wives have brought the divine
illumination into the House of Israel.

The wise and beautiful Rachel, daughter of the Jewish million-
aire [*Kalbo Shehvuo*], caused a great star to shine, the *Tanna* Rabbi
Akivo, along with 24,000 smaller stars, in the Jewish heavens.[13]

In our Mother Sarah's house the *Shabbos* illumination of the
Torah never departed from one *Shabbos* to the next. Women
should encourage their husbands on *Shabbos* (after one has rested
from weekday labors) to study. This is the spiritual illumination
that carried over from one *Shabbos* to the next [in Mother Sarah's
house].

Not in vain did a famous Sage liken the Torah to a capable
woman [traditionally translated as a woman of valor], for such a
woman is priceless. This is also the meaning and intent of our
Sages when they say [The soul which I have placed in you is called
a lamp . . . ].[14] As the verse says: [The soul of a man is the lamp

of the Lord—Prov. 20:27]. A lamp needs a wick. That is to say, the soul needs a body and, in order for it to shine, it must have a flame. A lamp without a flame is dark. It is the wife's duty to light the *Shabbos* candles so that the home will shine. The wife observes this by bringing the light of Torah into her husband's lamp and into those of her children. Where husband and children are devoid of Torah, their lamp is without flame. . . .

## 35. *Techinno* before Taking *Challo*[1]

Beloved Father and great King, I come now with happiness and joy to fulfill the *mitzvo* that You have decreed for us in Your holy Torah [The first fruit of your dough you shall set apart as a gift . . .—Num. 15:20], to set aside *challo* from our dough. In the old days, when we lived in our land, we set aside a goodly portion of dough and baked it for the young priests who studied in the *yeshivos* [sic]. Today, however, since we are unclean [*tohmay*] and the priests are prohibited from eating it, we set aside a small olive-sized portion (and burn it). We do this to remember the *mitzvo* of *challo* (which teaches us) to support *yeshivos*, so that great scholars [*talmeday chachomim*] and geniuses [*geonim*] in Torah and good deeds will be produced by them [by the *yeshivos*].

May the merit [of support for *yeshivos*], compassionate Father, persuade You to send Your blessing wherever we may be. Bless the labor of our hands and bless all our endeavors.

May our children not be scattered far from home so that we shall be able to feed and sustain them.

May the *mitzvo* of taking *challo* be reckoned before You, as I have consciously fulfilled it, along with all the other *mitzvos*. *Omayn*.

[The blessing is now recited, followed by a Hebrew passage found in the traditional *Siddur* at the end of the *Amidah* prayer in the Morning Service:] May it be thy will, O Lord our God and God of our fathers, that our Holy Temple be restored [in Jerusalem] quickly and in our time, and grant us our portion [among those

who devote themselves to] Your Torah. May we be able to worship You there [in the Holy Temple] in awe as in the days of old,
in ancient times.

## 36. The *Mitzvo* of Candlelighting (*Licht-Benshen*)[1]

1. It is a *mitzvo* to light at least two candles for the *Shabbos*,
one because of [*Observe* the Sabbath Day to keep it holy—Deut.
5:12], that is, illuminate the mind (with understanding) so that
we know what we should not do on the *Shabbos* and avoid doing
it; the other because of [*Remember* the Sabbath Day to keep it holy—
Exod. 20:8], that is, illuminate the mind (with understanding) so
that we know what the holy *Shabbos* means and know what to do
in order to maintain it.

2. On Friday, at least ten minutes before sundown, light the
candles and recite the blessing. It is essential that the husband
ready the lamps and set up the candlesticks. Before the first
*Shabbos* of her lying-in she should say to her husband: "Be my
emissary [*shohlee'ach*], light the candles and recite the blessing."
In so doing, she becomes a partner and shares in (the reward of)
the *mitzvo*.

3. It is a *mitzvo* to wash oneself and dress in festive clothes
before a candlelighting. However, in the event that it is late, light
the candles and say the blessing and then attend to your person.[2]

If it happens to be a moment before sundown and the husband
sees his wife has not yet returned home,[3] he should light the
candles himself and recite the blessing. If, upon arriving home,
she is displeased with him for having lit her candles and taken
her *mitzvo*, let him gently explain to her that she would have in
any event been unable to earn the reward of the *mitzvo* because
of her tardiness. On the contrary, it would have been a transgression amounting to *chillul Shabbos* [profaning, desecrating the Sab-
bath]. When spoken to thus with kind words and quietly, an

understanding woman will calm herself and remember in the future to make every effort not to arrive home late.

## 37. Sabbath Candle Blessing (Version 1)

Our God and God of our fathers. . . . May it be Your will that I be remembered for good. . . . Remember Your servant . . . listen to my prayer as You listened to and accepted the prayer of our Mother Channo, may she rest in peace. She had been barren, but You destined her for good, pious children; from her would be born the righteous prophet Samuel, a man of the quality of Moses or Aaron. As it is written: [Moses and Aaron were among His priests and Samuel among those who invoke His Name—Ps. 99:6].[1]

Regard my prayer favorably, mercifully, and with good will by virtue of the merit of the three holy *mitzvos* You have bidden us women to observe, namely *niddo*,[2] *challo*,[3] and *hahdlohkas ha-ner* [candlelighting], and which I have observed. May they be advocates before Your Throne of Glory so that through them I may have good, pious children who will be [Jewish] scholars. Open their hearts to understand the secrets of Your Torah and learn for the sake of Your holy Name. May they be fresh and healthy and whole in all their limbs, without blemish in the entire body. May they be neither too tall nor too short, neither too pale nor too dark, neither overly clever nor foolish. May they be as intelligent as necessary. May they find favor in Your eyes and impress others favorably. May I and my husband be worthy of raising them with honor, riches, and long life, and may none of them die in our lifetime.

May we receive an honorable livelihood from Your faithful, abundant hand and not from a human hand so that we may be able to perform benevolent acts and give alms. May we be worthy of seeing our children and grandchildren studying Torah and busy with good deeds. . . . *Omayn*.

## 38. Sabbath Candle Blessing
## (Special for America) (Version 2)

I beg of You, merciful God, heed the prayer of one who stands before the holy candles. Accept my prayer for the sake of the merit of the (*Shabbos*) candle blessing that I have just done [and do not dismiss us empty-handed from Your presence].[1]

Almighty God, You have given us, Your people Israel, the present of the holy *Shabbos*, guarded in Your treasury since the [six days of creation]. You have also given us the holy festivals [*yomim tovim*] and cautioned us not to perform any labor on those days; also, to enhance them with good foods and fine dress and avoid weekday conversations. I beg of You, *Ribono shel olom*, if I have somehow failed to observe something properly in connection with Your *Shabbosim* and *yomim tovim*, forgive me and do not allow it to prevent the angels from bringing my prayer before Your holy Throne of Glory.

[Because of our sins we were exiled from our land . . .[2]] where we dwelt in peace and tranquillity, each one [beneath his own vine and fig tree[3]], and were able to observe Your *Shabbosim* and festivals in all their detail as well as all the *mitzvos* of the Torah.

Today we are in exile, where the trouble of making a living, the worry for a livelihood, is great. Circumstances are often such that we cannot keep the *Shabbos* and *yom tov* according to the *halocho* [Law]. Kind Father in heaven, it is almost two thousand years that we have been wandering, driven from land to land without rest. We have always carried Your holy Torah with us; wherever we have been, it has also been with us.

The persecutions we have endured in other lands have driven us here to America, a refuge for the persecuted and suffering. Making a living here is very hard and [because of our many sins] Jewish children have no choice but to desecrate the *Shabbos* and *yom tov*. I accuse no one, heaven forbid, of doing this simply to anger You, to blaspheme Your holy Name. But time and circumstances have brought this about. They do it first out of need and later out of habit, as the holy *Gemoro* says: When a person transgresses once and then again, it appears to him almost as something permitted.

I beg of You, God of Abraham, Isaac, and Jacob, guard and protect me, my husband, and children from *chillul Shabbos* [desecration of the Sabbath] and *yom tov*. Permit us to gain our *parnoso* [livelihood] easily and without sorrow, without transgression, so that because of the need for a livelihood we shall not be compelled to profane the *Shabbos* or *yom tov* and be able to rest on the holy days and serve You wholeheartedly.

Help me, Your servant, see to it that my husband and children are never absent from the *Shabbos* or holy day table. May Your holy days never be disturbed. May the angels of peace, the ministering angels, the angels of the Exalted One, who come each Friday evening into every Jewish home, not be shamed.[4] May they find a properly prepared *Shabbos* in the home and always bless us with [May it be thus on the coming *Shabbos*]; may it be the will of God that the coming *Shabbos* shall be likewise. May Your holy angels who come on each holy day remain in my house and not, heaven forbid, go away shamed. Protect us, *Gottenyu*, with Your great loving-kindness [and lead us not into temptation nor into disgrace[5]]; do not lead me, my husband, and children to the temptation of *Shabbos* and holy day desecration so that we be not shamed [in the eyes of God and man]. Grant also to all Jewish children an abundant livelihood so that they will not have to diminish Your holy days and we shall all merit the blessing of a [day that will be entirely *Shabbos* and rest].[6] *Omayn*.

## 39. After Lighting Sabbath Candles (Version 1)

*Ribono shel olom* [Lord of the universe], I praise and thank Your beloved Name for having been found worthy to perform the great *mitzvo* You have bestowed upon us women . . . to bless the candles on Friday before sunset.

May Your mercy illuminate my eyes to perform this *mitzvo* for many years. Protect me so that I shall never be late and light candles after sunset, thereby committing the greatest transgression of *chillul Shabbos* [profaning the Sabbath]. It is a most important precept of the Torah, for the *Shabbos* is the [spiritual] heart of Judaism.

As a reward for my faithfulness in fulfilling this *mitzvo*, I hope and pray that the children You have given me, and in Your kindness may yet give me, will never profane the *Shabbos*. May my life not be darkened through them in the world-to-come. May the light of the Torah illuminate their eyes so that they never stumble through transgressions. As King David says [Your words are a light for my feet—Ps. 119:105a]: Your Torah illuminates my step so that no transgression can cling to me [it is a light for my path—Ps. 119:105b]; it illuminates my entire way of life.

Because I kept the beloved holy *Shabbos* in its proper time with honor and caused it to shine with beautiful candles, bless me with children who will be scholars [*talme-day chachomim*] and luminaries for all Israel, that I may have *naches* [pleasure] and *kovode* [honor] in both worlds. *Omayn.*

## 40. After Lighting Sabbath Candles (Version 2)

You are my light and salvation [Ps. 27:1], great God. I have honored the holy *Shabbos* with my candlelighting [*licht-benshen*] at the proper time and observed the *mitzvo* of setting aside a portion of the *challo* [The fruit of your dough you shall set apart as a gift . . . —Num. 15:20] as is proper. I have also observed the cleanliness that we women are required to observe. By virtue of these acts, I pray You correct the damage that Mother Eve did for, through her, the dough of the world [as it were] was made unclean [*tohmay*].

(The Creator mixed earth with water like dough and, as it were, set aside a portion of *challo* from which the first man [*ohdom rishon*] was created. He admitted him to *Gan Ayden* [the Garden of Eden] to serve the holy Name in sanctity and purity. But, through her [Eve], he was driven out of the Garden of Eden, extinguishing his light and spilling his blood, for he was condemned to mortality. And we were condemned to suffer in pregnancy, in childbirth, and in raising children.)

Therefore do I pray for Your compassion. May the merit of the observance of the three *mitzvos* [of *challo*,[1] *niddo*,[2] and candle-lighting] serve to restore that which was damaged by sin.

In the holy *Gemoro* [*Shabbat* 31b] it is written that a Galilean sage taught Rav Hisda: The Holy One blessed be He says: "Israel was holiness to the Lord, the *first* fruits of his harvest" [*rayshis tehvu'osee*—Jer. 2:13]; therefore, I gave you the *mitzvo* of *challo*, which is called "the *first* of your dough" [*rayshis ahreesosaychem*— Num. 15:20].[3]

Since I have given man a *rehvee'iss* of blood,[4] I have therefore given you the *mitzvo* of removing yourself from the blood of a menstruant [*dahm niddo*] (so that you will be able to protect your *rehvee'iss* of blood from contamination).

The soul is referred to as a candle [*ner ha-Shaym nishmas odom*— Prov. 20:27]; "the spirit of man is the lamp of the Lord." I have therefore given you the *mitzvo* of the *Shabbos* candle [*ner Shabbos*].[5] The *Shabbos* candle [*licht*] will illuminate your souls with faith in the renewal of the world [*chiddush ho-olom*], which is the meaning of *Shabbos*. If you keep and observe this *mitzvo* as one should, everything will be in order. Your name [Israel] will be great in the world [i.e., respected]. For no nation or language can lay claim to such sanctified family life.

If not, heaven forbid [*chohleelo*], I shall reduce your *rehvee'iss* of blood and your [collective] light (the soul) will be extinguished. Your great name will become as nothing. Which is why the three *mitzvos* were given to us women to be properly observed, to correct the wrong so that the world will be restored to its proper function to serve as a Garden of Eden for man and achieve once more life everlasting, eventually reaching that happy time when we shall enjoy a "day which will be completely a *Shabbos*."[6]

Just as, until today, I have observed the three *mitzvos*, so may You grant light to my eyes and enable me to live a hundred years, I and my daughters and my daughters-in-law. By merit of the *mitzvos*, may You bless me with the three blessings of good health, a livelihood, and pleasure from my children [*naches fun kinder*]. *Omayn*.

# 41. Before *Havdolo*[1]

*Ribon kol ho-olomim* [Lord of all the worlds], who come with love and mercy for all Your creatures whom You have created, hear the prayer of Your servant who comes before You on the threshold of the new week with a full heart but heavy spirit. The beloved holy *Shabbos* is departing, and with it has gone our [*Shabbos*] calm. Who, other than You, heavenly Father, knows the hard life of Your people Israel? [Who knows] their bitter spirit, how hard it is for every Jew to earn his piece of bread? With what worry and heartache, with what fear and hardship he gathers his bleak living! Who among all the nations of the world regards a new week with such trepidation as Your poor, driven children?

We face the new week with new worries and cares, new fears and sorrows. All that remains for us is our hope and faith in You. Merciful One, You have given us the strength to face our troubles and bear them patiently.

May it therefore be Your will, Almighty One, that You open for us the doors of compassion in the coming week. Enable us to gain our livelihood easily and without sorrow. Grant us a full measure of sustenance. As King David, may he rest in peace, says: [You open Your hand generously and feed every creature to its heart's content—Ps. 145:16]. May the new week bring good news, salvation, and comfort[2] upon us and upon all our brethren. Comfort our broken hearts and heal our wounds; gladden the hearts of Your scattered children wherever they may be and send Your righteous Redeemer quickly, in our time. *Omayn*.

## 42. After Lighting Chanuko Candles

Merciful Father, [remember the merit] of the righteous priest
Mattathias, who was the first to sacrifice his life [*moser nefesh*] and
slew Antiochus's officer who had persuaded Jews to eat unclean
foods; [remember the merit] of the righteous woman Judith whom
You designated to deliver Your children and behead Holofernes.

May they be advocates on our behalf to persuade You to grant
us the ability to understand and appreciate the Chanuko lights,
that they may shine proudly and courageously in our hearts.

The tiny flame of each Chanuko candle is like a star in the heavens. It seems small, but in reality it is a great world.

The story of the cruse of olive oil showed that the Holy Temple
was a sound indicator of the state of the people. The fact that all
the containers of oil but one were impure shows how much
Antiochus and his army of occupation succeeded in misleading
the masses. The majority no longer observed dietary laws, and faith
was defiled by impure thoughts.

One small cruse of oil, those few Jews who had held firmly onto
the holy Torah under the protection of the priest Mattathias, remained [faithful]—just enough to illuminate the menorah for a day;
it would be dark again the following day. The few elderly Jews
would soon die and the younger generation would remain mired
in dark and evil ways. But You wrought miracle upon miracle and
the few weak Jews imbued with the flame sacrificed their lives for
the honor of God and Torah. They overcame a multitude of strong
oppressors and achieved a great victory physically, since they were
freed from the iron-handed rule of Antiochus, remaining indepen-
dent for some two hundred years under their own kings. Spiritually, they shone a long time until there was again pure oil; that is,
they encouraged extinguished darkened hearts and blew into them
holy sparks until it came about that [ . . . all the children of Israel
had light in their dwellings—Exod. 10:23].

Help us likewise to kindle our lights proudly and courageously
in memory of that great victory, clean and pure in body and soul.
Help us to keep Your holy days, not to defile them with irrespon-

sible merrymaking and cardplaying.[1] May we praise Your holy Name joyfully and with holy thoughts. *Omayn.*

## 43. *Yohrzeit* (Anniversary of Parent's Death) (Version 1)

Heavenly Father, in the Ten Commandments that You gave us with great circumstance on Mount Sinai is found [Honor your father and mother]. Aside from the fact that the reward thereof is great in the eternal world, You have in addition promised a good wage for it in this world, namely, [length of days]. . . . You hold this *mitzvo* in high esteem, having placed it on a par with Your honor. When one honors parents, it's as though one honors You, and when one has respect [for them], it's as though one shows You respect. Our Sages have interpreted this to mean that when people honor their parents, the Holy One, blessed be He, says that He regards it as though He were dwelling among them and they honor Him. When, heaven forbid, one causes grief to his parents, He says, "I did well not to dwell among them, they would have brought me grief as well."

Our Sages also say that the *mitzvo* of honoring father and mother continues even after death, when they are already in the true world. We must treat them honorably, as children who pursue the right way [in life], perform *mitzvos* and good deeds, and thereby enable people to say, "Blessed are the parents; may they who have raised such good religious children occupy a sublime place in Paradise." In the other world, parents have much (spiritual) pleasure [*naches*]. Through the children's *mitzvos* and good deeds, parents are correspondingly elevated in Paradise.

Dear God, when I consider how much time and energy parents invest in children, I see how I have failed my parents. It is, in addition, an obvious *mitzvo* that *saychel* [reason] would compel us (to perform) even if You had not given it. You simply granted it in order to be able to bestow upon us the reward for its performance. The fact is that one can derive it [the obligation of honor of one's parents] through common sense. Such was the case with Esau, who acted criminally in all things except honor of his father. He observed this *mitzvo* scrupulously. When he had to serve Isaac, he dressed himself in beautiful, splendid garments entrusted to his mother, Rebecca, for safekeeping and never to his wives.[1]

Our Sages tell many stories of how nations of the world honored their parents.[2] Aside from the fact that I understand it rationally, I have also been given it in the Ten Commandments, but I have failed to observe it as I should have. Which is why I pour out my heart to You, Father in heaven, and pray for Your guidance in understanding and acting properly in honoring my parents. All the more so since today is their *Yohrzeit*, a holy day, the day when they left this dark and foolish world for the illuminated world of truth . . . help me to increase their joy, to illumine their souls in Paradise by my prayers with a warm heart. I donate a candle, that others may pray and study by its light and illumine their souls in Paradise. I also give *tzedoko* [charitable contributions] from which to make a fitting holy garment for their souls, as the prophet says [He has clothed me in a coat of righteousness—Isa. 61:10]; through the alms one gives, they are dressed in holy garments in Paradise.

Help me this day with pure and holy thoughts to think only of my beloved parents and how to increase their honor and pleasure in Paradise.

May their merit and that of all pure souls in Paradise enable me to lighten the burden of making a living in order to devote more time to *mitzvos* and good deeds, by means of which I shall always be able to bestow honor on them.

May I be worthy of seeing them face to face in the great joy of the resurrection of the dead, speedily, and in our own time. *Omayn*.

# 44. *Yohrzeit* (Version 2)[1]

*Author's note: It is proper for a woman observing a* Yohrzeit *to go to* bays ha-midrosh [*the house of study, which also served as a small*

*synagogue] to pray and, before [the prayers of]* Ashray[2] *and* U-vo
l'tzion,[3] *should recite this* techinno. *Also, before reciting this
techinno, she should contribute charity* [tzedoko] *according to her
means.*

*Ribono shel olom* [Lord of the universe], I come before You with a
contrite heart and humble spirit. This day is one of woe and lament.
Fallen is my crown. On this day my [father/mother], who was
called [name of the deceased], died. This day is one of woe and
each year I am reminded of my misfortune . . . and am incon-
solable. I do not inveigh, Heaven forbid, against Your acts, and I
lovingly accept [the fact] that You are a God of mercy and loving-
kindness. You do what must be done. All that You do is for the
best.

When I recall on this memorial day my [father's/mother's]
passing, tears flow from my eyes to plead that you deal mercifully
with me and not send more misfortune my way—neither to me
nor to my family.

Hear my voice, Lord of the universe; listen to my weeping,
behold my tears and contrite heart, and grant my request. You
smite, yet You also heal and console. I hope only in You and for
Your compassion. Hear my prayer and bestir Yourself on my behalf
because of the *z'chus* [merit] of the holy soul of my [father/mother],
who died on this day. May his/her good deeds stand me in good
stead on this day and every day.

I also pray, dear God, and pour out my heart to You that You
arouse Your compassion on behalf of the soul of my [father/
mother], who died on this day. Raise up [his/her] soul to a lofty
plane so that it may [eventually] repose beneath Your Throne of
Glory [*keesay ha-kovode*] and shine as the firmament. May [his/
her] soul dwell among the souls of righteous men and women,
bound up in the bond of eternal life. Forgive the sins committed
and remember all the righteous acts performed.

Remember also the *z'chus* [merit] of the *tzedoko* [charitable con-
tribution] that I donate today. May this *tzedoko* stand the holy soul
in good stead and enable it to be raised ever higher [in order to

be closer to You]. May it be restored to life [eternal] at the Resurrection of the Dead [*techeeyas ha-maysim*], when our Messiah will
come, and [may that day be] quickly and in our time. *Omayn*.

And you, O holy and pure soul for whose sake I pray today; do
you intercede on my behalf with the Holy One, blessed be He, to
lift up my *mazel* [good fortune] and that of my husband and children; increase [the number of] our years, bless us with health and
honorable livelihood. Spare us from serious illnesses, overwhelm-
ing misfortunes, untimely deaths, and calamities.

As you were faithful to me in life, so be faithful to me now. Forget
me not by [virtue of] the merit of the charity that I donate today
on your behalf and by [virtue of] the merit of the prayers that I
recite. May I deserve to behold the day when you rise up at the
Resurrection to life [eternal]. *Omayn*.

## 45. An Orphan Bride's *Techinno* on Her Wedding Day[1]

*Ribono shel olom* [Lord of the universe], I come before You this
day with contrite heart and tears and pray You accept my bitter
tears as though they were a sacrifice [offered You in the Holy
Temple]. This is a day of judgment [*yom ha-din*] for me. Today I am
judged for happiness or, heaven forbid [*choleelo*], unhappiness.
The day of judgment on Rosh Ha-shono and Yom Kippur is only
for the coming year, whereas the present one for me is for a lifetime. I am frightened and tremble because I know I have nothing
[to my credit] with which to approach this critical day of judgment. I am so filled with sins that I am unworthy to have my parents lead me to the *chuppo* [bridal canopy]. I am an unhappy and
miserable orphan. What an unfortunate wretch I am not to have
my parents present at my wedding!

For the first time [in my life] I am fully aware of my loneliness.
If I'd had any *z'chus* [merit] to my credit, my parents would have

been here to declare the statement found in our holy Torah: [I have given my/our daughter to this man as wife—Deut. 22:7].

I beseech You, Lord, to be as a father to me, for You are the Father of orphans. [It is written of You that] [As a father has compassion for his children . . .—Ps. 103:13]. Likewise, may You have compassion for me this day. Bring me under the wedding canopy with Your right hand; lead me to happiness, to a successful marriage, to pleasure [naches], to a lasting marriage. . . .

Forgive my sins; I hope only in You. Other than You, *Ribono shel olom*, I have no one to whom I can turn. Although I am unworthy, remember on this day the *z'chus* [merit] of my dead parents, the merit of their good deeds that they performed throughout their lives. May the merit of their holy souls stand by me always, especially on this crucial day of judgment. Open the doors of compassion for me and enable my wedding day to become one of enduring happiness, that it become known to all that You are the Father of orphans and are concerned for their welfare.

Remember the soul(s) of my [father/mother] and lift them up [that they may dwell] among all the righteous men and women. *Omayn.*

Holy soul(s) of my [father/mother], although I was unworthy to have you at my wedding while you were alive, I pray you will at least be present in spirit, at my right hand, under the *chuppo*. Bestir yourselves today and remember me, your orphaned daughter, whom you left behind. Pray to the Holy One, blessed be He, that He act as my [spiritual] father, protect me and take pity on me, that He lead me to lasting happiness on this day, that He be with me all my life.

[*U-reeno, heesohr'reeno*]² Awake, awake, O holy soul(s), and arouse *z'chus* for me on this day of my judgment so that I may be spared unhappiness. May the sun shine continuously upon me in purity and brightness; may my life's light never be dimmed. Bring my tears before the Holy One, blessed be He, and say to Him: Here is the sacrifice offered up by our orphan daughter. With it she seeks atonement for sins and improvement of her chances for happiness in her forthcoming marriage. May it be an honorable one and enduring. *Omayn.*


## 46. A Childless Woman's Lament[1]

My God and God of my ancestors, You have created me from clay and given me a soul, a life in this world, and everything with great mercy. But You have made me into a vessel that, unfortunately, is somewhat useless since I have not been blessed with children. How bitter my life is! I am like a full-grown tree that bears no fruit. A great sorrow rests upon me and there is no one to share it with. I beg heaven and earth to lament on my behalf[2] because my years slip away like [a trail of] smoke. Still, I don't blame the world for my sorrow. Should I not come [to You] with my great sins, seeking forgiveness, so that I may [at least] merit the world-to-come?

Woe is my life! Tears flow from my eyes: how mournful is my heart! I cannot be happy. I lament and bemoan my years and the day I was born. What can I speak or say? . . . Who can heal my woe and set aright my bitter life?

You have shown me much loving-kindness and compassion. You have raised me, though I am useless. . . . Consider my sad life, dear God, and forgive me my sins. If I do not merit the blessings of this world, then at least let me be worthy of the world-to-come so that my soul will not be ashamed there.

*Ribono shel olom*, I must talk out my bitter heart before You. By whom am I to be offended? Whom shall I blame? My mother, who dressed herself and made herself attractive to my father so that I might be born? Her intention was for the sake of heaven, to do Your will so that the world would not be an empty wasteland, but populated. Shall I blame the bad *mazel* [luck, fate, constellation] under which I was born? All the fates must do Your bidding, for all the hosts of the heavens bow down to You and obey Your orders. . . . Shall I blame the midwife? Maybe she failed to

straighten out my limbs. Shall I fault the angel who oversees preg-
nancies? No, each one performed his and her role to which he or
she was assigned by You. They fulfilled their roles and saw to it
that I was properly created to serve You and bear children [in
order] to increase [life] in the world.

It is God's will because of my many sins [ba-ahvonosy ho-rabim]
that I am so completely alone. I cannot be angry at anyone, only
at myself, for having sinned. How sad is my heart! The waters have
covered my house![3]

I look about me and see no one but You, my Creator, to whom
I can turn. I shall place myself and my soul in Your hand when
my time will come. Receive me with great compassion and mercy.
Accept my confessions [veeduyim] and my hot tears with which I
bemoan the day of my birth. Deliver my soul from severe decree
and from Gayhenom. May it [my soul] be protected from Satan and
find eternal shelter under Your wing. Omayn.


## 47. Parental Support

Ribon ho-olomim [Lord of all worlds], all of us are Your children,
as we refer to You in our prayer "Our Father, our King" [Oveenu
Malkaynu]. We are duty-bound to obey You, fear You, honor You,
and carry out Your commandments as You instructed us in Your
holy Torah. It is Your will that we honor our human parents who
brought us into this world through Your great mercy, as You have
declared in Your holy Ten Commandments: [Honor your father
and mother].

I do not know whether I have met my obligations to You and
to my father and mother who begot me and were concerned for
my welfare and raised me to adulthood. I am, after all, a mere sinner with the yetzer ho-ro [Evil Inclination] who misleads one. Perhaps I have stumbled and not fulfilled the mitzvo of honoring father
and mother properly. Perhaps I have caused them grief, or disgraced them. I beg of You, Ahv ho-rahchamim [compassionate
Father], do not punish me now measure for measure.

I, who stand before You now, must depend upon the mercies of my children, be supported by them. Without them my life and existence are impossible. I beg of You, good Father in heaven, strengthen them so that they will be sound and able to earn enough for their sustenance and mine. Enable them to treat me honorably, give me food and clothing in kindliness and friendliness, wholeheartedly. And may I never be a burden to them.

We live in a time when many children do not honor parents. Perhaps it is the place (and not the time) but, I beg of You, enable my children and grandchildren to love me as I love them. May they not be ashamed of me, nor I of them. Inspire them [to understand and discern[1]], to honor me and do nothing against my will, nor against Your holy will. May I never become burdensome or superfluous at their table, as they never were at mine. Permit me to enjoy my portion with them. May I not be grieved by them, nor they by me. Let peace and calm prevail in their homes and let no evil befall them.

If, heaven forbid, they should stumble and fail to hold me in proper esteem or treat me respectfully, I beg of You [compassionate and forgiving Father], forgive them and do not punish them on my account. May the time never come when my children or grandchildren will be punished because of me. Dear Father in heaven, punish me instead so that no evil will ever befall them. *Omayn.*


## 48. Peace of the Kingdom[1]


Great King of the world, whose dominion extends over all the world and has given a portion of His glory to the kings of the world—protect, make happy, and elevate our Master and Czar, Nicholas the Second,[2] together with his family. With the good-heartedness for which You are known, grant him long life and protect him from misfortune; cause his enemy to submit to him and may good fortune befall him wherever he turns . . . pour sympathy into his heart and into the hearts of his counselors and

officials to deal kindly with us and all the Children of Israel who
are under his protection. May the pure truth become known in
his time, that Jews are always faithful subjects. May we dwell in
peace and safety until the Redeemer will come. *Omayn.*

## 49. All Israel Are Brethren[1]

Communal worship [*tefillo b'tzibur*] is important and every prayer
is more effective when said in a congregation. Common sense tells
us that when communal [*b'tzibur*] is used it means I love my fellow Jew, my fellow Jew loves me, and so forth. This is (successful) communal worship [*tefillo b'tzibur*]. When, however, I dislike
the other fellow and he dislikes me there is no community, no
congregation [*tzibur*], and it's everyone for himself. Therefore, the
holy Rabbi Judah, *z"l* [*zichrono leevrocho*], may his memory be for
a blessing, writes that a Jew before praying should take upon himself the *mitzvo* of [Thou shalt love thy neighbor as thyself–Lev.
19:18], to think consciously of loving every Jew, to be concerned
for his (fellow Jew's) honor and fortune, so that each individual
prayer will be joined to the collective prayers of the community
of Israel [*klal Yisroel*]. And, since the prayers of the many are always
acceptable (to God), we wish to write a (brief) chapter on the
subject of friendship between people.

The holy *Tanna* Rabbi Akiba says: [Beloved is man, for he was
created in the image of God–*Ethics* 3:18], that every person is
precious to God since He has created him in His shape. And how
great is God's love for man can be seen in the fact that God said
to Noah [. . . for in the image of God made He man–Gen. 9:6],
referring to all men and not just Jews. Now, while Jews are more
highly valued by the Creator since God refers to them as (His)
children, as *Moshe Rabenu* says to us in God's name [You are the
children of the Lord your God–Deut. 14:1], we must love all persons and common sense also forces us to this conclusion. Each
one helps in the work that the world requires–plowing, sowing,
reaping the grain. Mundane tasks are performed by people. Thou-

sands of ships cross oceans. Who are the sailors? People. The world has been so created that all men must work for one another, help one another in time of need. From birth to death, one needs human help. When a child enters the world naked and unable to grasp anything with its hands, unable to stand on its feet, unable to move, it sees and hears but understands nothing; it is soiled, in need of someone to cut the umbilical cord, to bathe it and wrap it, to keep it warm, to suckle it; to teach it to eat, to speak and, later, to teach it Torah, wisdom, manners, a craft (in order to make a living).

The first piece of bread that he takes into his mouth—how many have worked on this bread, worked on the iron to make the plow? And how many instruments were needed before being able to make the iron for the plow? . . . How were those tools made? And tools for those tools? . . .

Should he happen to fall ill, who will nurse him back to health? In old age who will assist him, give him food? Finally, when he dies, he must rely on others to prepare his corpse for burial, dress it in shrouds. In sum, all people are collectively as one, just as the body is composed of 248 limbs and 365 veins,[2] all interdependent. Pain in even a small finger is felt and suffered throughout, which is why one takes care of the entire body and protects it from even the slightest injury, nourishing and maintaining all parts in the event of illness. Similarly, one should love others and protect them from the slightest harm, feed and cure them from illness, and attend to their slightest need. The Torah said it in three words [You shall love your neighbor as yourself—Lev. 19:18], you should love your friend. Every person is your friend. Each one has a part, through his labor, in your welfare. He is one of your limbs, like you. As you are built of limbs and veins, so are all men, which is why a person should be appreciative of any kindness done him and thankful for the good done him. One of the things that the Holy One, blessed be He, dislikes is when one fails to appreciate a good done to him. Such a person is referred to by the disgraceful term of *k'fui tovo* [an ingrate].

The verse [You shall love your neighbor as yourself] may be understood by a story of two men, Moshe and Shmuel, who swore a bond of eternal friendship for as long as they both would live.

They would never hide anything from one another; they would share their joys as well as their sorrows. And so it was for a long time.

It happened once that Moshe traveled to England on business. He stayed at an inn at the time that a princess was murdered. The (real) murderer got away, but Moshe was falsely accused (of the crime) and thrown into prison. He was tried and sentenced to hang.

Meanwhile, back home, the family was grief-stricken (at his failure to return). No one knew what had happened to him. Shmuel sought tirelessly night and day to find out what had befallen his friend. Eventually, he learned of the false accusation. Saying nothing to his wife and Moshe's wife, he announced that he had to set out on urgent business. He took with him a large amount of money in case of an emergency.

When he arrived in the city where Moshe was imprisoned, he inquired about Moshe's fate and was told that not even millions could save Moshe from death. He was destined to be hanged in several days' time. Shmuel was frantic and wept miserably at the thought of his friend being hanged. Each day he went to the prison and tried to gain entrance and each day he was turned away. Once, however, a sympathetic guard was persuaded by Shmuel with a bribe to sneak him in at night. The friends embraced and wept on each other's shoulder.

After a time, when both had calmed down, Moshe spoke: "I have a great favor to ask of you, my friend. Will you consent to take my place here and act as guarantor for me? Your remaining in prison in my stead will enable me to return home for a final leave-taking from my wife and family. I would come back as soon as possible."

"Yes," answered Shmuel without hesitation, "I will do this for you!" He hurried to the court and pleaded for Moshe's release, adding that he was volunteering to remain hostage until Moshe returned. The senior judge warned Shmuel that his life would be forfeit should Moshe fail to return by the appointed day for his execution. Shmuel responded that he understood. Moshe was released from prison and went home.

There was much rejoicing upon Moshe's return by wife, children, and friends, although no one could understand his sadness. (Soon thereafter) he sent for the notary and had his will drawn up. At this, his wife and children were dismayed and he had to tell them how he'd managed to come home. . . . His wife and children were determined not to let him return. Since it was winter and there was a great cold (upon the land), they hid his winter garments until he would promise not to return. However, he stole away one night from home and traveled swiftly by stage. Time was short. One day remained. Were he to arrive (even) a minute late, Shmuel would be dead. He arrived early on the morning of the appointed day and saw many people coming to witness the (public) hanging. Shmuel was led forth to the scaffold.

"I am here! I am here!" Moshe shouted. The senior judge was informed of the criminal's return. "Free that man and take me in his stead, for I am the murderer of the princess!"

The judge ordered Shmuel released, but Shmuel refused to descend (the scaffold): better that he die and Moshe live! To which Moshe replied: "I left you as a guarantor until my return. It is for me to die." Neither man would permit the other to be hanged.

The judge was at a loss. Since he had never witnessed such a thing before, he had both men remanded to prison for the king to decide their fate.

Informed of the situation, the king ordered the men brought before him. He asked why they were willing to give up their lives for one another. They told him of the bond of friendship they had sworn to one another. How could either one witness the death of his beloved friend and continue to live? Death or life—but together!

"This cannot be," mused the king, "that both shall live since one of them has slain the princess. But both cannot be executed since, of a certainty, Shmuel has not slain the princess. How can an innocent man be executed?"

"Your majesty," said Moshe, "please believe that, just as Shmuel has not slain the princess, so am I innocent of the charge."

"I believe you," replied the king, "and I set you free. However, I wish to ask you something. Would you be willing to accept a third party into your bond of friendship?"

"If that third party would agree to be as faithful as we two are, he would be acceptable and we would willingly give our lives for him."

"I wish to be that third party," said the king, "and you shall henceforth live in my palace. I shall protect you and you will protect me."

And so it was. The king appointed them to the highest positions at court and they became his counselors and protectors.

This is what the Holy One, blessed be He, meant when He said to the Jews [You shall love your neighbor as yourself]: If a Jew loves his fellow as himself in sorrow as in joy, is willing to give his life for his fellow man, then the Holy One, blessed be He, says [I am God]—to such a loving relationship I wish to be a third party. I shall protect you and [I shall be with him in his sorrow]; when times are bad, heaven forbid, for Jews, then God suffers too. As it is written [And His soul grieved for the miseries of Israel—Judg. 10:16] and He helps them; and the Jews have to be ready to sacrifice their lives [*moser nefesh*] for the love of the Holy One, blessed be He, as is written in the verse [You shall love the Lord your God with all your heart, with all your soul, and with all your might—Deut. 6:5][3]

## 50. Deliverance from Bad Neighbors

Creator of the world, You have made Your world so that man should inhabit it. I am going out now to look for a dwelling in which to settle with my husband and children. Please help me, God, send me to a nice, appropriate [*kosher*] place where I shall not have to haggle about the rent or fall in among bad neighbors. Our Sages say: [Keep far from a bad neighbor[1]] so that he may not corrupt my character; all the more so, from a neighbor corrupted in his faith, so that he may not infect my children with heresy, nor mislead my daughters into lewdness, debauchery, and profligacy. Help me get to know good, religious neighbors and learn good qualities from them. As our Sages say: [What is the good way to which a man should cling? . . . Rabbi Jose says: A good neighbor—*Ethics* 2:13].

May we also be found worthy of dwelling in our own land in our own houses, quickly and in our own time.[2] *Omayn.*

## 51. A New *Techinno* for *Parnoso*[1]

This holy *techinno* was *composed* by a righteous man, one who always kept fear of God in *mind.* Whoever reads it with *kavono* and takes it to *heart* assuredly will be spared evil happenings. One may read it by day and by *night.*[2]

May it be Your will, my God and God of my ancestors, to cleanse my thoughts; prepare good responses to the words of my mouth, and purify the thoughts of my heart. May it be Your will, when I pray to You with my hands and feet, indeed, with all my 248 limbs, that my thoughts reach You; conversely, may that which Satan would have me think be held in check. Rebuke him severely so that he may not rule over me, my children and grandchildren. Help me to avoid evil dreams. Permit no *yetzer ho-ro* [Evil Inclination] *ah-yin ho-ro* [evil eye], no evil thought to dominate me, my husband, my children and grandchildren. *Omayn.*

May it be Your will, my God and God of my ancestors, compassionate One, who generously clothes everyone[3] and renders good to all His creatures and populates the earth; who filled the world on the third day [of creation][4] and prepared food for all with His compassion—that You may in like manner feed me; grant us an honorable *parnoso* [sustenance] so that we shall not be distracted from serving You wholeheartedly. Do not allow our *parnoso* to be obstructed by any failings on our part. Let it [our *parnoso*] not be cut off, heaven forbid, and grant us a full portion.

Protect us and all travelers [who must travel for their *parnoso*], including those who travel in the wilderness; protect them from wild animals and all manner of evil happenings, from anguish, from thieves and robbers one is liable to meet on the roads or at home. It is written that You order Your angels to protect us on all the highways and byways [of life][5] so that Satan may in no way be able to harm us—me, my husband and children, and Your people Israel. . . . Praised be He who listens to all prayers! *Omayn*. May it be so.

I beg of You, O God, who prepares *parnoso* for each and every one, from the mightiest to the worm beneath the earth, who prepares raiment for all His creatures and sends them food, send good health and nourishment to me, my husband and children, to my entire household. And grant us those needs that we have not voiced, as well as a livelihood to which there will be attached no shame, so that we need not rely upon the gifts or loans of mortals, but [rely] only upon Your open and generous hand.[6] Let it be a *parnoso* that will enable us [time in which] to study Your pure and holy Torah.

Grant us decent clothing so that we may walk with dignity among righteous people unashamed. And enable me, my husband, my children and grandchildren to live among them without shame. May our lives be good and come to a good end. Help us bring our hopes to fruition. Bless the fruits of our labor along the highways and byways of life—ours and those whom we love. Grant us well-lived lives: good lives, peaceful and blessed. Deal kindly with us, for we know not what is good for us and You do. Bring us good fortune and fill our hearts with blessing. Protect and defend us and lead us forth from darkness into light. Protect us and all Israel from sorrows and unfortunate events, from evil decrees this year and in all the years [to come], in this month and in all the months, in this week and in all weeks, in this day, in this moment, and in all moments [to come]. *Omayn*.

## 52. Far from Home

Dear God, Our Sages write that he who has no livelihood in his town should seek it elsewhere.[1] *Ribono shel olom* [Lord of the universe], because we have no livelihood here, my husband has gone to seek it elsewhere. I pray for Your compassion; lead him in the right way. May the merit of his small children who are free from sin stand him in good stead. Grant him good fortune that he arrive safely and find work or business and be able to send money for my little ones so that I shall be able to raise them in Torah and fear of heaven [*yirahs shomyim*].

Just as he kept the holy *Shabbos* here, protect him there from profaning the *Shabbos*. Keep him from bad company so that he not be misled into evil ways, into debauchery, into cardplaying, or other foolish activities.

When he finishes work, let him associate with good friends and study Your holy Torah, as our Sages say: ["What is the good way to which a man should cling? . . . Rabbi Joshua says: A good friend"–*Pirkay Ovos* 2:13].[2] May the exile into which he has been thrown by adverse circumstances atone for our sins.[3] May he soon return home unharmed and may we all be nourished from Your generous hand in dignity and happiness. *Omayn*.

## 53. New Month of *Shevot* (*Rosh Chodesh Benshen*)[1]

*Ribono shel olom* [Lord of the universe], as we come before You to pray for the holy month of *Shevot*, on the fifteenth day of which falls the New Year of the Trees when we thank You for the fruits of the trees, please bless the trees so that they will blossom fully and yield their fruit to refresh all men.

Protect Your people Israel so that the cold at this season will not harm them, that those who must travel the roads will not die from its severity.[2] May the roads be smooth and straight so that the travelers will not get lost. Protect the little children in the towns and villages from the cold so that they will not fall asleep in it (and die).

We shall recite the blessings over the many fruits in praise of Your holy Name and pray that You send Your blessing for peace and good *parnoso* [sustenance] and redemption for us and all Israel. *Omayn.*

## 54. The New Month of *Odohr*[1]

Arise, *Moshe Rabenu* [Moses our teacher], and open the gates of heaven to admit the prayers and requests we now express. Behold your sheep (Israel) whom you fed in the wilderness and because of whom you suffered so much. They stand now with bitter hearts and contrite spirits to beg you to plead on their behalf before the King of kings, the holy One, blessed be He, that He bless the month of *Odohr* with all that is good. May He open for us the gates of compassion and favor, the gates of life and health, of livelihood and success. As it is written: [The Lord will open for you His good treasure . . .–Deut. 28:12].[2]

May God do all this because of your merit, for you were His envoy who led us out of Egypt and brought us to Mount Sinai and gave us the holy Torah in order to learn the holy *mitzvos* contained therein. We caused you much trouble and pain but, when the Jews sinned, you pleaded with God on their behalf (Exod. 32:10).

Stand up now before Him and plead on behalf of all Israel that the month of *Odohr*, which we now bless, shall be blessed by Him.

Just as, because of your merit, God caused the manna to rain down upon us, so may He rain down upon us now an abundance of blessing and success in all our endeavors. May we never, heaven protect us, need to come to a stranger's table. May our storehouses be full and our hands full of God's blessing. *Omayn.* (The prayers for the new month are now read.)

## 55. A Purim *Techinno*[1]

[Look down from heaven and see . . . –Isa. 63:15], dear God, the merit of Your beloved Jews. Much charity do they give on

Purim, each according to his ability, to fulfil the *mitzvo* of [ . . . gifts to the poor—Esther 9:22]. *Ribono shel olom*, may the verse be fulfilled for us that [Zion shall be redeemed with justice, and they who return with righteousness [*tzedoko*—Isa. 1:27], that Zion will be freed from its captivity (exile) through the merit of charity [*tzedoko*]. And may the *mitzvo* of charity be an atonement for our sins. As Daniel said to Nebuchadnezzar: [ . . . break off your sins by almsgiving—Dan. 4:24].

Forgive us our sins, *Ribono shel olom*, for the sake of the merit of charity so that we may be freed from exile speedily in our days. *Omayn.*

# 56. The Three Pilgrimage Festivals[1]

## PASSOVER

It is the way of the world for each nation to commemorate important events in its history. And what nation has so rich and marvelous a history as we Jews? As our teacher Moses [*Moshe Rabenu*] says [ . . . inquire about bygone ages—Deut. 4:32]: seek in the history of the world since the time that God created *odom rishon* [first man] from one end of the world to the other, whether such great things have ever happened or, perhaps, something similar? [*ha-shoma ohm*—Deut. 4:33]. Has any nation of millions of people heard the voice of God when He appeared with His glory [*kovode*] in public and spoke to them face to face [*pohnim el pohnim*—Deut. 34:10] as we Jews have heard?

Where did it ever happen that one of the gods, whom the nations serve, saved them as did the God of Abraham, Isaac, and Jacob, appearing in Egypt with great wonders and wars against the Egyptians until He brought out the seed of Abraham as a nation? What god ever led his people forty years in a desolate wasteland, where one cannot survive, and sustained them with food, clothing, and dwelling as though they were in a habitable land?

Usually, it would be appropriate to commission a marble statue of Moses and set it up on an attractive boulevard (if we were in our own land) as a memorial to this worthy person through whom all the wonders came to be, who brought down the light of the Torah without which the world would have stumbled about in darkness for thousands of years.

But our Torah has superseded such material things as monuments. Besides, since they are immovable, they are limited in function. Furthermore, when one becomes accustomed to them, there is always a danger that common people will make gods of them. That is why the Torah prohibited them [You shall not make for yourself a sculptured image or any likeness . . . —Exod. 20:4]: You may not set up any likeness. King David says: [He has made a memorial for His wonderful works, God is full of compassion—Ps. 111:4]. He who would achieve eternal happiness, let him have faith in the Creator of the world and observe the precepts of the Torah for, when he sees that there is a Creator, he knows he must be upright and observant.

With this in mind, God made spiritual memorials of the miracles He wrought when He chose us as a people. By means of these spiritual memorials love and fear of Him are implanted in our very blood.

Thus, in commemoration of the historical exodus from Egypt, He established *chag ha-matzos* [the Festival of Unleavened Bread] . . . and the Passover *seder* . . . telling the children of the great wonders, of how God settled accounts with Pharaoh and the Egyptians who caused us much pain and suffering. This is a great [educational] device for implanting the *Shema Yisroel* . . . in the Jewish heart.

## SHOVUOS

Consider this wonderful thing, that the Name, blessed be He [*ha-Shaym yisborach*], appeared before the entire people on Mount Sinai and spoke the sweet Sayings to us [the Ten Commandments] face to face [*pohnim el pohnim*], the flavor of which rests upon the lips of our souls to this day (for all the souls yet to be born were also present). Our souls still yearn for it, as it is written: [Let him kiss me with the kisses of his mouth . . . –Songs 1:2a].[2] How may we again be worthy of hearing the sweet words from His mouth? [ . . . for thy love is better than wine–Songs 1:2b], for such a relationship is pleasant and more dear than any other pleasure in the world. It is why God has given us as a legacy the holy festival of Shovuos. When the Jew is spiritually prepared by the night of Shovuos,[3] he will experience the following morning, through hearing the *Akdomos*[4] and the reading of the Giving of the Torah [*mattan Torah*], something of that divine bliss.

## SUCCOS

Because of great wonders we were preserved forty years in the wilderness. It means that Israel will have the good fortune to continue to survive. Therefore, the Creator gave us the spiritual memorial of the festival of Succos, the time of our rejoicing [*z'man sim'chosaynu*]. Just as for parents the greatest joy is that a child grows up and celebrates its birthday, so too was the festival of unleavened bread [*chag ha-matzos*] the time of our rejoicing [*z'man sim'chosaynu*] for Israel. We were freed from the house of bondage as a child is brought forth from the prison of the womb. For Israel, it was a dark and narrow tomb in which he was confined many years until, like the child, he was brought forth [a nation from the midst of a nation–Deut. 4:34]. For little Israel [i.e., the child], Shovuos means that he has had the good fortune to begin studying in *cheder* [the one-room school], which is the time of the giving of our Torah [*z'man mattan torosaynu*]. But the joy has not come to fruition yet, for how can we know whether the tender child, barely out of the womb, will be able to survive the rigors of Torah study? Especially in view of the fact that he might be adversely affected by wicked children who do not want to learn (anti-Semites). They would gladly devour him with their wolfish eyes.

This is why we were given the festival of Succos [*chag ha-succos*], the true time of our rejoicing [*z'man sim'chosaynu*], because it reminds us of the forty years' wandering in the wilderness in which no human can survive on his own. The Creator sustained us with all kinds of blessings, as the prophet says: [ . . . have I been like a wilderness to Israel?—Jer. 2:31]. Did the Jews ever feel as though they were in a wasteland? While Israel is busy with the study of Torah, two fire-breathing serpents blow upon him. Israel will nevertheless continue to flourish until the entire world realizes that he was created to illuminate it and teach it to recognize the Creator [*ha-koras ha-boray*]. Thus, when Israel's train is on track (as the Torah ordained for him), he will progress. But should he depart from the straight course, he will become hopelessly mired. He will have no choice but to return to the way of Torah. This in general is the lesson of the pilgrimage festivals.

One should study such holy books as *Menoras Ha-mo'or* and *Ma'aseh Alfes*. The Jewish woman should joyfully and with fear of heaven [*yirahs shomyim*] observe the *mitzvo* of lighting the candles [*licht-benshen*], for they are the entryway into the holy festivals [*yomim tovim*]. If she does this, she will be found worthy to enlighten her children's eyes so that they will never depart from the path of Torah and she will derive *naches* [pleasure] in both worlds.

# 57. After Candlelighting—Pesach (Version 1)

Great King! I thank and praise Your beloved Name for having given me the precious *mitzvo* of candlelighting with which to illuminate this *yom tov* [holy festival]. . . . You took unto Yourself a nation on whose behalf You wrought great wonders (the ten plagues upon the Egyptians) on this night, smiting their firstborn while Your firstborn Israel You led out of the house of bondage proudly, with great honor.

Dear God, just as You protected Israel on this night long ago, please care for us so that nothing unfortunate will happen in my house. . . . Accept favorably the great effort and expense to which we have gone in preparation for this festival—cleaning the house of *chometz* [leavened food] and bringing in all the (necessary) things for Passover.

Help us clean out the *yetzer ho-ro* [Evil Inclination] that *sours* [i.e., makes *chometz*] our heart so that we not, heaven forbid, transgress the prohibition of *chometz*, so that I shall not by foolish behavior steal, as it were, the *afikomen* from my husband throughout the year.[1]

Grant us enough good cheer and liveliness so that we do not fall asleep at the *seder* and shall be able to relate to our children the wondrous deeds You wrought for our ancestors at the Exodus. Implant in our hearts and in our children's hearts the pure belief in Your holy Name so that we may travel the road of life happily in both worlds. *Omayn.*

## 58. After Candlelighting–Pesach (Version 2)

Dear God, as I have illuminated my home with my candlelighting in honor of the holy *seder*, so may You illuminate the darkness enveloping our holy land and rebuild the Holy Temple, that we may be able to make the thanksgiving offering (the Passover sacrifice) as You instructed us in Your holy Torah.

You brought Joseph out of prison darkness and made him second in the land after Pharaoh, in which capacity he served for eighty years. May You in Your great compassion deal with us in like manner and bring us out of the imprisonment of exile and return our monarchy to us (the kingdom of the house of David).

You protected our ancestors throughout the night [of servitude and exile] in Egypt so that even a dog did not bark at them [but against any of the children of Israel not a dog shall bark–Exod. 11:7]. Protect us likewise on this festival so that the barkers will not fall upon us with their falsehoods of blood libel.

In Queen Esther's time You poured Your grace upon her generously because she endangered her life pleading her people's cause. You helped her so that the enemy of the Jews was requited with what he sought to do to them. As she found favor in the eyes of her husband the king, enable us to find favor in the eyes of the king and his officials in our time. May the sorrows that Haman's descendants seek to visit upon us in our time rebound upon their heads. Let there be light and joy for the Jews, let it be bright and cheerful for them because of You. *Omayn.*

## 59. Intermediate Days of Pesach

Almighty God, I have lit the candles that illuminate the *yom tov* [holy festival]. On such a night as this did You with Your spiritual flame illumine Your holy people Israel when Pharaoh overtook them at the sea. They were so miserable, hemmed in on all sides: the sea ahead of them, the wilderness with its serpents and lizards to the right and left, Pharaoh with his mighty army behind them. Your children cried out to You and You told *Moshe Rabenu* [Moses our teacher] to split the sea and the spiritual fire lit the way. Your children went through the sea on dry land as winds held back the water, but Pharaoh and his army drowned.

Your children today find themselves confronted by sorrow-laden times. From behind they are driven out, deprived of every means of livelihood. Roundabout are barriers preventing entry into other countries. The only alternative would seem to be to throw themselves in desperation into the sea, heaven forbid!

*Ribono shel olom* [Lord of the universe]! Command the sea of sorrows to dry up for us. May our pursuers drown and salvation come to us so that we shall be able to sing to You the hymn of praise and thanksgiving as Moses and Israel did in the Song of the Sea [*Oz yoshir*]. [Terror and dread befell them . . . —Exod. 15:16.] May terror and dread befall our oppressors so that they become as dumb as stone until we pass through the sea of exile and arrive quickly in our holy land to serve You in Your Holy Temple [*bays ha-mikdosh*]. *Omayn.*

## 60. Sabbath of Intermediate Days of Pesach

*Ribono shel olom*! I thank and praise Your beloved Name for having granted me the precious *mitzvo* of *licht-benshen* [candlelighting]
with which to brighten the holy *Shabbos*. As I have brightened my
home in honor of Your holy Name, so may You brighten my soul
with Your Torah's light. May the Torah's light resurrect me when,
as we hope, the resurrection will come during the intermediate
days of Pesach,[1] as we shall read tomorrow in the *haftorah* [the
prophetic portion chanted after the Torah reading in the syna-
gogue] that the Creator revealed to the prophet Ezekiel the resurrection of the dead. He saw a large field with dry bones and God
told them to prophesy [Ezek. 37:4]. There was a great commo-
tion [*ra'ash*] and the bones came together and were complete
skeletons. After this, sinews and flesh and skin came upon them.
Ezekiel prophesied and the breath of life was blown into them,
and a great number arose and stood on their feet. Then God said
to him that these bones represent all of Israel [Son of man, these
bones are the whole house of Israel—Ezek. 37:11]. . . .

Grant me a good heart so that I shall be able to love the Torah
and raise my children in the ways of Torah and obtain virtuous,
observant sons-in-law who study Your Torah.

Enable me, my husband, and my children to hear the words of
Torah and ultimately be found worthy to hear the sound of the
holy spirit calling the dead to rise . . . at the resurrection.

This is as *Moshe Rabenu* suggested indirectly in the song
*Ha'azeenu* [Listen, O heavens and I will speak—Deut. 32:1]: when
you listen attentively to what the Torah says while you are yet in
the sense of "heavens" [*shomyim*], you still have your divine
creation of a soul within you, then will you be worthy of hearing
[Let the earth hear the words I utter!—Deut. 32:1] although you
be only earth (just a body) and the soul is no longer in it—worthy
of hearing the soft, delicious words of [Awake and sing, you who
dwell in the dust!—Isa. 26:19].

May this come to be quickly and in our own time. *Omayn*.

# 61. Memorial Service for the Dead—*Yizkor* (Version 1)[1]

*Author's note:* [*This is a "preliminary" techinno*] *to be recited before the Memorial* [Yizkor] *Service.*[2]

*Ribono shel olom* [Lord of the universe], and Creator of mankind, You created man's body out of the earth and the soul from beneath Your holy Throne of Glory. They separate at death and each returns to the place [whence it came]. The body is placed in the grave and decomposes, whereas the soul flies to its holy resting place. If accepted, all well and good for the one who acted righteously during life on earth. That person has fulfilled what You enjoined in Your holy Torah, the observance of Your *mitzvos*: He acted piously toward God and man. That soul returns directly to its place of origin. There are no obstacles and it is not restrained, for You send Your holy angels to welcome it and bring it straight to You. You take comfort in it as a father who has managed to see his dear child after long separation. It is all well and good for such a soul, and its bliss is indescribable.

But, as is written, it is impossible for one to do only good and not sin [ . . . there is no righteous man on earth who does (only) good and never sins—Eccl. 7:20]. Sins form an ironlike wall after death and are an obstruction for the soul. They block the way and cannot be surmounted [in order for the soul] to come to its [spiritual] repose.

Some people are taken from this world in youth. Had they lived the full span of their lives, they might have [been able to] set straight what they had made crooked [as in Deut. 32:5— . . . a *crooked* generation]. Because of that, their souls are unable to return to their sacred place of origin and remain restless.[3] But You are merciful and compassionate and awaken Your compassion four times in the year, on Yom Kippur, Shemini Atzeres, Pesach, and Shovuos, to remind the souls, so that they will not be cast down into the abyss [*tehom*]. At these four times, Your compassion is powerful enough to raise them up and seat them among the holy souls of the *tzaddikim* [righteous].

We come before You with broken hearts and impassioned tears and beg of You, Lord of all souls, to accept our *Yizkor* prayer.

Open the doors of compasssion and raise them up, grant them repose among the holy souls of righteous men and women by virtue of the *z'chus* [merit] of our prayers, the *z'chus* of the sacred Torah we have read [today], and the *z'chus* of the charity that we pledge to give [to the needy]. Regard favorably the tears shed today in all the *shuls* [synagogues] and houses of study. . . . Should I prove unworthy of praying for the repose of my [father/mother] called [name(s)], do not allow my sins and evil deeds to move You to judge my parents' souls with the quality of justice [instead of with the quality of mercy]. May my sinfulness not be a barrier preventing their holy souls from rising upward [to repose among the holy souls of the righteous]. Consider our good deeds, the merit of our *mitzvos*, and the merit of our little children on behalf of our parents who brought us into this world. . . . Accept my prayer with compassion. *Omayn.*

## 62. Memorial Service for the Dead—*Yizkor* (Version 2)[1]

Dear holy souls, for whose sake we pray today, we ask that you remember us. Forget us not as we forget you not. Remember that you have left behind in this world your children whom you raised with great difficulty and watched over constantly. Watch over them today also. Remember us, our husbands, and children. Bestir yourselves in your lofty and holy repose. Be good intercessors on our behalf before the Name, may He be blessed. Plead with Him not to judge us solely according to the law [*din*], but also with mercy and compassion, that He forgive us our sins. May our prayers be accepted so that He will help us and grant our needs. Pray to Him that He inscribe us for life on Yom Kippur, that He lengthen [the number of] our years and those of our husbands and children, our brothers and sisters, relatives and good friends, that we not be torn untimely from this world.

May our children not [have to] be raised by another, may we not be widows and our children orphaned. May we never know of woe and disaster. May no one ever be missing from our home. May God be a father and protector for widows and orphans, healing the brokenhearted.

May He send us an honorable livelihood so that we shall not be humiliated and need to turn to a stranger, for that is a great mortification. May we be allowed to raise our children in [knowledge of] the holy Torah so that they will act piously toward God and dutifully toward man.

Because we give charity on your behalf, dear souls, strengthen us to achieve the right way and not drown in the lusts of this world. Let us not be led astray by the Evil Inclination. By the z'chus [merit] of our Forefathers Abraham, Isaac, and Jacob and the merit of all righteous men and women, may we be found worthy of beholding the reconstruction of the Holy Temple and the resurrection of the dead, speedily and in our time. *Omayn.*

## 63. After Candlelighting—Shovuos

Lord of the world, I thank You and praise Your beloved Name for having given me the gift and opportunity to fulfill the beloved *mitzvo* of candlelighting for the holy and magnificent *yom tov* [holy festival]. Through this *yom tov* You caused Your great glory to appear on Mount Sinai, to teach Your people the illustrious Torah and *mitzvos.* You enabled them to hear Your magnificent voice and holy words in flames of fire. With thunder and lightning You revealed Yourself over them and, with a shofar blast, as is recorded in the holy Torah.

Great and holy Father, I pray for Your compassion. May the merit of my candlelighting stand me in good stead so that You send Your holy angels to bestow upon me a crown of spiritual beauty, such as You bestowed upon Your beloved people Israel at the giving of the Torah [*mattan Torah*].

Grant my husband and children a great desire to study Your Torah diligently whenever they have time.[1] Enlighten their eyes to appreciate its profundity and sweetness.

Dear Father, bless the fruit of the trees[2] that You judge on this holy day, that they have in them good juices with which to refresh the heart. Bless our children, the fruit of their parents, that they too possess good juice, that is, good thoughts and qualities [*middos tovos*] with which to refresh their parents' hearts. And may we merit a second time to hear Your words when You will reveal Yourself to us as You did to our ancestors. . . . As Moses was watched from afar by his sister Miriam and delivered from the Nile River[3] since he was destined to receive the Torah from You . . . so may we be delivered from the river of sorrows in which we now struggle to survive. And as he was brought to the royal palace, so may we be brought into Your holy palace of Zion and Jerusalem quickly. *Omayn*.

## 64. The Second Day of Shovuos (Before Reading Psalms)[1]

Great King! Inasmuch as today is the anniversary of our holy King David's death, I come to render *naches ruach* [spiritual pleasure] to his pure soul and recite the songs and praise in his holy Book of Psalms. May he be a good advocate for us. May our children experience the sweetness of the Torah[2] that he felt. As he says: [They are more desirable than gold and fine gold, and sweeter than honey and the drippings of the honeycomb—Ps. 19:11]. [How I love Your Torah! I speak of it all day!—Ps. 119:97]. In whatever company they find themselves, may they express their love of Torah. As he says: [I shall speak of Your testimonies before kings and not be ashamed—Ps. 119:46]. Enable us the merit to behold the monarchy of the House of David restored in Zion and Jerusalem quickly and in our time. *Omayn*.

# 65. A *Techinno* for Tisho B'Ov[1]

*Author's note: This* techinno *is to be said on the ninth of Ov, both in the evening and morning, to the accompaniment of much weeping.*

God, full of compassion, You are the merciful One and Judge of all the world and all Your laws are truth.

On this day [the ninth of the month of *Ov*] our ancestors, whom You brought out of Egypt into the wilderness, were unwilling to accept the good thing You had prepared and promised them through Abraham, Isaac, and Jacob [i.e., the Promised Land].

After hearing the report of the spies [we were as grasshoppers in our own sight and so were we in their sight—Num. 13:33] and [all the congregation lifted up their voice and wept—Num. 14:1, the Talmud tells us:] "That day was the ninth of Ab; the Holy One, blessed be He, said: They are now weeping for nothing, but I will fix [this day] for them as an occasion of weeping for generations" [*Sotah* 35a, Soncino trans., p. 172, and *Ta'anit* 29a, Soncino trans., p. 152]. On this day, their descendants suffered the loss of both temples. The temples were our beauty and our crown.

Now we can no longer bring sacrifices to be offered up on Your holy altar, nor can we observe the three pilgrimage festivals annually [by going up to Jerusalem] to behold the beauty of Your holy *Shecheeno*, happy that Your *Shecheeno* rested between the cherubim.[2]

Woe is us! On this day our Holy Temple was burned by heavenly fire.[3] Because of Israel's great sins committed against You, going in evil ways and troubling You, almighty God, You destroyed their sovereignty, their monarchy, and their happiness. You handed them over to their despoilers. Well-loved and gentle wives and daughters were taken captive and forced to do course, hard, physical work. They were fettered and shackled and heavy neck chains were put on them. They walked with great difficulty. They suffered hunger, thirst, and many troubles that the nations of the world beheld and applauded, saying: This was Jerusalem, choicest of all the cities of the world. How she had lorded it over them! Now her sovereignty is destroyed by enemies. . . . They took pleasure in her downfall and cursed her with harsh words.

*Ribono shel olom* [Lord of the universe], I stand before You today with bitter heart and weeping. Tears flow from my eyes and sorrow grows in my heart when I recall the beauty of Your exiled children and Your Holy Temple burned. Priests once served in Your House and Levites sang and played sacred songs on musical instruments, but they do so no more. The altar, the table of the showbread, the laver, and sacred utensils have come into the possession of the unclean hands of Jerusalem's despoilers.[4] My eyes are swollen from weeping and my heart weak from moaning and mourning. My very entrails do sigh and groan. My body is weak. My limbs are worn out with lamentation over the calamity that has befallen Your Children of Israel.

But You are a gracious God of compassion, merciful, concerned with men's well-being. For the sake of Your great Name, incline Your ears and eyes to hear and see our devastation and that of Your holy city of Jerusalem, which you once allowed to be called by Your Name. See how Your beloved children have been brought to shame and yearning. See how much their blood has been spilled. Consider their righteous deeds, dying for the sake of *kiddush ha-Shaym* [sanctification of the Name, martyrs' deaths]. . . . The blood of parents mingled with the blood of children, brothers and sisters, brides and grooms, scholars and wives, humble Jews and their families, cantors and *dayonim* [judges], scribes, teachers, and schoolchildren, all were slain together.

Remember these altars of the slain, merciful God, and help us. Gather us from the four corners of the earth and build for us again, with sacred fire, Your city of Jerusalem. Deliver us from our sad estate and send us Your *Mohsheeach* [Messiah] to bring us back to the Land of Israel so that on this very same day we shall rejoice and praise Your Name and tell of Your wonders, how You brought Your people Israel out of Egypt [i.e., out of our present exile].

May the words of the prophet soon be fulfilled, that the month of *Ov* will be changed into joy and there shall be no more mourning and crying. May it come to be soon, in our own time. *Omayn* and *omayn*.

## 66. *Techinno* for the Month of *Elul*[1] (Version 1)

*Author's note: This* techinno *was composed for the entire month of* Elul *in order to awaken people's hearts to do* teshuvo *[return, repentance] and purify their thought so that they may merit life in* olom ha-bo *[the world-to-come].*

*Ribono shel olom* [Lord of the universe], in Your holy books it is written that You gave the month of *Elul* [as a time in which we should try] to rectify past acts through which we have sinned. [It is also the time when] You took *Moshe Rabenu* [Moses our teacher] into heaven, keeping him there until Yom Kippur and teaching him that these forty days are a good time in which to have our sins forgiven when we do *teshuvo* [return, repentance]. Which is why I struggle against the *yetzer ho-ro* [Evil Inclination]. . . . my limbs tremble, I cannot speak, much less lift up my eyes, as we approach the Day of Judgment to stand before the King of kings, the Holy One, blessed be He.

You don't need to listen to any testimony before Your judgment of me. You know all the hidden things, good deeds and bad ones, that I have committed throughout the year. I am in great fright when I think of how You will demand an accounting from my soul and fortune: Have I covered the [year's] distance correctly and in righteousness?

What can I answer? How can I raise my face before You, King of kings, when I have soiled my soul's garment with sins? Woe is me! What can I do? How can I seek Your pardon when my limbs have committed so many vile deeds? My tears flow endlessly as I seek release from my suffering. . . . I must not wait until the Day of Judgment. My heart must turn again to You now. May many good angels speak my good deeds on behalf of my soul. May they succeed in preventing countercharges from being brought before You on the Day of Judgment. I want to confess my sins ahead of time during the month of *Elul* for, as it says in Your Torah, when one confesses voluntarily, You deal compassionately with him and he is freed from severe punishment. Which is why I want to make confession in the month of *Elul* so that Satan and the Evil Inclination will be ineffective when You sit on the Throne of Judgment and the angels will be lined up before You on both sides. . . .

May my blood loss due to fasting be reckoned as a sacrifice on the altar upon which blood was sprinkled for You . . . I have dishonored Your holy Name. With my sins I have broken all those laws [*dinim*] through which accrue to Your holy people Israel abundance and blessing. . . . Heaven forbid that I be consumed by Your great punishing flame, for I am Your creation. Be merciful unto me and don't take Your wrath out on me. Do not requite me according to what I justly deserve. Be merciful and hear my prayer. Turn Your heart and ears to me and accept my prayer and *teshuvo*. . . .

You [must] know that all I have thought was not in order to anger You. I was born a flesh-and-blood sinner. In Your Torah it is written that when one has a mind to do good but cannot [carry it out], it is regarded as though he had done it. Therefore, regard it as though I had acted rightly in spite of the fact that I have sinned. You know full well that our intelligence is limited and cannot always right the wrongs we have done. Woe for my soul that You have made and I have damaged and that I cannot undo!

*Ribono shel olom*, see how deeply my heart is moved by the great fear and trembling that have come upon me because I have sinned before You.

I recall the sins of my youth when I did not think to protect my old age, but committed more sins than there are hairs on my head. Remembering these things today, I afflict my body so that my soul may not stand ashamed on the Day of Judgment before Your Throne of Glory when You judge all creatures.

Respond, dear God, today. I sorrow greatly, for my sins overwhelm me. I am in deep water and about to drown. All Your creatures, myself included, must give an accounting. Angels are aligned on both sides [of Your throne]. All the books are open, the books of life and of death. My sins have been written down by my own hand. How can I respond [in my defense]? How am I to justify myself before You?

I beg of You, *Ribono shel olom*, with a contrite heart, support me with Your right hand and incline Your ear to me sympathetically when I confess my sins before You. Command Satan not to denounce me. Before You alone have I sinned and before You alone shall I admit to and confess my sins:

I have eaten forbidden foods, causing blemishes [to appear] upon my soul.[2]

I have not washed myself,[3] for which the abundance and prosperity[4] of Your people Israel have been diminished.

I have eaten leaven [*chometz*] on Passover. I was not careful. Therefore, my soul must transmigrate [after my death] into the body of a domestic animal, heaven forbid! I have not properly observed my *mitzvos*.

I have failed to count the *Omer*.[5]

I have not recited the *Shema* with proper concentration.

I did not bless the *lulov* earnestly.

I did not listen [attentively] to the blowing of the *shofor*.

I have been haughty, for which my soul will enter into a bee.[6]

I have slandered, for which my soul must enter a dog.

Woe is me, for I have thought of strange men when I copulated with my husband. . . . I have shamed good people. It is as though I had shed their blood, for which my soul must flounder about in a river.

I have carried things outside my house on *Shabbos* in public. I deserve to be stoned.

I have shown great anger to others. It is as though I worshiped idols.

I have spat on people and driven them away, for which my soul will enter a pig.

I have worn cloth made of mixed linen and wool [*shatnes*],[7] for which my prayer was unable to enter heaven.

I have sworn falsely.

I have made a vow and failed to keep it, for which little children will die.

I have gone about in *Shabbos* clothes on weekdays.

I have done prohibited things on festivals [*yomim tovim*] and on the intermediate days [*chol ha-moed*], for which one is denied entrance into the world-to-come [*olom ha-bo*].

I have committed prohibited acts on Yom Kippur.

I did not hold my father and mother in high esteem.

I closed my hands when it came to giving charity [*tzedoko*]. My soul is destined to enter a raven that treats its young cruelly.[8]

I have copulated with my husband by light [instead of in the dark] and have diminished the light of the Divine Presence [*Shecheeno*]. Therefore my soul will be reborn, heaven forbid, in a goat.

I have drunk unkosher wine and my soul must transmigrate into a gentile's body.

I have eaten improperly [ritually] slaughtered meat. From that comes a plague, and my soul will be reborn in the leaves of a tree.

*Ribono shel olom*, I cannot correct so many wrongs by myself, whether or not I have committed one or all of them. May it therefore be Your will that, as soon as I have made confession and done *teshuvo* [repentance], they be accepted by You along with my tears. May the transgressions be wiped out. Cast them into the deepest ocean.[9] I greatly repent of my misdeeds. When the time arrives, may my soul return to that place from which it originated.

May the words of my mouth and the thoughts of my heart be acceptable to You, my Creator and Redeemer. *Omayn. Selo.*

## 67. *Techinno* for the Entire Month of *Elul*[1] (Version 2)

Serel: I rely upon Your many compassions to beg of you . . . [2]
God: Before You call out [to Me] I respond.[3]
Serel: Deal with me according to Your great loving-kindness.[4]
God: I shall act with loving-kindness
for I remember the fathers' merit
on children and children's children.[5]

Serel:  Have Your loving-kindness comfort me.[6]
        Make us a favorable sign
        that our enemies will see
        and be discomfited;
        for You, God, have helped and comforted me.[7]
        You bind up the brokenhearted[8]
        who stand for judgment today.[9]
Serel:  You have compassion for babes and sucklings.[10]
        Though all the gates are closed
        the gates of tears remain open.[11]
        With all my heart I call upon You:
        Remove Your fierce anger from me.
        What can we say? For what can we ask?[12]
        I give thanks with all my heart.[13]
        Do not rebuke me with Your anger.[14]
        Although I've been far from good deeds,[15]
        Fulfill Your loving-kindness to Your maidservant.[16]
Serel:  Remove Your fierce anger from me
        although I've clung to evil deeds,[17]
        for You open the Book of Records . . . [18]
        Were it not for Your mercy[19]
        what could I rely upon?
        I suffer because of my evil deeds,[20]
        Have mercy upon Your children![21]
Serel:  With mercy bring upon us
        the earth-shattering Day of Judgment.[22]
        I know I've turned from Your *mitzvos*[23]
        and it's time to stand for Your judgment.
        Listen to us and heed our cry,[24]
        for You are near to those who call on You.[25]

# 68. A *Techinno* for the Courtyard of Death[1]

*Author's note: This prayer should be said word for word as one goes
about[2] the House of Life [cemetery].*

I have come to go around the graves of the righteous men and women buried here, to benefit from the merit that, in their lives, they have amassed.

You souls, who are buried here, may God grant you permission to pray for me, for my husband and children so that we shall be protected from evil and sorrow, from every unhappiness, from every sickness, from all the sufferings of the world, from a violent death [*miesseh m'shuneh*, lit., a strange, an extraordinary, death].

Dear God, deal with us as a father with his children and grant us long life with happiness. Enable us to retain the mental powers of our youth [to meet life's difficulties firmly and courageously] and the understanding that You have given us. May none know poverty.

*Ribono shel olom* [Lord of the universe], with fear in my heart I have acted uprightly according to Your will. May I be worthy of receiving the blessings of Your holy Torah.

You know I have determined to do good, whether the *mitzvos* be easy or difficult, so that I shall not *chas v'sholom* [heaven forbid], be shamed in the world-to-come.

May I, through prayer and Your loving-kindness, be safely delivered from hell [*Gayhenom*] and the suffering of a dead sinner in the grave [*cheeboot ha-kever*].[3] *Omayn*.

## 69. A *Techinno* for the Angelic Advocate of Justice[1]

Dear God, permit me soon to enjoy the merit of the righteous men and women buried here who, in their lifetimes, performed good deeds.

May the angel over those buried here bring my prayers to the Name, may He be blessed, in *Gan Ayden* [Paradise] where the righteous will intercede on behalf of me, my husband, and my loved ones. May the Holy Father of all the earth not remain silent in heaven at the sight of my tears flowing like a stream of water. As King David says: [I melt my couch with my tears—Ps. 6:7], tears with which I bewail my misdeeds and my sleep, which dissolves into nothing. Dear God, [permit] the z'chus [merit] of the righteous to protect me. Omayn. Selo.

## 70. To the Righteous Dead[1]

Holy souls, who lie here in the Eternal House [of life], I have come to greet you at your gravesites.[2] I know my request that you be advocates of justice [m'litzay yosher] will be acceptable so that my prayer in turn will be acceptable to the Name, may He be blessed. Let it be a time of compassion and grace during which He will hear my prayer. May He not judge my sins judgmentally, for I am but dust and ashes and have no strength with which to contend against the fiery angel, the yetzer ho-ro [Evil Inclination], who misleads one into depraved ways.

Therefore do I, submissively and with many tears, bow before the King of kings, the holy One, blessed be He, [and pray] that He deal mercifully with me, forgiving the sins of my youth, which I deeply regret [having committed].

From this time on, I shall know how to walk in the right path and, with God's help, avoid the yetzer ho-ro [Evil Inclination], [thus] enabling me, my husband, and my children to live long lives and do good in the eyes of God and man, and our name [and the memory of our righteous lives] shall evermore be remembered. Omayn.

## 71. Before, during, and after Rosh Ha-shono[1]

Author's note: This techinno should be said during the entire month of Elul and Erev Rosh Ha-shono at the cemetery [the bays chayim—the House of (Eternal) Life],[2] as well as in the shul [synagogue]. It is also good to recite it every day of one's life.

Dear God, at this season of the year all the heavens are open and You render judgment for the entire world.

You are our Father and we are Your children.

At this time, You sit on the throne of judgment and judge the entire world with great mercy.

If, heaven forbid, something evil has been decreed for me or my children, please erase it and make it null and void.

On this day, have mercy upon me, my husband, and my children for the new year about to come upon us.

May I, my husband, and my children be inscribed this Rosh Ha-shono for a good year and may we be found worthy of giving our children in marriage honorably. *Omayn.*


## 72. *Selichos Techinnos*[1] (Version 1)

*Author's note: Say this* techinno *early in the morning before Rosh Ha-shono.*

Lord [Master] of the world [*Adon olom*], You reigned even before You created the world. You created everything according to Your will. There is none to compare with You. Who can tell of Your greatness or describe the esteem [in which You are held], the dominion and might that are in Your hand? You alone are God.[2] You gladden me when I call upon You. In Your hand I place my soul [for safekeeping] when I go to sleep, and You return it to me upon my awakening. If You are with me, I fear nothing. Our Father, look kindly upon us from Your holy [dwelling] place and help us.

When our Holy Temple stood, we had few sins because they were mostly forgiven. . . . The sacrifices were an atonement.[3] But today [since we have no Temple and no sacrifices], with what may we come to You? Therefore, accept [as a substitute for the sacrifices] our contrite hearts and pain [at having sinned]. Accept our prayer as though it were a burnt offering. Hear our outcry and plea: rebuild the Holy Temple quickly in our time. *Omayn.*

*Ribono shel olom* [Lord of the universe], I come before You with contrite heart and spirit, at a loss what to do in view of the coming great and awesome Day of Judgment. Our Sages advised rising very early several days before Rosh Ha-shono to read the *selichos* prayerfully and with concentration so that they would be acceptable by You. But [surely] they meant only those persons [relatively] free of sin who could pray to God to grant them their needs; surely not such as the likes of me, for I know that I have sinned much. How can I ask that You grant me goodness? My needs are many, yet I am of little worth.

Nevertheless, I have risen early with much fear and trepidation to pray. I know not what to do to seek Your forgiveness . . . but if, with *teshuvo* [return, repentance] and *vidui* [confession], I may make myself acceptable, then I surely repent and confess I have sinned and transgressed. You, dear God, are merciful and forgiving. Forgive me, for I pray and plead that You accept my humble prayer.

If shedding tears and sighing are acceptable, I do these willingly. Woe unto my body for my sins! But You do not require excessive weeping and wailing before receiving the contrite of heart. *Ayleeyohhu ha-nohvee* [The Prophet Elijah] said of the false prophets: Cry aloud to your god; perhaps he will hear you,[4] whereas You accept our prayer immediately.

*Ribono shel olom*, I pray that You be merciful to me and personally be my defender at judgment time. Gladly would I possess this world and the world-to-come but, with my previous conduct, I have not earned them. . . . The [daily] concerns for making a living hindered us from properly serving You. While I seek to attain both this world and the other one, I do not know which one to pray for first so that it will be acceptable to You. May the merit of our Forefathers stand by me on the Day of Judgment. I beg of You to open the doors of heaven as You did when Israel stood at Mount Sinai and received the Torah . . . so that my prayer may enter.

When Abraham sought to offer up his beloved son, Isaac, at the *ahkaydo* [binding], an angel's tears fell upon the knife and he was unable to slaughter the lad. As those tears came down, so may ours rise up before You on the threshold of the New Year.

When Esther came before King Ahasuerus to plead for the lives of Your people, an angel accompanied her and she found favor in his eyes and he received her. Likewise, dear God, at our judgment send such angels as will cause grace and mercy from Your holy eyes to trickle down upon us, and I shall be confident that You in Your great mercy will help me. For there is no righteous person in the world who does not sin.

At the creation of the world, You foresaw those generations destined to be evil and which people You would need. Those You needed were destined to be created; those for whom You would have no need You destined not to be created. [Since You created me and have need of me,] I beseech You to be merciful in the coming year, for You are our merciful God and we are Your beloved people, as it is written [ . . . who is like Your people Israel . . . −2 Sam. 7:23a].[5]

You are our God and You alone should judge us. It is appropriate that You alone judge Your people so that it will come to be, as it was written, that God will give a sign for good,[6] for You are our God and our comforter. May You send us our Righteous Redeemer this year. *Omayn. Selo.*

*Shema* [Listen], dear God, to my prayer that I speak with riven heart and accept it as though I had brought a burnt offering.[7] As it is written: A broken and contrite heart is exactly like a sacrifice. [The sacrifices of God are a broken spirit; a broken and contrite heart, O God, Thou wilt not despise−Ps. 151:19.][8] Do not therefore shame my contrite heart. Accept my stammering [out of fear?] favorably, as though I had brought a burnt offering. May it be acceptable before Your Throne of Glory and treat us with kindness. Keep me from rotting away although my sins are great, for everyone lives because of Your kindness and mercy, which You freely grant. Enable me and all my friends to live without sin and shame. It is written that God is merciful over all His creatures.[9] Since we are Your children, be gracious and bestow upon us some

of Your luster so that we shall not be held in low esteem by others.
*Omayn.*

*Yehhe rohtzone milfonehcho* [May it be Your will], my God and
God of my ancestors, that this present time be one of good fortune as I stand before You to pray for my welfare and that of my
husband and children. Protect us from all illness and degrada-
tion. May we not be disgraced by extreme poverty. And send us
the Righteous Redeemer soon. *Omayn.*

Although this world is a small one, if we have no good luck in
it, we cannot achieve the other one also. Do not shame my prayer,
but gladden my heart. My woes are so great that I cannot express
them all. Besides, how could I confide them to someone [other
than You]? How could I be sure he would understand and be
kindly disposed [toward me]? Perhaps [unknown to me] he might
be my enemy. Then he would rejoice in my sorrow. There is no
one but You to whom I can turn. Do not allow them who rise up
against me to rejoice. Consider the heavy troubles I bear upon
my heart and inflict punishment upon them who seek to do me
harm, for You are all-powerful. Remember on my behalf the *z'chus*
[merit] of the Mothers [Sarah, Rebecca, Rachel, and Leah] so that
I shall have no more sorrow. Permit me to enjoy only goodness at
the hands of my children and friends.

May we be dealt with honorably by Your hand so that we shall
not have to depend upon any human agency. Allow us to enjoy
the merit of our Mother Channo who entered the Tabernacle to
pray when Eli the priest was there and he saw her lips move but
heard no voice. He thought she was drunk and ordered her out.
She answered him and said, "No, my lord, I am a woman of sor-
rowful spirit," and he interceded for her and You helped her.[10]
May You, dear God, answer me likewise. Do not inflict punishment on me. Although I have sinned, I pray You be merciful and
judge me with the quality of compassion [*middas ho-rahchamim*]
and not with the strict quality of law [*middas ha-din*].

Our Father Jacob, *ohlov ha-sholom* [may he rest in peace], prayed
that You forgive the transgressions of his children should they

happen to err; he asked You to remember what sorrow he underwent before finally managing to raise them. I pray that I shall have no sorrow in raising my children.

I know that I ask a lot and am not fit to stand before You, but You desire that one should pray to You and You will act mercifully toward him. For that reason, I pray that You cast me not off in old age; when my strength is gone,[11] dear God, do not let me fall into human hands, for there is no greater sorrow than to have to depend upon others. May I, my husband, and my children find favor in Your eyes and may we want for nothing, so that our children and grandchildren will be able to study Torah day and night. May we live in this world honorably and, when my time comes, may no Satan have power over my soul. Send angels of mercy and grant my portion among righteous women, both in this world and in the world to come. . . . *Omayn.*

## 73. *Selichos*: A *Techinno* of *Teshuvo*, *Tefillo* and *Tzedoko*[1] (Version 2)

*Author's note: This sweet, beloved* techinno *comes out [is based on, was translated from the Hebrew text of]* Sefer Chasidim *[Book of the Pious].*[2] *It is good to say it on every fast with much weeping so that the prayer will be accepted by the Name, may He be blessed.*[3]

*Yehhe rohtzone* [May it be Your will], my God, that my tears, which I shed for the transgressions I have committed, extinguish those transgressions. May my heart, which is, as it were, saturated with water, extinguish the hot coals of those transgressions. May my tears turn away Your wrath. . . . Accept my not having set the table today as a sacrificial offering to You. May my not having set the pot over the fire [to cook] be like the altar's flames [in the Holy Temple]. May the blood lost today [by fasting and afflicting the soul] be like the blood sprinkled on the altar. Let the suet we went without today be like that offered up on the altar. Let my tears be like the wine poured on the altar. May the sound of my weeping be reckoned as the sound of levitical song during the ceremonial sacrifice. May the shine that has left my eyes because of the fast be reckoned like candles burning in the Holy Temple. . . .

Shame not my broken heart. . . . As I afflict myself during prayer, so may my sins be torn from the book in which they are recorded. May the prayer I recite now silence the mouths of all my enemies. Do not allow my prayer to leave Your presence empty-handed and my heart shall rejoice. May the repentance [*teshuvo*, return] that I do now not be thrust away from You empty-handed.

I deeply regret the transgressions I have committed intentionally or otherwise. I beg of You now, *Ribono shel olom*, who are compassionate and gracious, accept my repentance [*teshuvo*, return to You] so that my prayer not be delayed [in reaching You].

Help me to sin no more. May those good thoughts and deeds that I yet intend to do be prepared before You and used for my benefit and the benefit of all Israel to help us to repentance. *Omayn.*

*Ahv ho-rahchamon* [Compassionate Father], You know well my limitations: You know well my needs. The *yetzer ho-ro* [Evil Inclination] inhibits me and induces me to evil. You know hidden things and are an examiner of hearts. You know what is in contrite and heavy hearts, what weighs heavily upon them, things one cannot reveal to others—only to You. You know the hidden wounds I carry in my heart. Where shall I find a physician who understands my sorrow and, if he should understand, will be able to help me? You help those who call upon You. You accept our prayer and are a father to orphans and a judge for widows [seeking justice]. You can enrich the poor, raise up him who has been cast down. You do no wrong and give each his due. All is within Your power.

I beg of You, do not abandon me in my middle years and, especially, in my old age. Do not allow my enemy to rejoice in my low estate. As King David, *ohlov ha-sholom* [peace be upon him], once said: There is no greater pain than an enemy who rejoices over one's downfall.

I beg of You to hear my plea and grant me an abundant *parnoso* [livelihood] and success in my life's endeavors so that I shall be able to help the poor with my *tzedoko* [charity, aid]. May I and my children not suffer want, nor may I have any need to depend upon them.

I know that I ask much of You and am undeserving of what You already have done for me until now, but cast me not off in my old age so that I shall not be shamed in the eyes of the world. May my portion be among good and pious folk. And [when my time comes to leave], draw me forth in joy from this world into *olom ha-bo* [the world-to-come]. *Omayn.*

*Ribono shel olom . . .* open the gates of heaven . . . so that my prayer, together with all the other prayers, will be admitted. May my prayer serve as a crown for You, and I, my husband, and all my dear friends will be able to bask in its efficacy as though we had offered up sacrifices in the Holy Temple. *Omayn.*

# 74. *Selichos*[1] (Version 3)

*Ribono shel olom* [Lord of the universe], I come before You as a penitent with contrite heart and soul. Our Sages have ordained that in the days before Rosh Ha-shono we should rise early and read the *selichos* with great feeling and pleading so that they will be acceptable to You. The Sages must have had in mind persons free of sin who could ask You to fill their needs. Certainly not the likes of me, for I am full of sin. How can I ask You to grant my many needs when I am so unworthy? Nevertheless, I have risen early in fear and trembling to pray. I don't know what to do or how to persuade You to forgive me. If by means of *teshuvo* and *vidui* [confession] I can make myself acceptable to You, these I gladly do.

Though I have sinned, You are compassionate and forgiving. Please forgive me and accept my *tefillo* [prayer] and my urgent *techinno* [petition]. You require tears and sighs? I give them. Woe is me for my sins. . . .

*Ribono shel olom*, I beg of You to pity me and be my advocate in judgment. Gladly would I possess both worlds but, with my misdeeds, I have not earned that. Yet the one without the other is impossible. Worries about making a living have hindered us from serving You properly. . . . May the merit of our Fathers [Abraham, Isaac, and Jacob] stand by us on the Day of Judgment and persuade You to open the heavenly doors as You did when the Children of Israel stood before Mount Sinai and received the Torah. You opened the heavens so that they could behold Your oneness over all worlds. In like manner, permit my entreaties to open them for my prayer.

. . . Almighty God, grant life to me and those dear to me, a life without sin and shame for, as is written, [You are good to all and Your tender mercies extend over all Your works—cf. Ps. 145:9] and we are Your children. We pray for compassion, for the sake of Your beloved Name. Let us not be held in low esteem by anyone.

Lord God of Israel, I beg of You, compassionate One, have pity on me. *El molay rahchamim*,[2] [Merciful God], do not let my children or grandchildren die during my lifetime. You are compassionate. It is written in Your holy Torah, for example, that when one finds a bird's nest one should send the mother away before taking the young [Deut. 22:6-7]. . . . You have shown compassion for animals; how much more do we need Your mercy! With much effort have we raised our children under Your divine guidance. Enable us also to raise them in service to You so that the verse [Grandchildren are the crown of their elders, and the glory of children are their parents—Prov. 17:6] shall apply. Even if I have not deserved it [because of my sins], nevertheless do I beg You to grant it.

*Ahv ho-rahchahmon* [Merciful Father], grant us a livelihood from Your hand and not from human hands, for the gift of humans is as nothing. How can a person meet another's needs? And, when he finally does give something, it's never given when needed. But

You, beloved God, know a person's needs at any moment. May we therefore be fed by Your holy hand.

. . . As it is written: You open Your hand and satisfy with food every living thing through Your goodness.[3] Do not abandon me, Father of the entire world, so that I may be able to serve You until my time comes to die, for then I shall no longer be able to do so. . . . May my limbs not weaken, so that I may continue to be able to serve You as is fitting. When my time comes to die, may it be at Your pure hand. May my death be a *kaporo* [an atonement] for my sins. May the words of my mouth and the thoughts of my heart be acceptable to You, God, my Creator and my Redeemer, forever.[4] *Omayn.*

Dear God, do not shame my prayer. Gladden my heart, for my wounds are so great that I cannot express them before any person. How could one possibly help me even if he should pity me? And what if he turned out to be an enemy who would take pleasure in my sorrow? Before whom but You, dear God, can I lament?

Behold the suffering I bear in my heart. May the merit of our Mothers (Sarah, Rebecca, Rachel, and Leah) stand by me so that I shall not have any more sorrow from my children and from my good friends. May we be fed honorably from Your hand and not have to depend upon anyone else.

Dear God, enable us to enjoy the merit of our Mother Channo [1 Sam., chapters 1–2]. . . . As You helped her, answer my prayer also. Although I have sinned, do not punish me . . . judge me with compassion [*middas ho-rahchamim*] and not strictly according to the law [*middas ha-din*]. . . .

I know full well that I ask too much and am unworthy of standing before You, but You regard it as fitting and proper that we plead our cause to which You are sympathetic. Cast me not off in my old age, when my strength is gone.[5] Dear God, do not allow me to fall into human hands, for there is no greater sorrow than to have to depend upon others. Deliver me from such a fate.

May my husband and I and my children find favor in Your eyes

. . . that we live without want, that our children and grandchildren study Torah day and night, that we live out our days honorably. And when my time comes, let no Satan have control over my soul. Send angels of compassion and may my portion always be with righteous women in both this world and in the world-to-come. . . .

Help me to sin no more and strengthen me to walk in Your paths, to give charity and do good deeds, to live a righteous life. . . . Dear Father, be compassionate with me as a father is with his children [k'rachaym ov ahl bonim]. If I should err, heaven forbid, remind me to do teshuvo . . . heal my imperfections, for You are the physician who heals broken hearts.

Our Father in heaven [Oveenu sheh-ba-shomyim], cause good fortune to shine upon me and my husband; bless me with good children and let me not know sorrow through them. For this is all the meaning in life for man in this world and in the world-to-come. Enable us to earn our bread and clothes honorably. Permit us to live out our years with a goodly measure of happiness. And may we be found worthy to behold our Messiah of Righteousness quickly and in our time. Omayn, may it be Your will.

Ahv ho-rahchahmon [Compassionate Father], You know well my limitations; You know well my needs. The yetzer ho-ro [Evil Inclination] inhibits one and induces him to do evil. You know all hidden things and are an examiner of hearts. You know what is [found] in contrite and heavy hearts, what weighs heavily upon them, things one cannot reveal to others—only to You. You know the hidden wounds I carry in my heart. Where shall I find a physician who understands my sorrow and, if he should understand, will he be able to help me? You help all those who call upon You. You accept our prayer and are a father to orphans and a judge for widows [seeking justice]. You can enrich the poor, raise up him who has been cast down. You do no wrong and give each his due. All is within Your power.

I beg of You, do not abandon me in my middle years and, especially, in my old age. Do not allow my enemy to rejoice in my low estate. As King David, peace be upon him [ohlov ha-sholom], once said: There is no greater pain than an enemy who rejoices over one's downfall.

I beg of You to hear my plea and grant me an abundant *parnoso* [livelihood] and success in my life's endeavors so that I shall be able to help the poor with my *tzedoko* [charity, aid]. May I and my children not suffer want, nor may I have any need to depend upon them.

I know that I ask much of You and am undeserving of what You already have done for me until now, but cast me not off in my old age so that I shall not be shamed in the eyes of the world. May my portion be among good and pious folk. And [when my time comes to leave] draw me forth in joy from this world into *olom ha-bo* [the world to come]. *Omayn.*

*Ribono shel olom* . . . open the gates of heaven . . . so that my prayer, together with all the other prayers, will be admitted. May my prayer serve as a crown for You, and I, my husband, and all my dear friends will be able to bask in its efficacy as though we had offered up sacrifices in the Holy Temple. *Omayn.*

## 75. *Techinno* for Forgiveness[1] (Version 1)

Lord of the universe, You are the Compassionate and Forgiving One, merciful and gracious. I come before You with bowed head and contrite heart, with great fear and trembling to pray for Your pardon and forgiveness for sins I have committed during the past year intentionally or unintentionally. I do know that when one comes before You, one's good deeds must be advocates [in his defense]. But I have no more good deeds, nor righteous acts, uprightness, or repentance [*teshuvo*]. I have only the hope that the doors of Your precious compassion will open [for me] in time.

You have given us Yom Kippur [as a means by which] to forgive our sins.[2] On this Day of Atonement, You forbade us to eat or drink, to bathe ourselves, to use cosmetics or fragrances, to wear [leather] shoes,[3] and to have [sexual] contact with our husbands.

[May] these abstentions be an atonement for the sins we [may] have committed during the [past] year.

We have eaten and drunk forbidden things. By means of the fast, a spiritual fire enters us. May our souls be purified thereby. May the painful fast atone for all our misdeeds of the year. With our transgressions we have prevented abundance and prosperity [*shefa* and *brocho*] from descending [upon all Israel].

May the pain and discomfort we endure from being shoeless as we stand [during Yom Kippur] atone for our sins of having run after evil things. . . .

May the discomfort of [sexual] separation from our husbands atone for those times when we conducted ourselves improperly in [the marriage] bed. Because of them and our other sins, the exile has been prolonged.

Dear God, bestir Your mercy and bring us into our Holy Land during this coming year. May our lament be turned to joy and happiness. . . . You understand all and know full well my unhappy condition. Accept my tears, see how my very heart weeps. Silence the mouths of our enemies. Do not allow me to be dishonored in my old age. Accept my prayer and grant me righteous advocates. Do with me as You did with Manasseh, King of Judah, for whom You made a hole beneath Your Throne of Glory and thereby enabled his prayer to reach You.[4]

Show me Your mercy as You do with all Your creatures. Accept my prayer and do not allow us to be shamed. Grant me an honorable livelihood so that I shall not need to rely upon the gifts of mortal men, nor upon their favors.[5] May I receive my food and dwelling from Your generous hand until the day of my death. . . .

Enable me to serve You wholeheartedly. Grant me the ability to express through my prayer, fervent tears and confusion before Your holy Name . . . as a maidservant before her mistress, my eyes are raised up to You . . . my Father. My heart weeps and beats within me, my breath is short. I fear greatly because I know I have sinned. I beg of You, merciful Father, be compassionate and forgive me on this Day of Judgment. Inscribe me for a *chayim tovim* [good life] and for *sholom* [peace]. *Omayn.*

## 76. *Techinno* for Forgiveness[1] (Version 2)

Lord of the universe, how long will You not have mercy upon Your
people Israel? We have had enough sorrows. Like a rose among
thorns, we are pierced [attacked] on every side, yet we remain firm
in our belief, suffering all forms of unnatural deaths for the sake
of Your holy Name. Why should the nations [of the world] feel
that You cannot help us? You promised to bring us into the Holy
Land. As You are truth, so is Your word truth. We pray that You
will soon make it so. Inscribe us in the Book of Life [*sefer ha-chayim*]
on this Day of Judgment for all good things, free of sorrows, so
that Your children will not be driven away from their Father's table.

Ohveenu Malkaynu [Our Father, our King], when we sinned in
the wilderness Moses, *ohlov ha-sholom* [may he rest in peace], stood
before You and prayed for us, saying: "*Ribono shel olom*, forgive
Your people Israel about whom You bragged and referred to as
[*b'nee b'choree Yisroel*—Exod. 4:23] 'Israel is *My son, My firstborn.*'"[2]
You accepted his prayer and replied: [*sohlachtee kee-d'vorehcho*—
Num. 14:20] "I have pardoned as you asked."[3]

Today, we have no one to intercede for us. We must rely upon
our own resources. . . . I pray that You forgive me my sins. Please
do not take it amiss that I rattle on like this before You. I know
how great Your compassion is and that You will accept my *teshuvo*
[return, repentance] and my bitter heart on this Day of Judgment,
for You are a Prober of hearts.[4]

I beg of You, dear God, let me not stumble in old age when my
strength will have left me and I shall be unable to do *teshuvo*
wholeheartedly. Pardon me and protect me from further transgression, as it is written: "If one comes to cleanse [i.e., purify] himself, he is helped" [*Shabbat* 14a]. Do not allow my enemies to rejoice
over me. King David, *ohlov ha-sholom* [may he rest in peace], asked
of God: Shut the mouths of my enemies so that they will be unable to do me any evil.

May compassionate angels bring my prayer before You and may
You in Your mercy put me in order[5] for the Day of Judgment. May

my judgment be blended with mercy and compassion, but not
with anger.

*Ribono shel olom*, deal with me as it says in the verse: "Before I
shall call upon You, You will answer; before I shall speak You will
hear me"[6] and will not abandon me, as until now You have not
abandoned me. *Omayn, kayn yehhe rohtzone* [so may it be Your
will].

# 77. A *Techinno* for the Ten Days
# of Repentance[1]

[These things do I remember as I pour out my soul . . . –Ps. 42:5].
When I remember thus, I weep disconsolately for having had only
practical purposes as my goal in life. I failed to bear in mind that
I shall be brought to the bar of justice and have to account for all
my actions in the world-to-come. It did not occur to me that a
person's life in this world is so insignificant [For a thousand years
in Your eyes are like a single yesterday–Ps. 90:4]. How can one
not be concerned with the fact that he must be ready for death
each day? [Until his return to the dust he will not rest.][2] Night
and day one worries about how to obtain his food and, because
of the hardships of making a living, he is unable to serve You,
dear God.

Therefore, I beg of You, inscribe us for the New Year with an
easy means for a livelihood. May it come from Your gentle and
faithful hand and not by human agency.

Woe is me for the years I have spent in suffering! The morality
books say: [It is better not to have been born than to have been
born[3] to a day of sorrow and wrath[4]]; it is better not to have been
created than to have been created for a single day of suffering.
For man's days are few and pass quickly[5] as in a moment and, in
the end, he is held accountable for all his actions. He cannot deny
anything: his deeds have been recorded in his own hand. He may
be called at any moment to the other world and, if he has failed
to provision himself [with *mitzvos* and good deeds] for the long
trip, he will be naked and bereft because he can take no worldly

goods with him. It is written: [Naked came I out of my mother's womb and naked I shall return there–Job 1:21]. He came out naked from his mother's womb and he will return to the earth naked. He is suddenly overwhelmed by an evil web, the dark day of his death, the day when God makes a final accounting of what man has done in this world, when man must leave his illuminated home and enter the dark grave, when the eyes can no longer see and he recognizes neither family nor friends.

If he bears this in mind, he will not associate during his lifetime with the *yetzer ho-ro* [Evil Inclination]. He should also remember that he comes from a putrid drop of seminal fluid [*tippo s'rucho*]; each day he should picture to himself the grave to which he will be brought, a place of worms and maggots [*reemo v'solayo*].[6] He should also remember that he will have to give an accounting [*din v'cheshbon*] for all his sins from the time of his birth until the day he leaves this world. . . . Even if he should live a hundred years, they are as nothing. They pass in sorrow and suffering; he has no peace of mind until he sleeps in the grave.

But it is well with him who spends his time in study of Torah and performance of *mitzvos* and good deeds, for they will accompany him in the true world [to come]. Therefore, dear God, I implore You not to take me from this world before my time so that I may return [repent, do *teshuvo*] from my transgressions. May I be able to do some good in this world so that I will not be shamed in the other world. Show me Your mercy while I yet live. [Will Your mercy be recounted in the grave, or Your faithfulness in the place of destruction (*sheol*)?–Ps. 88:12] What are we, what is our life?[7] What is our life to have been created for a single day of suffering? . . .

It is written: [Man in his splendor will not last . . . –Ps. 49:12]. Even if he is very rich, he may not last the night. One amasses a fortune but knows not who will inherit it [He heaps up riches, and knows not who will gather them–Ps. 39:7]. Today my hope is but that You [Deliver me from all my transgressions . . . –Ps. 39:9]. I hope unto You, dear God, for [You listen to the needy . . . –Ps. 69:34]. You hear their cry. Consider my poverty and disregard my sins. . . .

Inscribe us for life. You sustain the entire world with Your great compassion. Grant us the livelihood that will enable our husbands and children not to lose Torah study time, that we shall be able to serve You, *Ribono shel olom*, with a happy heart. Grant each and every one of us our sustenance from Your gentle hand so that we need not depend on others.[8] *Omayn. Selo.*

## 78. A Prayer by the Writer Noam Elimelech[1]

May it be Your will, our God and God of our ancestors, who hears our voices and prayers with compassion, to purify our hearts, mend our thoughts, and approve our prayers. Hear the pleas of Your servants who pray to You contritely. You, God, are gracious and compassionate. With Your acts of mercy, forgive us and erase our sins together with those of all Your people Israel.

We have sinned and distorted and committed wrongs before You. Not out of a sense of defiance and wickedness, heaven forbid, have we rebelled against Your Torah and *mitzvos*. It is due to the powerful *yetzer ho-ro* [Evil Inclination] who burns constantly in us. He never lets up until he brings us around to lusting for this world and its vanities. He jumbles our thoughts. Even when we pray before You and plead for our lives, he muddles our thoughts with his trivia. We cannot resist.[2] Our *saychel* [intellect] is weak and our brains exhausted by the sorrows and troubles and bothers of the world.

Do with us as You said to Your faithful *Moshe Rabenu*: "I will be gracious to whom I will be gracious" [Exod. 33:19]. Concerning this, our Sages added: "Even if one is not at all worthy [of Your compassion, You will show him compassion], for it is Your way of dealing with the wicked as well as with the righteous. You know full well our bitter sorrow, our moaning and groaning at being unable to draw near in worship, unable to unite our hearts with You truly and uprightly" [cf. Judg. 9:19]. Woe unto us and our souls!

Our Father in heaven [*Oveenu shehba-shomyim*], we implore You to bestir Your great compassion and mercy on our behalf; shout at the Evil Inclination to stop and leave us alone. . . . Do not permit him to lure us away from service to You. May he be unable to cause evil thoughts to enter us while awake or asleep; especially when we are about to pray or are studying Your holy Torah, or when busy with Your *mitzvos*—may our thoughts be pure, clear, and strong with truth and courage and a whole heart. . . .

Move our hearts and the hearts of all Israel to declare Your unity in truth and in love. . . . May our faith in You be as firmly set in our hearts as the nail is firmly driven home [in a piece of wood]. Remove all barriers that separate us from You.

Our Father in heaven, deliver us from all temptation and error. Do not abandon us. Do not allow us to be seduced [by the Evil Inclination]. Do not shame us. Be ever at our side when we speak and act and think. . . .

Our Father in heaven, unite our hearts and thoughts, our speech and actions . . . to serve You in truth, with integrity, without base thoughts. Purify our hearts and make us holy. . . . Sprinkle us with pure water[3] and cleanse us with Your love. May fear[4] of You be ever in our heart in every time and place, wherever we may go, whenever we lie down and rise up.[5] Implant Your holy spirit in us. May we continue forever to rely upon You, upon Your greatness and love, upon Your written and oral Torah, both hidden and revealed, upon Your *mitzvos*. . . . Deliver us from evil thoughts, from pride and anger, from irascibility, depression, slander, and all the other failings that dishonor [us and You]. Cause Your holy spirit to flow over us so that we may always be bound to You and be loved by You.

Raise us up so that we may approach the level of our Forefathers Abraham, Isaac, and Jacob. May their *z'chus* [merit] enable our prayers to be accepted and answered [regardless of] whether [they are] for ourselves, for others, or for all Israel [*klal Yisroel*]. May You be proud of us and pleased with us. May our deeds strike root and bear fruit. Remember not the sins of our youth. As King David [*ohlov ha-sholom*], may he rest in peace, used to pray: [Remember not the sins of my youth,[6] nor my transgressions—Ps. 22:7]. . . .

Move us to remember *teshuvo* [repentance; literally, return to God's way] and to do *teshuvo* before You wholeheartedly in order to correct that which we have perverted. . . .

Deliver us from jealousy of one another. May we consider one's good qualities and not his faults. [Help us] not to retain ill will against anyone. Enable us to give sound advice to a friend. May our love for one another be so firm as to give You pleasure [*naches ruach*]. . . .

Should we lack the *saychel* [good sense] to direct our hearts to You, teach us to know how to serve You honestly.

Above all, *El molay rahchamim* [God full of compassion], we entreat You to accept our prayers willingly and compassionately. *Omayn, Kayn yehhe rohtzone* [so may it be Your will].

# 79. A Blessing for Children before Yom Kippur

*Author's note: It is a holy custom to bless the children before going to shul since that time before Yom Kippur is one of great holiness and the gates of compassion are open.*[1]

[May God make you as Ephraim and Manasseh]; may God, blessed be He, help you to be as important as Ephraim and Manasseh (as great a person in Torah as Ephraim and in worldly matters as Manasseh). [The blessing for daughters is nonbiblical: May God make you as Sarah, Rebecca, Rachel, and Leah.] May it be the will of our Father in heaven to instill in your heart a love and awe-filled respect for Him reflected constantly in your countenance, so that you will not sin and your desire shall ever be for Torah and *mitzvos*. May your eyes be enlightened with Torah, your mouth speak words of wisdom [*divray chochmo*], your heart be concerned with fear of heaven [*yirahs shomyim*], your hands with giving charity, and your feet run to do the will of the Creator, blessed be He, and help the needy.

May He bless you with righteous sons and daughters who will study Torah and be imbued with it all their lives . . . and send you a kosher livelihood, earned honorably and easily so that you may possess the calmness of spirit with which to serve your Creator. May you be inscribed and sealed for a happy year and peaceful life among all the righteous ones of *klal Yisroel* [all Israel]. *Omayn.*

*Author's postscript: After this, one should go to* shul *with great humility and full awareness of the sanctity of Yom Kippur.*

## 80. *Techinno* for the *Olaynu* Prayer[1]

*Olaynu* [It is our duty to praise the Master of all]. It is incumbent upon us to love Your holy Name in dread and benefit from Your kind heart although I am full of sin. [You are called the Compassionate One Who has taught *teshuvo*:] You are, after all, kindhearted and have taught us the way of repentance [*teshuvo*, return]. Thus, I come before Your venerable Name [to pray for my soul and for my family], to pray for myself, my husband, and my children, bending the knee, bowing, prostrating myself in fear to beseech of Your holy Name, King of kings, the holy One blessed be He, that the kindness that You have done me, my husband and children from our youth until this day, God full of compassion, that You do not permit me to extinguish Your mercy since the present time is one of grace before Your Throne of Glory. May You forgive our transgressions, as You have assured *Moshe Rabenu* in the holy Torah [I have pardoned as you requested—Num. 14:20],[2] may You forgive the sins that we have confessed and accept our prayers, as was Channo's prayer when she said to Eli [I am a very unhappy woman—1 Sam. 1:15]: "I am a woman with a troubled, bitter heart." [And do not enter into judgment with us. . . . ] Do not judge us [for before You no creature is in the right—Ps. 143:2], no person is free of transgressions. And when, heaven forbid, Satan is the accuser,[3] allow us to partake of Your kindness and compassion. Arise from the throne of judgment and sit on the throne of compassion. Dear God, deal kindly with me, my husband, and my children and cleanse us of our sins—but not with suffering or illness.

Lord of the universe, my heart breaks when I recall the Holy
Temple that once stood, when the High Priest carried out the
Avodo[4] in the Holy of Holies, the red thread turned white,[5] and
all Israel knew their prayer(s) had been found acceptable. These
days, because of our many sins, we have no Temple, no High Priest,
no sacrifice to atone for us; we have only our prayer. Therefore,
accept our prayer with compassion and grant the means whereby
I shall be able to assist students of the Torah and give tzedoko to
the poor and needy, not to use our wealth as a means to dominate them. [You open Your hand . . . –Ps. 145:16a.][6] Open Your
gentle hand and feed, compassionate Father. [May the words of
my mouth . . . be acceptable to You . . . –Ps. 19:15a.][7] Please
accept my thoughts and when, heaven forbid, on occasion I may
say something improper [Grace me with understanding],[8] test my
contrite and saddened heart. Permit my tears and pleading to be
my defense, for my husband and children as well. If I am already
unworthy to plead for myself, my husband, and my children, You
have nevertheless assured us that [You do kindness to thousands];[9]
You will turn Your mercy upon many thousands of Your creatures.
Accept my prayer and do not let my tears fall in vain. Rebuild the
Holy Temple quickly in our day so that the High Priest will once
again be able to officiate at the Avodo Service. Omayn.


# 81. A *Techinno* before *Neilo*[1]

Merciful God, open Your holy eyes and see how broken my heart
is, how tears flow from my eyes as though from a fountain. Behold my pain and my grief. May my burning tears convey my
prayer through the gate known as [the Gate of Tears] straight to
the Throne of Glory.

The sweet day of Yom Kippur will soon be over. The sun is
sinking, its brilliant rays are fading. These final moments are so
precious. There is yet time to beg for Your mercy, that You bestir
Your compassion for us. I cry out with all my remaining strength,
my every fiber entreats You despite my extreme weariness brought

on by the fast. Almighty God, seal us [in the Book of Life] for a good life, all of us [who are] the Children of Your Covenant.

May my tears wash away the [spiritual] stains upon my holy soul. Watch over these tears until they arrive at Your Throne of Glory. Welcome them with great compassion. Hide them away in the vault where You store the holy prayers of righteous and pious people. May their prayers stand by us so that we may find fulfillment of that for which we hope and pray: *L'shono ha-bo'oh berusholoyim* [Next year in Jerusalem]. *Omayn.*

## 82. After Candlelighting—Succos

*Ribono shel olom* [Lord of the universe], I thank and praise Your beloved Name for having given us the *mitzvo* of candlelighting to illuminate the *succo*,[1] commemorating the great wonders You wrought for our ancestors during their forty years of wandering in the wilderness. You protected them with a great cloud from scorching heat, harsh weather, and sudden downpourings of rain where there were no buildings in which to take refuge. You supplied their needs—manna from heaven, water from a spring . . . cared for them as one does the apple of one's eye [He kept him as the apple of His eye—Deut. 32:10].

Kind God, I beg of You to have compassion upon me as when You protected our ancestors with the clouds of glory [*ahnehnay kovode*] from the rains and the sun's severe heat, and from the great serpents and lizards of the wilderness. Shield our festival of Succos from rain so that bad weather will not prevent us from fulfilling the holy *mitzvo* of [dwelling in] the *succo*. By virtue of this *mitzvo* that we fulfill, protect us from the debility that comes from [exposure to] severe heat and bad weather. Protect us, too, from those two-legged serpents (the enemies of Israel) who seek to consume Your divided and dispersed people.

Remember our dwelling in the *succo* and leaving our houses. Ease the sufferings in exile that were decreed upon us; gather our scattered brethren from all the corners of the earth. Lead us to

Your holy land and rebuild King David's fallen *succo*,[2] which is
the Holy Temple. For that will be our true joy. May it come speedily
in our day. *Omayn*.

# 83. The Four Species[1]

The festival of Succos shows the world that we will exist [survive]
forever despite our enemies—as experience has proven. Great
nations such as Assyria, Babylon, Amon, and Moab, rulers before
whom the entire world trembled—all have been removed. There
is no memory of them, whereas we, weak sheep among many
wolves and tigers with gaping jaws about to swallow us—we have
survived. By what merit has this come about?

When we sit in the *succo*, what do we learn [understand] from
the heavens (which we see through the branches covering the
*succo*)? We rely not upon human strength but upon our Father in
heaven, submitting all our limbs to His will. King David, may he
rest in peace, says [on behalf of all Israel]: [All my being shall say:
Lord, who is like You?—Ps. 35:10].[2] With all my limbs I testify that
You alone are One and no other. With that thought in mind, we
take in hand the four species on Succos. They represent the main
parts of one's body.

The *esrog* [citron] is the heart (i.e., it is shaped like one). The
*lulov* [palm branch] is like a man's spine, the *hadassim* [myrtle
leaves] are like the eyes [To You I lift up my eyes . . . —Ps. 123:1][3]
that we raise up to our Father in heaven. The leaves of the *arovo*
[willow] are shaped like the [lips of the] mouth; with them we sig-
nify by shaking the four species in the four compass directions
that we move ourselves and all our limbs in the service of God.
May they ward off all sorts of [*ruchos rohos*] melancholy spirits,[4]
all storms and winds raging round about us throughout the world.
[In the last two directions] we raise them [the four species] up and
lower them in the hope that no evil vapors befall us from on high
and none rise up against us from the earth to harm us and en-
danger our existence.

Although not every person has such a noble feeling as to say and observe [All my being shall say: Lord, who is like You?], the holy One, blessed be He, has suggested a solution. During the Exodus, Jews merited receiving the Torah because they were united as one [ . . . and Israel encamped there—Exod. 19:1[5]]: those of high standing influenced those in lower (social) strata. *Ba'ahlay bohsim* [houseowners] who have performed good deeds but are deficient in Torah learning resemble the *lulov* [in that it bears fruit but lacks a nice odor]; those who have acquired Torah learning but lack good deeds resemble the *hadassim* [myrtle leaves], which have a nice odor but bear no fruit; finally, there are the humble, simple Jews who lack Torah learning and good deeds but who resemble the *arovo* [willow]. They should form holy societies [groups] to study Bible, *Mishnah, Ayn Ya'akov, Menoras Ha-mo'or*, a psalms group, or a *Chevra Shas* [Talmud study group] and obtain a scholar who has in him both Torah learning and good deeds and is like the *esrog* [which bears fruit and has a good odor]. He [the *talmid chochom*, the scholar] should be able to unite the Jews into a cohesive group, as it is written: [And who has founded His *vault* upon the earth—Amos 9:6][6] to study daily, to bring them close to Torah and *yirahs shomyim* [fear of heaven].

The lesson of the bundle [*ahgudo*] of the four species is emphasized by King Solomon, who says: [He who keeps company with the wise becomes wise—Prov. 13:20], he who binds himself to a study society of scholars and virtuous Jews, the merit of the many shall influence him, ennoble his feelings, and strengthen his faith so that he will be able to rise to the degree of [All my being shall say: Lord, who is like You?]

## 84. *Techinno* for *Hoshano Rabbo* before *Hallel*[1]

I pray now, great, strong, and awesome God, as I come before You in fear and trembling with great *kavono* [concentration] on this day. It is the final day on which judgments are sealed for each person, decisions made as to what is in store for him during the coming year, whether he will live or die; whether he will perish by water or by fire, by sword or by wild beasts, by hunger or by thirst, by storm or by murder; who will be strangled or stoned; whether he will be at home or wander about, will live quietly or be robbed, live peacefully in good health and be strong; will be afflicted with suffering, impoverished or enriched, [cast down or] raised up.

*Ribono shel olom* [Lord of the universe], on this day of *Hoshano Rabbo* when we receive our written judgments for better or worse, I come to plead before You for a good judgment for myself, my husband, and my children, for life and health and an honorable *parnoso* [livelihood] for us as well as for all the people of Israel, that You bless them with a good *parnoso*, with abundance and success and all manner of good.

*El molay rahchamim* [Merciful God], when we have acted foolishly, please act in keeping with Your nature and forgive us despite the fact that we have repaid Your goodness with evil. Compassionate Father, requite us with good; what benefit is there in casting us down into the hole of *Gayhenom* for our sins?[2] Are You not known for Your mercy and compassion?

Compassionate Father, consider the rectitude of Your servants who in former times gave their lives and those of their children unhesitatingly, scorning their existence in this world, submitting their wills to Yours and, sanctifying Your great Name, stretched forth their necks to be slaughtered. Their [shed] blood has come before You. It is the [shed] blood of fathers and children, mothers with infants, sisters and brothers, brides and grooms, men and women. They died for *kiddush ha-Shaym* [sanctification of the Name; martyrs' deaths]. Earth, do not cover their blood until God first sees it!

*Ribono shel olom*, remember these things and reconsider. Destroy Your anger, [do not pour out] the burning wrath upon Your people Israel. Bring us forth from trembling into radiance and grant us a good year of redemption for the sake of the *z'chus* [merit] of our holy Fathers Abraham, Isaac, and Jacob. *O-mayn.*

*Ribono shel olom,* grant us a good life.

*Ribono shel olom,* grant us a good *parnoso* [livelihood].

*Ribono shel olom,* do not destroy us.

*Ribono shel olom,* fulfill the prayers of our hearts for good.

*Ribono shel olom,* put an end to our downcast spirits.

*Ribono shel olom,* grant us the end of our captivity.

*Ribono shel olom,* grant us the day of our salvation.

*Ribono shel olom,* behold the poverty of Your people Israel.

*Ribono shel olom,* hear our outcry.

*Ribono shel olom,* grant a good and long life to the monarch in whose land we dwell.

*Ribono shel olom,* implant in his heart and in the hearts of his counselors and officials the compassion with which to be kindly disposed toward us.

*Ribono shel olom,* grant peace in his kingdom.

*Ribono shel olom,* bless this land and the entire world.

*Ribono shel olom,* give bread as needed to the poor of Your people Israel, that they not depend upon the mercy of others.

*Ribono shel olom,* do not take my *parnoso* from me.

*Ribono shel olom,* bless with success the endeavors of my hands.

*Ribono shel olom,* help me to have good and religious children.

*Ribono shel olom,* enable me and my husband to raise our children in [the ways of] Your holy Torah.

*Ribono shel olom,* prevent all illnesses from coming upon us.

*Ribono shel olom,* accept my bitter tears.

*Ribono shel olom,* hear the sound of my weeping.

*Ribono shel olom,* remember us for the sake of the *z'chus* [merit] of our Fathers Abraham, Isaac, and Jacob.

*Ribono shel olom,* remember us for the sake of the *z'chus* of our [Mothers] Sarah, Rebecca, Rachel, and Leah.

*Ribono shel olom,* remember us for the sake of the *z'chus* of all righteous men and women.

*Ribono shel olom,* accept the prayer that we shall recite in the *Hoshanos* and seal us [in the divine record] for a good and blessed year. *Omayn.*

## 85. *Techinno* for Simchas Torah¹ (Version 1)

Torah, Torah! Regard your dear children who come to kiss you
out of their great love for you. See the great affection they hold
for you in their hearts. See how they dress themselves in their fin-
est clothes out of respect for you and in your honor. Requite us
by putting in a good word with the Name, may He be blessed,
that He give us a good year filled with blessings and financial
independence.

May we merit the good fortune to be able to come and kiss the
sacred Torah in the Holy Temple, quickly, in our [life] time. *Omayn.*

## 86. *Techinno* for Simchas Torah¹ (Version 2)

*Ribono shel olom*, as we are about to depart from Your holy synagogue, we reflect on how happy we are to have been here and
[with great affection] kiss Your precious, holy Torah.

Strengthen our hearts so as to be able throughout the [com-
ing] year to fulfill all that is found in the holy Torah. Because of
the merit of all the saintly *tzaddikim* and pious [*frume*] people, may
we be found worthy next year at this time to gather together in
the holy city of Jerusalem. As the holy *Gemoro* says, in that time
all the synagogues will come up to the Land of Israel [*Eretz Yisroel*].
May we at that time merit the Redemption [*ge'uloh*]. And may it
take place speedily in our [life] time. *Omayn.*

## 87. *Techinno* for Simchas Torah¹ (Version 3)

*Author's note: This techinno is to be said on Simchas Torah when
one comes into shul [synagogue] to kiss the Torah.*

*Yehhe rohtzone milfonehcho* . . . [May it be Your will], our God and
God of our ancestors, that the hour when we come to *shul* and open

the holy ark [*ohron ha-kodesh*] to kiss Your beloved holy Torah, be a favorable hour, one of mercy and forgiveness. May the *z'chus* [merit] we earn by coming now to kiss Your holy, beloved Torah open for us the gates of life and health, the gates of a good *parnoso* [livelihood] and good fortune, the gates of happiness. Grant us happiness in all of life's ways and enable us everywhere to keep Your holy Torah and its *mitzvos*.

Because we rejoice in the beloved *yom tov* [holy festival] with Your Torah, cause our hearts to rejoice in all good things. Do not permit any sadness to come upon us and spare us from harm.

Torah, behold your beloved children who come to kiss you. They have great love for you in their hearts and are dressed in festive clothes in your honor. Speak on our behalf to the Name, may He be blessed, that He grant us a good year with many *b'rochos* [blessings], with riches and honor, that we shall merit kissing the holy Torah in the *bays ha-mikdosh* [Holy Temple] quickly in our time. *Omayn.*

When kissing the Torah, recite this verse three times: "May he kiss me with the kisses of his mouth/for your love is better than wine" [Songs 1:2].[2]

*Ribono shel olom* [Lord of the universe], we now prepare to leave Your beloved and holy *shul*, happy [in the knowledge] that we have been here and kissed Your beloved holy Torah. We ask, dear God, that You strengthen our hearts so that in the coming year we shall be able to fulfill all that is in Your Torah. For the sake of the merit of all the righteous and pious people everywhere, may we be found worthy of being able to come again [on Simchas Torah] into Your holy *shul. Omayn, omayn.*

# 88. Flee, My Beloved[1]

Dear God of Israel, have pity on Your sheep [who dwell] in the wilderness [of exile], seventy thousand of whom (in Morocco and

Romania)² have had their wool torn from them from all sides [by
their enemies] with sharp teeth, despoiled right down to the skin,
so that blood flows. It is unbearable. Our brethren no longer have
the strength to withstand the onslaughts in those distant lands of
exile and we are unable to help them, neither with good deeds
nor with the study of Torah and [the performance of] *mitzvos*.
The *yetzer ho-ro* [Evil Inclination] strives mightily against us
because we have not served the holy Torah properly. Our children go in corrupt ways. We are guilty of all this. It is the *yetzer
ho-ro* who has misled us. We were blinded [by his temptations].
Pity Your children, descendants of holy Forefathers Abraham,
Isaac, and Jacob. Remember their *z'chus* [merit] in our favor. Remove the Evil Angel [the *yetzer ho-ro*] from us so that we may serve
You heart and soul.
Lighten the heavy burden of making a living. It is as difficult
for us as the splitting of the Sea of Reeds, since we must rely on
the generosity of our enemies [even for our livelihoods].
*Ribono shel olom* [Lord of the universe], pity us and gather us
from the four corners of the earth into Jerusalem. Let us be worthy of rebuilding the Holy Temple in which we shall serve You
wholeheartedly forever. *Omayn.*

## 89. Rachel Weeping for Her Children¹

*Ribono shel olom* [Lord of the universe], although we are exceed-
ingly sinful and unworthy of appealing to You for pity and we
know we are impertinent, for we have not rendered the honor due
You as the one and only God of the world before whose glory the
angels, *serofim*, *ofanim*, and holy *chayos*,² do tremble, [please] bear
in mind that we are merely flesh and blood. Only Your sacred
promise comforts us. We stand like a poor man at the door [seek-
ing charity]. May the merit of righteous martyrs who died for the
sake of Your great and holy Name . . . whose blood flowed [like
water], erase the [spiritual] blemish of our sins.
Remember Your holy promise made to our faithful Mother

Rachel. When the Jews were being led out of Jerusalem into exile (for their many sins) and they were passing her grave [a voice from Ramah was heard—Jer. 31:14], a terrible voice was heard from heaven [lamentation and bitter weeping—Jer. 31:14]. Her weeping rent the heavens. The voice, as recorded in the Midrash, was that of a sheep among seventy wolves. And God replied [to her]: "Moderate your weeping. There will come a time of Redemption when they will return joyfully from foreign lands to their own borders in the Land of Israel and will serve God in sanctity and purity. The Holy Temple will be rebuilt and they will be righteous people [tzaddikim] once again." For it is written in Your holy Scripture that [Your people shall all of them be righteous—Isa. 60:21].[3]

Your promise is eternally sacred. Accept, therefore, the weeping of holy Rachel, together with our tears, so that we may merit [the good fortune] to behold the [return of the children to their border—Jer. 31:16b],[4] quickly and in our own day. *Omayn veomayn.*

# 90. Embarking on an Ocean Voyage[1]

Great Creator of the world, You created heaven and earth and all therein in six days. On the third day, You commanded waters covering the globe to be gathered in one area. And so it was. The water was gathered together and became a mighty ocean. You created in it all sorts of creatures.

Everything on land is found in the ocean except the mole—to teach man that when he is tranquil, wallows in earthly pleasures, collecting endlessly like the mole, not knowing for whom he's collecting [ . . . amassing and not knowing who will gather in—Ps. 39:7], since he's confused by the bustle of the world and fails to hear Your voice (the divine element in his soul), he mistakenly thinks his entire purpose is to eat and drink.

On the ocean, however, the tumult of the world is driven out and he hears Your voice, as King David says [The voice of the Lord is upon the waters—Ps. 29:3]:[2] Where does man hear God's voice?

Upon the waters. [And the spirit of God was hovering—Gen. 1:2.]
Where does God's spirit move? Where does man sense Him? [. . .
over the water—Gen. 1:2.] Man is often more aware of Him when
traversing the great ocean, as is written in the psalm beginning
with the words [The Lord reigns . . . above the noise of the
mighty waters . . . —Ps. 93:4], which is the tumult of the world;
[more majestic than the breakers of the sea] more powerful than
the waves of the great sea [is the Lord, majestic on high]; there
(on the ocean) one notices how strong and mighty divinity is, as
King David says [They who go down to the sea in ships—Ps.
107:23]: those who travel the ocean in ships, [who do their business on the mighty waters] the sailors and merchants who work
on the great waters [they have seen the works of the Lord—Ps.
107:24], they behold God's work and His wonders of the deep
[by His words He raised a storm wind—Ps. 107:25a]. Through His
word a storm is raised over the ocean [that made the waves surge—
Ps. 107:25b] and its billows surge. [They mount up to the heaven,
plunge down to the depths—Ps. 107:26a.] The storm's waves
sweep over the ship as high as the heaven and cast it down into
the deep; [their soul is dismayed by the terror—Ps. 107:26b], their
soul is filled with fright. [They reel and stagger like a drunkard—
Ps. 107:27a.] They are hysterical and reel about like one intoxi-
cated [and all their nautical skill is useless—Ps. 107:27b], all their
knowledge (of running a ship) is as nothing. [They cry out to the
Lord in their distress—Ps. 107:28a.] They cry out to God in their
need [and He delivers them from their afflictions—Ps. 107:28b].
He brings them out of their crushing situation and emergency.
[He reduces the storm to a whisper—Ps. 107:29a.] He converts
the storm to silence [and the waves are stilled—Ps. 107:29b] and
the waves are quiet. [They are happy when the waves are quieted—
Ps. 107:30a.] They are happy when they remain quiet [and He
brings them to their haven—Ps. 107:30b]. He brings them to the
place they desired. [May they give thanks to the Lord for His loving-kindness—Ps. 107:32a.] They ought to thank God for His
mercy and tell of His wonders to all men.

   Beloved Father! With my present ocean trip I am able to see
some of Your might and great mercy that You have bestowed upon

man, how You have given him the know-how to make his way over the ocean. As the prophet says [ . . . Who makes a way in the sea . . . —Isa. 43:16a], You are the One who has made a way in the sea; You led Your people Israel over the sea as easily as one travels a straight post road [and a path through the mighty waters—Isa. 43:16b], as though leading a train [sic] through the mightiest, most tumultuous waters, You have given man the understanding to overcome those forces that You created in nature, that he might make great engines to drive the ship as the locomotive drives the train.

As You have done man many kindnesses, so do I beg of You to have my trip succeed. May the ocean be calm and the ship reach its destination. May it not be struck below the waterline nor run aground. Let not the sailors sleep during their night watch so that ships will not collide; protect us from all misfortunes that might happen at sea, for Your supremacy is over all. As the prophet says [ . . . Who stir up the sea so that its waves roar—Isa. 51:15]. You quiet the roar of the waves, as on that (seventh) night (of Passover), when Pharaoh chased the Israelites and overtook them at the sea. You caused a windstorm to come over the sea in the midst of which was a calm, where it split into twelve paths and each tribe crossed individually, pursued by their enemy. At that moment, You signaled the sea to flood over them, and rider and horse drowned while Your children were delivered.

Bring me to a safe landing, uninjured, with nothing to prevent my disembarking. May I find all those (to whom I go) healthy and happy.

As You silence the ocean in the midst of the storm, so may You silence all the enemies of Israel who stew and fret about us. Pour out Your spirit over all Your creatures that they may acknowledge Your oneness. May they be filled with divine knowledge so that the holy words of the prophet Isaiah be fulfilled [For[3] the earth shall be full of the knowledge of the Lord—Isa. 11:9b], the land will be full of the recognition of God [as the waters that cover the sea—11:9b], as the waters covering the sea. May it be speedily and in our time. *Omayn*.

# NOTES

## INTRODUCTION

1. Yudel Mark, "Yiddish Literature," in *The Jews: Their History, Culture and Religion*, ed. L. Finkelstein, vol. 2 (Philadelphia: Jewish Publication Society of America, 1949), p. 864, refers to the *techinnah* as a "prayer of entreaty" as found in Joseph Bar Yakir's first Yiddish prayer book, *Shmuel-Buch*, published in Augsburg, 1544.

2. Solomon Freehof, "Devotional Literature in the Vernacular," *Central Conference of American Rabbis* 33 (1923): 375-423.

3. Nevertheless, a *techinnah* collection was published recently by one Rabbi Moses Greenfield: *Techinno Kol Bo He-chodosh* (Brooklyn: Ateres Publishing, 1969). The book is mainly a reprint of earlier editions and follows earlier formats. There is a considerable increase in the use of vowels; typeface is clear and legible; pagination is inaccurate in a number of places, probably due to straight copying from earlier editions. Plagiarism was a nonexistent concept in this genre—even though this edition does indicate a copyright.

4. Freehof, "Devotional Literature," p. 379.

5. Ibid., p. 390.
6. Emanuel S. Goldsmith, "Yiddishism and Judaism," *Judaism: A Quarterly Journal* (Fall 1989): 527-536.
7. J. Biguenet and R. Schulte, eds., *The Craft of Translation* (Chicago: University of Chicago Press, 1989), p. xii.
8. Ibid., p. 528.
9. Ibid.
10. G. Scholem, *Major Trends in Jewish Mysticism* (New York: Schocken Books, 1946), p. 44. See also Ezekiel, chapter 1.
11. B. L. Visotzky, *The Midrash on Proverbs* (New Haven: Yale University Press, 1992), p. 46.
12. Ibid., pp. 56-58.
13. Scholem, *Major Trends*, p. 111.
14. *Language of Faith*, 2nd ed., ed. N. N. Glatzer (1947; New York: Schocken Books, 1967), p. 26.
15. Fanny Neuda, *Stunden der Andacht* (Prag-Breslau: Verlag von Jakob B. Brandeis, 1916).
16. Michael Gluzman, "The Exclusion of Women from Hebrew Literary History," *Prooftexts* 11:3 (1991): 259.
17. *Mekor Dimoh Shas Techinno Hadosho* (Vilna: Rosenkrans & Schriftsetzer, 1922).
18. *Shas techinno Rav Peninim* (New York: Hebrew Publishing, 1916).
19. *Encyclopaedia Judaica*, vol. 2, col. 604 (henceforth: *EJ*).
20. I learned subsequently that "various collections were combined into one larger extended work containing about a hundred and twenty *tkhines* . . . usually under the title *Seder tkhines u-vakoshes* (order of supplications and petitions). This collection became very popular and was reprinted with only minor variations. . ." (Chava Weissler, "Prayers in Yiddish and the Religious World of Ashkenazic Women," in *Jewish Women in Historical Perspective*, p. 162).

## 1. TO OUR ESTEEMED WOMEN

1. Translator's Comments (henceforth: T. C.).
This threefold section (To Our Esteemed Women, More Understanding in Women, Prepare Yourselves in the Vestibule), properly understood, is not a *techinnah*. It is, rather, an attempt to convey a mental orientation to the woman reader, to heighten her awareness of her self-worth as a

person in the Jewish world, and convey an appreciation of the contributions her female predecessors have made throughout history to the Jewish people. The Jewish woman's world was a circumscribed one outlined by many generations of living within a religious tradition. It was, as the Germans put it, one of *Kinder, Kirche,* and *Küche*–(raising) children (and seeing to their religious and moral upbringing), church (preserving and transmitting the received religious tradition and its values), and kitchen (presiding over the household and seeing to the physical well-being of family members). Study of Torah and practice of *mitzvot* enabled one to maintain spiritual health in this transitory world as well as ensure admission into the world-to-come.

2. Exodus 2:18-22. On verse 21: "... because the midwives feared God, He made them *houses.* Rashi: That is, "dynasties of the priesthood and Levites . . . from Jocheved (Shifrah) . . . and a royal dynasty from Miriam (Puah) . . . as stated in *Sotah* 11b."

3. Rashi on Exodus 38:8 says that the daughters of Israel had mirrors into which they looked when they adorned themselves. "They did not hesitate to bring these as a contribution for the Tabernacle. Moses wanted to reject these since they were made for vain purposes. . . . God said to Moses to accept them for, through them, the women raised many children in Egypt . . . the laver was made of them [the mirrors] to promote peace between a man and his wife."

4. The story of Judith and the beheading of Holofernes is found in the *Apocrypha.* The story was generally retold at Chanukah because it dealt with Israel's deliverance from the Assyrian threat. The story of Chanukah, dealing also with the deliverance of Israel from mighty conquering oppressors, is found in the *Scroll of the Hasmoneans.* See Birnbaum, *DPB,* pp. 713-725. Also known as the *Scroll of Antiochus,* it has come down to us in both Hebrew and Aramaic. During the medieval period, this scroll (*megillah*) was read in Italian synagogues on Chanukah as the *Scroll of Esther* is read on Purim. The English version of the Judith story is available in an edition published by Oxford University Press, London, n.d.

5. *Prozdor,* hall, is "the Hebrew transliteration of a Greek word for a dining hall, and may have been chosen because the Happiness of the World to Come is conceived under the image of a banquet" (Hertz, *ADPB,* pp. 677-678, footnote). See also footnote to *Avot* 3:20 on "everything is prepared for the feast" (Hertz, *ADPB,* p. 662).

6. Which add up to the traditional 613 commandments.

## 2. UPON ARISING IN THE MORNING

1. Found in the *Adon olom*, which may have been composed by Solomon Ibn Gabirol (11th century, C.E.); part of the Weekday Morning Service since the 15th century; often sung at the end of the Sabbath Morning Service.
2. Hertz, *ADPB*, p. 663, footnote: "Unless the body is adequately nourished, the brain will not function properly, and study will be ineffective." Also, ad loc: "Man's duty is to feed his mind and spirit, as well as his body. 'Man doth not live by bread alone, but by everything that proceedeth out of the mouth of the Lord doth man live'" (Deut. 8:3).

## 4. BEFORE GOING TO SLEEP

1. From *Ahnaie Shas Techinno* (Vilna: Rochel-Esther Bas Avi-chayil, 1930?), p. 47. JTSAL: BM 675 74 A3.
2. The surname *Bas Tovim* will be found again in the "Three Gates Techinno," (#33) by Sarah *Bas Tovim*. It seems that both ladies sought to attach themselves to (rabbinically) distinguished families. See *EJ* 4:318.

## 5. A LITTLE WITH *KAVONO*

1. *Kavono (Kavvanah)*: ". . . the motivation of the act, or the spirit in which it is performed. . . . It connotes intention, devotion, dedication, single-minded concentration . . ." (Garfiel, *Service of the Heart*, p. 138). Cf. ". . . the means by which a fixed liturgy eludes routinization and retains vitality" (Mintz, "Prayer and the Prayerbook," in *Back to the Sources*, ed. B. W. Holtz, p. 426).

## 6. STRONG AS A LION

1. The words Rabbi Jacob used on the first page of his *Tur Orach Chaim* are a quotation from *Ethics of the Fathers* 5:23—"Judah son of Tema said: Be bold as a leopard, light as an eagle, swift as a deer, and strong as a lion, to carry out the will of your Father in heaven." Rabbi Joseph Caro in his *Shulchan Aruch* shortened it in his opening section to the volume *Orach Chaim* to "One should be strong as a lion to arise in the morning and do the will of his Creator. . . ." The Evil Inclination's summer and winter arguments in this *techinnah* were also borrowed from the *Tur Orach Chaim*, p. 2a.

## 7. *TECHINNO MODEH ANI*

T.C.: While the opening words of this *techinnah* begin with the opening words of the prayer *Modeh Ani*, it differs in content from the actual contents of the prayer. The author of this *techinnah* appeals to God to forgive all the woman's sins previously committed, including those done inadvertently, concerning which all women are enjoined to observe, namely, those concerning *challo, niddo*, and candlelighting. (See "Three Gates *Techinno*, #33, for explanation of these terms.) The hope is also expressed that, when her time comes to leave this world, her death may serve as a *kaporo* (atonement) for her sins. The section concludes with a final plea that God hear her prayer.

The Hebrew *Modeh Ani* prayer deserves further attention. The most attractive translation of the *Modeh Ani* Prayer is found in *Siddur Sim Shalom: A Prayerbook for Shabbat, Festivals, and Weekdays*, p. 2:

> I am grateful to You, living, enduring, King,
> for restoring my soul to me in compassion.
> You are faithful beyond measure.

Historically speaking, it is of relatively recent vintage, its first appearance in print dating from the publication of the prayer book *Seder Ha-yom* in 1695. However, its origins probably go back to the *Elohai Neshamah* prayer found in the tractate *Berachot* 60b, which was to be recited as one performed the acts of dressing and washing after rising from sleep. Eventually, the *Elohai Neshamah* prayer came to be recited in the synagogue and not in the home as originally intended. Abraham Millgram (*Jewish Worship*, pp. 143-146) has pointed out that

> there were people who objected to reciting this prayer upon awakening. How can one, they asked, utter a prayer with God's name in it before washing one's hands? The prayer was therefore transferred along with the morning blessings to the synagogue services. . . .
>
> But the transfer of the *Elohai Neshamah* prayer to the synagogue service left a void in the religious life of the people. They missed a prayer to recite upon waking from sleep. Another passage was composed, known by its initial words *Modeh Ani* (I thank [Thee]). . . .
>
> Every Jew who was brought up in an observant home remembers this brief morning prayer which his mother taught him in his early childhood, and many a Jew has continued to recite it for the rest of his life.

In preparing this English translation, three Yiddish versions of the *techinnah* were available: the 1853, 1904 (*Shas Techinnos* [Lemberg: David Balaban Publisher, 1904], pp. 10-13) and 1916 (*Shas Techinno Rav-Peninim* [New York: Hebrew Publishing, 1916], p. 9ff.) editions. Some stylistic variations were immediately evident. Despite the typographical clarity of the 1916 version and the ease with which it could be read, thanks to later anonymous editorial hands, there is something to be said for the 1853 version. Although it sometimes shows a cruder style, one occasionally discovers a depth of emotion that has been perceptibly toned down in the 1916 version. For this reason, I chose to rely mainly on the 1853 edition.

It was called the *Techinno Modeh Ani* probably because the reader was supposed to read it soon after reciting the *Modeh Ani* prayer and then wash his/her hands, since God's name is mentioned in it and one would not be expected to read it without first having washed the hands.

The connection between the contents of the *Modeh Ani* prayer and the *Techinno Modeh Ani* is tenuous at best. The contents are not closely related. One example will suffice: The 1904 version includes Maimonides' Thirteen Principles of Faith. These do not appear in the *siddur* at the beginning of the Weekday Morning Service but at its end (Birnbaum, *DPB*, pp. 153-155).

1. The following information has been furnished on the title page: *Techinno Modeh Ani*, by Mistress Sarah, daughter of R. Yukil S"gl Horowaitz, Chief Rabbi of the *Bays Din* [ecclesiastical court] of the holy congregation of Greater Glugoh; wife of R. Shabsi, Chief Rabbi of the *Bays Din* of the holy congregation of Krasni (Russia-Poland). [In Russian:] Printing permitted, Kiev, 9 June, 1853. Censor: [name unclear]. JNUL: R. 71 A 96B:296.319.1.

2. It is surprising to come across these kabbalistic elements in a humble *techinnah*. Specific reference to the worlds or realms is explained in *EJ* 10:580. The article on Kabbalah in *EJ* is extensive. It deals with the subject according to the outline in 10:489, and continues through column 649. For a briefer treatment, see Seltzer, *Jewish People, Jewish Thought*, pp. 436 ff. See also essay by L. Fine, "Kabbalistic Texts," in *Back to the Sources*, ed. B. W. Holtz.

3. The 1853 edition used Isaiah 5:7—"Let the wicked person abandon his way./ and the sinful one his thoughts [plans?];/let him return to the Lord, and He will have compassion on him." That is, He will accept his *teshuvo*, his return to Him. This verse was familiar to traditional, observant Jews from the prophetic reading in the afternoon of the Ninth of *Ab*, the traditional date on which the first and second temples were destroyed.

The anonymous revision in the 1916 edition was probably made some-
time in the nineteenth century, doubtless by an anonymous *maskil*
(Enlightener) with an eye for style. In his opinion, we conjecture, the
Jeremiah passage (3:22), with only five Hebrew words and quoted in the
*techinnah*, had more impact and was less wordy.

## 8. A NEW JERUSALEM *TECHINNO*

T.C.: This *techinnah* reflects a careful previous examination of priori-
ties and an ordering of responsibilities. The petitioner makes four requests: (1) that God lead her in the "right way" in life, (2) that she and
her family merit "good years and long life," (3) that she be granted "good
and religious children who will be righteous, pious, and learned" and
she live to see them married, and (4) that He grant her family a livelihood.

Reflected here is what A. J. Heschel regarded as the Hebrew Bible's
concern for the problem of living rather than the problem of dying; and
not merely living, but living in the "right way," living in "holy service" to
God so that she will thereby be able to sanctify life.

1. "As a matter of fact this so-called new *Techinno* is found word for
word in the old German *Techinno* book. It is number 21 in the Sulzbach
*Techinnah*" (Freehof, "Devotional Literature," p. 389).

2. That is, a child, in 1 Samuel 1:1ff.

3. In the text: 100 years.

4. ". . . renew unto us the coming month *for good and for blessing*"
(Italics mine, N. T.). See "Prayer for the New Month," (Bokser, *PB*, p. 164).

## 9. UPON ARRIVAL AT SYNAGOGUE FOR MORNING SERVICES

1. From *Freger Techinno* (*A Book of Petitions*) (Lemberg, 1897). JNUL
S 6Z A948.

## 12. ACCEPTANCE OF THE YOKE OF THE KINGDOM OF HEAVEN

1. T.C.: This *techinnah* is more than prayer in the conventional sense.
While the petitioner does seek God's favor and blessing, the *techinnah*
also establishes a rationale for requesting them. This rationale serves to
make the petitioner aware of things she seeks within the framework of
her total life. This type of *techinnah* performs a function infrequently
recognized in considering literary prayers. Evelyn Garfiel wrote: "For it

is only when we pray that we can take the time to mull over the religious values of Judaism. And it is in the prayers that we find the most moving expression of those religious values which for the Jew constitute his normal experience" (Garfiel, *Service of the Heart*, p. 28).

A beautiful minor chord is struck in the final sentence of the *techinnah*: ". . . and have the good fortune to grow old along with my husband." It echoes a passage in Robert Browning's poem "Rabbi Ben Ezra," the opening lines of which encourage the beloved one to "Grow old along with me! / The best is yet to be. . . ." It is an attitude toward life not incompatible with the spirit implied in the closing words of the *techinnah* except that, in the prayer, the blessing comes from God.

2. "Kingdom" here means kingship, and "heaven" is merely a synonym for *God*. "To take upon oneself the yoke of the Kingdom of Heaven means, to recognize the rule of God in the heart and life of man" (Hertz, *ADPB*, pp. 112-113 footnote).

### 13. . . . WHO HAS NOT MADE ME A HEATHEN

1. T. C.: In the Morning Service we find a series of blessings following one immediately upon the other, to which Rabbi Hertz referred as "Individual Blessings." According to him, this benediction ( . . . Who has not made me a heathen) constitutes "the reawakening of self-consciousness as Jews, and as free men and women" (*ADPB*, p. 19). The following *techinnah* is an expansion of this idea framed in an historical awareness of one's connection with past and present by means of one's relationship with one's group and, through it, with mankind.

### 14. . . . WHO CREATED ME ACCORDING TO HIS WILL

1. T. C.: Among the "Individual Blessings" referred to by Rabbi Hertz is one in which the Jew gives thanks for not having been made a woman. Jews and non-Jews alike have been put off by this seemingly callous statement. This blessing, Rabbi Hertz pointed out (*ADPB*, p. 20), was an opportunity to "thank God for the privilege which is theirs for performing all the precepts of the Torah, many of these precepts not being incumbent upon women," as they were preoccupied with domestic duties and had the primary responsibility for the care and feeding of the young. The Jewish woman recognized this division of labor and responsibility, knew which precepts she could fulfill, and did so in the little free time available in her full family life; she sought to read (or be read to) inspi-

rational works calculated to enlighten and educate her in the ways of Torah in a broad sense, whether by parable or story, by legend or morality tale. What she really prayed for was the ability to learn and understand as a person in her own right.

## 16. YOU FAVOR MEN WITH KNOWLEDGE

1. The fourth benediction of the *Amidah* is the first of the individual petitions that, though of a personal nature, "voice the needs of all men" (Hertz, *ADPB*, p. 136).
2. Dr. Alfes is obviously including himself here. Is this merely a matter of public relations? Could he have authored this *techinnah* or is it a revised earlier (female) author's version?

## 17. TAKE GOOD CARE

1. T.C.: The above title in slightly different form is found in the weekly portion of the Torah in which Moses pleaded to no avail for permission to cross over to the Promised Land—*Vohes'chanan*.

In this section, Moses warns Israel to remain faithful to God and His Torah. The warning is couched in strong terms: "But take utmost care and *watch yourselves scrupulously* . . ." (*NJPS*) to observe the divine laws given you, and so on.

On a less heroic level, our author shaped this *techinnah* for the humble and modest daughters of Israel many centuries after Deuteronomy. Its purpose remains the same: to guide the daughters of Israel in time-tested paths that, according to him, befit the descendants of those who once stood at Sinai.

The second footnote by the author of the *Sha'aray Tzion* commentary is an example of what might also have been called a "minimanual" for the guidance of Jewish women. The ethical (*musar*) literature category to which it belongs was quite common in Yiddish, the earliest printed books of this type dating from the sixteenth century. Meyer Waxman (*WHJL*, vol. 2, p. 43) indicated their essentially folk character:

> They discuss the phases of actual life and go more into detail in depicting the conditions and circumstances of conduct, and consequently, we feel in them the actual pulsations of life as it was lived in the ghetto a few centuries ago.

2. The text in Proverbs is *derech rehsho'im* ka-*ahfay-loh* (*as* darkness). The author's quote here is: ba-*afay-loh* (*in* darkness). Is he perhaps misquoting from memory? More likely, he has "adjusted" the text to the idea he seeks to convey. This is one of many instances of the midrashic method wherein classic texts were adjusted or adapted to life's everyday situations.

3. *Sha'aray Tzion* commentary: The [author of the book] *Musar Haskayl* [*Moral Instruction*] writes that a faithful wife who wishes to earn the approbation "Most Honorable Woman" should assume the following responsibilities:

*a*) She should always go about clean and neat, never slovenly. Her clothes may be plain but never in need of repair; also, her children should be clean and their clothes not need repair.

*b*) At home all should be clean and neatly arranged, utensils in place. Slothfulness at home is misfortune at home. While things nevertheless do get broken, cracked or torn, a woman must be alert in managing her household.

*c*) Guard against excessive talk and chatter. Foolish talk is unattractive. King Solomon says: Even a fool, if he remains silent, is deemed wise [Prov. 17:28].

*d*) In a time of need, when things are difficult, she should not overly remind her husband of what is needed.

*e*) If she is slightly ill, let her not magnify it out of all proportion and take up with doctors and pills. She should avoid the current fad of going abroad for the baths [health spas]. Besides throwing away good money, one can really become sick. Rest and taking care of one's self can do much [for one's health, without the baths].

*f*) If her husband should happen to speak harshly, let it pass [without saying anything]. A man's anger ends quickly; he'll soon realize his error and try to make amends.

*g*) Avoid praising another man in his presence. So-and-so is clever; so-and-so is handsome, etc.

*h*) If he has suffered a [business] misfortune, don't blame him or throw it up to him. That's uncalled for.

*i*) Don't go around to the neighbors and bring home the latest news about dresses, furniture, and jewelry.

*j*) Better to pray at home alone before God than go to synagogue and look at someone else's pearls or jewelry and run the risk of covetousness or, heaven forbid, of *loshon ho-ro* [speaking ill of someone].

*k*) A wife should not distribute much charity without her husband's knowledge; she should also never get angry at poor people.

*l*) If her husband refuses to divulge some [business?] matter, she should not pester him to do so.

*m*) If one of her husband's friends visits him, she should receive him respectfully and with friendly mien.

*n*) She should not try to live beyond their means, especially in these times when luxurious living has become widespread. Failure to beware can lead, heaven forbid, to misfortune. As they say: "Live without reckoning, die before your time."

*o*) Raise children in piety and teach them to be polite. When someone gives them sweets, they should say "Thank you" and recite the correct blessing before eating. That's how they remember that reciting a blessing means giving thanks to the Eternal One for what He has created. Also, for this reason, teach children the appropriate blessings and see to it that they remember to say the *ha-motzee* blessing [over bread].

*p*) Always speak calmly and without anger; especially in one's relations with servants, never shout at them. Let her consider that her child may someday have to be a servant; she certainly would want an employer to treat her child well.

## 18.  REMEMBER THREE THINGS

1. From *Ahnaie Shas Techinno* (Vilna: Rochel-Esther Bas Avi-chayil of Jerusalem, 1930?), p. 47. JTSAL: BM 675 74 A3.

2. Based on *Sayings of the Fathers* 3:1.

## 19.  A PREGNANT WOMAN'S PRAYER

1. From *Ahnaie Shas Techinno*, p. 204. JTSAL: BM 675 74 A3.

2. The Hannah story is found in 1 Sam. 1:9 ff.

3. *Tiferes Yisroel* [He has cast down from heaven to earth the *beauty of Israel* . . . –Lam. 2:1]. The author of this *techinnah* has taken a term which, in its biblical context, represents a calamitous misfortune for the people and turned it into a reason for future hope in the child soon to be born.

## 20.  ON BEHALF OF A PREGNANT WOMAN

1. From *Ahnaie Shas Techinno*, pp. 205-206. JTSAL: BM 675 74 A3.

2. Huldah was the prophetess consulted by King Josiah concerning the *sefer Torah*, which had been discovered in the Temple in Jerusalem.

The entire story is told in 2 Kings 22:4-23:30. See also *EJ* 8:1063 for interesting aggadic material. As one of seven prophetesses mentioned by name in the Bible, she holds a not insignificant place in the history of the biblical and postbiblical periods.

3. Yael (Jael) slew Sisera in the aftermath of the war between Barak and the Canaanites while he slept in her tent (Judg. 4:17-22). The wife of Heber the Kenite, Yael was not an Israelite. Deborah (the prophetess and judge who persuaded Barak to go to war) praised her in the Song of Deborah (Judg. 5:6). See *EJ* 9:1247.

## 21. TO SYNAGOGUE THE FIRST TIME AFTER RISING FROM CHILDBED

1. [She shall bring a lamb in its first year for a burnt offering and a young pigeon, or a turtledove for a sin offering—Lev. 12:6]. According to the Talmud, the sin offering is incumbent upon her because during the anguish of childbirth, she foreswears any future relations with her husband, which she later regrets [*Niddah* 31b] (*EJ* 4:1050). "The burnt offerings, signifying complete surrender to God, were . . . associated with sin offerings in the process of atonement" (*EJ* 14:602). Spiritual affinity for the Jerusalem Temple and its sacrifices is evidenced by a powerful awareness of its absence. The yearning for its reconstruction is for a means through which to serve God better and more intimately.

2. Incorporated into the *Ma Tovu* prayer and recited at the beginning of the Weekday Morning Service. See Hertz, *ADPB*, pp. 4-5.

## 22. THE FIRST TOOTH

1. T.C.: The author of this *techinnah* was more picturesque in his title. He called it "An Ivory Tower" [based on Songs 7:5—Your neck is as a tower of ivory]. To this, the Soncino translator added a footnote: "A tower-like neck has always been considered beautiful." While we may or may not agree with such an aesthetic appreciation of female physiognomy, there is no denying the mother's enthusiasm at this stage in her child's development. Still, one might hestitate to regard that first tooth as a "tower of ivory." In English, at least, it seems a bit excessive.

## 23. YOUR MOUTH IS LOVELY

1. T. C.: The clause "Your mouth is lovely" is found in Song of Songs 4:3—[Your lips are like a crimson thread, / Your mouth is lovely]. This

text was familiar to Jews who observed the annual practice of reading the Song of Songs on the intermediate Sabbath of Passover before the reading of the Torah. The Hebrew *midborech* (Your mouth) is understood by Ibn Ezra as Your speech. In this sense, it has been fittingly expropriated by the author of the *techinnah* to convey the idea of the preciousness of the child's first speech. It embodies the ideal of verbal purity as an expression of spiritual probity, factors upon which, according to the author, depend the spiritual future of the Jews as a people.

2. That is, "Cautious speech may preserve life as rash talk can imperil it" (Soncino, Prov. 18:2, footnote, ad loc.).

3. The passage is found in Deuteronomy 33:4. It is part of Moses' blessing of the Children of Israel before his death. This verse is the first one that a father is obliged to teach his child: ". . . if he is able to speak, his father must teach him . . . Moses commanded us a Law, an inheritance of the congregation of Jacob." (*Sukkah* 42a, Soncino trans., p. 191). It is still recited today in many families.

### 24. A *TECHINNO* FOR GOOD CHILDREN

1. "Rabbi Simeon ben Yohai taught: He who leaves a son toiling in the Torah is as though he had not died" (*Midrash Rabbah: Genesis*, ed. and trans. H. Friedman, p. 424).

### 25. TO WARD OFF THE EVIL EYE

1. "The kindly eye, blessed with the quality of seeing the good in other people, and free from envy and ill-will . . ." (Hertz, *ADPB*, p. 638).

2. According to Rashi, Moses is the author of this psalm. This psalm was generally familiar to observant Jews since it is recited in the Sabbath Morning Service. See *ArtScroll Siddur*, pp. 380-381, footnotes to Psalm 91; also, footnote to Psalm 90, p. 378, regarding Moses' authorship of psalms 90 to 100, which David later adapted.

3. There follows a list of the kinds of evil eyes, which come in all sizes, shapes, and colors; for example, blue, green, yellow, round, dull, broad, narrow, protruding, or concave, and so on. They can be found in relatives, acquaintances, friends, old, young, male or female.

4. This verse is recited in the Prayer before Retiring (*ArtScroll Siddur*, pp. 294-295): "The Kabbalists find in this three-word prayer mystical combinations of letters spelling the Divine Name that provides salvation against enemies. . . ."

## 26. A *TECHINNO* FOR SICK CHILDREN

1. From *Freger Techinno* (Lemberg: Israel David Suss, Publisher, 1897), p. 5ff. JNUL: S 62 A 948: 296.319.1.

2. It is unclear whether reference is to chicken pox or measles. Chicken pox does form little watery blisters. Measles results in a red rash on head and body. "Measles is prone to lead to complications, the chief of which are pneumonia, bronchitis, phthisis and otitis media" (W. A. N. Dorland, *The American Illustrated Medical Dictionary*, rev. ed. [Philadelphia: W. B. Saunders, 1937], p. 794).

3. This is a long-standing practice with textual basis [in Prov. 10:2—Almsgiving delivers from death]. "The Hebrew word—*tzedaka*, 'righteousness,' quite early received the special sense of 'charity, almsgiving'" (Soncino trans. of the *Tanach*, p. 57, footnote).

4. This story has its basis in the *Midrash Rabbah* to the book of Esther, which generally, as Maurice Simon pointed out in his English translation, served the purpose of "showing how the Jews of Persia had undergone . . . suffering and had been delivered." This midrash had been done by the "Palestinian Amoraim of the fourth century, who unhesitatingly read the conditions of their own time into the biblical text."

> Having made the gallows, he went to Mordecai, whom he found in the house of study with the children. . . . He put chains . . . on them and set guards over them, saying "Tomorrow I will kill these children first, and then I will hang Mordecai." . . . They all wept piteously until the sound of their crying ascended to heaven and the Holy One, blessed be He, heard the sound of their weeping. . . . and He arose from the Throne of Judgment and sat on the Throne of Mercy and said: "What is this loud noise that I hear . . . ?" Moses our teacher . . . said: ". . . they . . . are the little ones of Thy people who have been keeping a fast now for three days . . . and nights, and tomorrow the enemy means to slaughter them . . ." At that moment the Holy One, blessed be He, took the letters containing their doom . . . and tore them and brought fright upon Ahasuerus in that night, as it says, ON THAT NIGHT, etc. (vi, I). (pp. 113-114)

5. The story of the mother (later known as Hannah) and her seven sons is found in 2 Maccabees, chapter 7. They were all executed after first being tortured for refusing Antiochus's command to prove their obedience by eating swine's flesh. (See *EJ* 7:1270-1271.) Nothing is mentioned of their death in their mother's arms. The poetic-dramatic imagination is at work here.

## 27. TO *CHEDER* THE FIRST TIME (VERSION 1)

1. Cf. "Even so did the Holy One, blessed be He, speak unto Israel: 'My children! I created the Evil Desire, but I [also] created the Torah, as its antidote; if you occupy yourselves with the Torah, you will not be delivered into his hand . . .'" (*Kiddushin* 30b; Soncino trans., p. 146).

2. The *Ma'aseh Alfes*, from which the following passage has been translated, is an extended footnote or commentary that elaborated on the implications of selected items in the *techinnot*. Such commentaries as the *Ma'aseh Alfes* were down-to-earth and unsophisticated, often furnishing practical suggestions on how to resolve specific problems. The passage selected here shows the woman how to go about keeping track of her child's progress in his studies. It is not, strictly speaking, part of the *techinnah*, but it does shed light on the domestic scene and the responsibilities mothers assumed willingly.

*Ma'aseh Alfes* commentary: It is important to hear the child [recite his lessons]. (The scriptural basis for this is Deut. 6:7. Also: [You shall teach them to your children . . . –Deut. 11:19]. And you shall teach them to your children, to speak of them when you sit in your house, when you are walking along the road, when you lie down and when you rise up.) It is a biblical injunction that a father teach his son Torah. However, not all fathers have the time or the ability to do so. For this reason the *melamed* is engaged as the father's representative. Nevertheless, the *mitzvo* is still incumbent upon the father [even though he engages a teacher] and the obligation [of teaching one's child Torah] is met when he hears the child recite his lesson.

This also motivates the child, since he knows his father will listen to his recitation. Thus, he will exert himself all the more to pay attention to the *rebbe*'s lesson since he knows his father will reward him if all goes well. If not, his father will be displeased. The *rebbe* is also motivated to see to it that the child is well prepared since this is also a check on him.

It is also a *mitzvo* for the mother to remind the father to quiz the child. When, however, the father is not at home she should ask a neighbor or a good friend [of the family] to quiz the child, in which case her reward [for the *mitzvo*] will be great, in addition to the trouble which she has taken [and for which she will also be suitably rewarded].

She should also encourage the *rebbe* to teach the child [as soon as possible] the correct blessings to be recited on various occasions; and also discourage the child from telling lies. By virtue of her constant proximity to the child, she is in a position to see to it that he be truthful and take care that he recite his blessings [at the proper time]. He who takes care of the sapling will ultimately enjoy its fruit.

## 28. TO *CHEDER* THE FIRST TIME (VERSION 2)

1. *Sha'aray Tzion* commentary: We find it necessary to mention here that there are some women who feel the study of *Chumosh* for a child is enough since he will at any rate never become a rabbi. We wish to explain to them a verse in which they have trained their children in order to show these women they are mistaken. [Moses commanded us the Torah; it is an inheritance of the congregation of Jacob–Deut. 33:5.] The Torah that *Moshe Rabenu* taught us was not for one generation alone; it was "an inheritance," something eternal, to be transmitted from elders to children and not "an inheritance for rabbis," by which we would (mistakenly) infer that only rabbis and learned persons had to study it. It is "an inheritance for the congregation of Jacob." All Jews must study and know Torah, each according to his ability. This is like the soldier who must learn his military manual; if he fails to do so, he's no soldier. The Torah is our manual, teaching us to be amicable in society and faithful subjects to the King of the world. He who learns no Torah is like the soldier who deserts. The main part of the Torah (study) is *Mishno* and *Gemoro*. Without study of these one will be, heaven forbid, like a Karaite [a member of a Jewish sect originating in the eighth century C.E., which rejected the Oral Law]. A wise mother will understand how correct this is.

The mother should also see to it that the child learns the entire *Chumosh* in proper sequence, as our forebears did, and from whom came forth the greatest *geonim* and *tzaddikim*; not [learn by] any [new-fangled] "methods" that use only bits and pieces from the *Chumosh*. Those [taught in this manner] will remain partially educated: a half of nothing is nothing. They should learn as did our great teacher *Moshe Rabenu* in his *cheder*–the whole Torah *k'seder* [properly].

## 29. AT HIS *BAR MITZVO*

1. *Ma'aseh Alfes* commentary: The mother who wishes her child to be diligent in the *mitzvo* of *tefillin* [phylacteries] and esteem them as is proper for such a sublime ornament. . . . should, on the day before the *bar mitzvo* (or the preceding *Shabbos*) read through with her son the introductory remarks in *Ma'aseh Alfes*, which we have written in the book *Talks on Tefillin*. There she will find many thoughts on the meaning of

the phylacteries, including the significance of the two letters *shin* (one with three and one with four stems). In short, one will find delicious food for thought to warm the heart and encourage him to put on *tefillin* always with pleasure.

(Note the difference in practice between European and American Jewry. In Europe, the boy who reached the age of *bar mitzvah* went to synagogue on that day [as he generally did on all other days]. What distinguished that weekday from others was the fact that he began to put on the phylacteries along with the other males thirteen years and up. In the United States, emphasis has been on Sabbath attendance and publicly demonstrating one's ability to chant the final Torah portion for that Sabbath nearest one's birth date according to the Jewish calendar or, at least, the prophetic section. The European practice was described in S. J. Agnon's short story "Two Pairs." The highlight of Agnon's religious maturity, he informs the reader, was when he went to the synagogue for weekday morning prayers with phylacteries his father had recently bought for him. On that occasion, his father "brought cakes and wine in honor of that day on which I graduated to the commandments . . ." for the congregation. It was a simple, uncluttered affair.)

### 30. A CONTRIBUTION TO THE ALMS BOX OF RABBI MEIR *BA'AL HA-NESS*

1. T. C.: *Ba'al Ha-ness* is someone to whom a miracle has occurred.

> Beginning with the eighteenth century a Meir *Ba'al Ha-ness* box was found in almost every Jewish home, and housewives dropped small change into it just before kindling the Sabbath lights. . . . it was customary to contribute money, candles, or oil for lighting as a specific protection against all kinds of ailments and dangers. . . . (*EJ* 11:1246)

The traditional site of Rabbi Meir's tomb (second century C.E.) is on the outskirts of Tiberias. It is covered by two buildings containing houses of study, one for Ashkenazim and one for Sephardim. The *EJ* article is accompanied by a photo of the buildings (col. 1246).

2. This prayer, almost incantatory in nature, appears in the story found in *Avodah Zarah* 18a-b, Soncino trans., pp. 93-94:

> Beruria the wife of R. Meir was a daughter of R. Hanina b. Teradion. Said she [to her husband], "I am ashamed to have my sister placed in a brothel." So he took a *tarkab*-full of *denarii* and set out (to release her). If, thought he, she has not been subjected to anything wrong, a miracle will

be wrought for her, but if she has committed anything wrong, no miracle will happen to her. Disguised as a knight. . . . He went to her warder and said, "Hand her over to me." He replied, "I am afraid of the government." "Take the *tarkab* of *dinars*" said he, "one half distribute [as a bribe], the other half shall be for thyself." "And what shall I do when these are exhausted?" he asked. "Then," he replied, "say 'O God of Meir, answer me!' and thou wilt be saved." "But," said he, "who can assure me that that will be the case?" He replied, "You will see now." There were some dogs who bit anyone [who incited them]. He took a stone and threw it at them, and when they were about to bite him he exclaimed, "O God of Meir, answer me!" and they let him alone. The warder handed her over to him.

This story, plus a few other details, is retold in Yiddish in an explanatory footnote by the author of *Ma'aseh Alfes*, ad loc.

3. The reference is to several marvelous adventures mentioned in connection with Rabbi Meir in the *Avodah Zarah* source, included in the above-quoted passage and repeated in the *Ma'aseh Alfes* so that the petitioner would know to what specifically the *techinnah* referred.

4. Cf. Bokser, *PB*, p. 47: ". . . He sows righteousness and causes deliverance to sprout forth. . . ."

### 31. A PRAYER AT THE WESTERN WALL

1. From *Shas Techinno, Rav Peninim*, pp. 127–130. JTSAL: BM 675 74 A3 1923.

2. "A stone lay there [beneath the Ark] ever since the time of the Early Prophets and it was called 'shethiyah'" (*Sanhedrin* 26b; Soncino trans., p. 155). ". . . foundation stone. . . ." Another view holds that it was the rock on which the Ark stood. Today, it is the "protruding rock on the Temple Mount in the middle of the Mosque of Omar. According to the *aggadot* of the Sages, creation of the world began with and emanated from the *Even shethiyah* . . ." (A. Even-Shoshan, *Ha-milon hehchadash*, vol. 1 [Jerusalem: Kiryath Sepher, 1972], p. 6).

The suggestion is that Zion was created first, and around it other clods, rocks, formations, continents, were formed until the earth was completed. (Soncino trans. to *Sanhedrin*, p. 257, n. 3)

3. "The Psalmist is evidently precluded from bringing an offering and hopes that his prayer will be an efficacious substitute" (Soncino, Psalms, p. 458, footnote).

4. Incorrectly attributed to David, it appears to be quoted from memory. In the original Isaiah passage God, speaking through Isaiah, is directly quoted: "All flesh shall come to bow down before Me." (Emphasis mine, N.T.)

An initially confusing but interesting "revelation" arose in connection with this quotation attributed to David. I could not locate such a passage in Psalms. There is, however, one with a similar ring in Isaiah 66:23 in which the prophet's book concludes on the universal note: ". . . all flesh shall come to worship before Me saith the Lord." (The Hebrew "to worship" is "to bow down.") This sounds like something our *techinnah* writer might have borrowed from the *Siddur* and attributed innocently to David. Unfortunately, a search of the *Siddur* proved fruitless.

My colleague Eliezer Slomovic recognized it immediately upon hearing the quote and referred me to the Birnbaum *Machzor* (*HHPB*), in the Yom Kippur Evening Service, just after the *Ya'aleh piyyut* on p. 523. At the end of the first line and beginning of the second we find: "All flesh shall come to bow down (worship) before You." In a footnote on the following page, Birnbaum refers the reader to Ps. 65:3—"Unto You all flesh shall come"; Psalm 86:9—"All nations . . . shall come and prostrate themselves before You, Lord." The remainder of the psalm references indicate to varying degrees the idea of universal worship of the Lord.

How does a *techinnah* mean? Forgive us, O ghost of John Ciardi, excellent poet and teacher (*How Does a Poem Mean?*), for stealing some of your thunder, but much of what you did over thirty years ago in basic textual analysis seems more significant and relevant than what Structuralists, Deconstructionists, and others have tried to do in the postmodern era. The word, the phrase, the verse must be understood in the light of history, as picture, as feeling, as form; as the stirrings of language, roots, and distinction—all are more important than reconstructing or deconstructing a text into chaos.

Somewhere in the great talmudic sea, a Sage once said: "If the text is meaningless to you, it is you who are at fault, not the text." (*Im rayk hu—me-kem hu!*) Text and context, yes, but never a pretext for one's ideas.

Whether the author of this *techinnah* was aware of what the *Machzor* editors had done in Birnbaum (*HHPB*, p. 523) may never be known. That he was a psalm-reading Jew, a *Tillim Yid*, is not to be doubted for a moment. But it is important to see how such a passage and countless others over many lifetimes and generations have blended into the collective memory of a people. It is humbling to stand on the threshold of a people's eternity.

5. The miracle of God's fire consuming the bullock, altar, and surrounding water-filled trench in 1 Kings 18:30 ff. took place "at the time of the meal-offering (*mincha*)"—v. 36. "It is understood . . . to correspond . . . to the daily afternoon sacrifice offered in the Sanctuary" (Soncino, 1 Ki. 18:29, p. 133, footnote).

## 32. UNTITLED

1. T.C.: This *techinnah* follows immediately after the preceding prayer, which was designed to be read at the Western Wall. It is untitled and, at best, is indirectly connected to the preceding one. Its content shows that it was written for the woman living outside the Holy Land, in the Diaspora, and apparently to be read at about the same time as the preceding one, on Friday afternoon before the beginning of the Sabbath. It reflects a custom (*minhag*) that probably developed some time in the Middle Ages, of placing a few coins in a charity box usually left in the home by emissaries from charitable institutions in the Holy Land. One of the better known boxes was for the study houses (Ashkenazic and Sephardic) at the tomb of Rabbi Meir *Ba'al Ha-ness* in Tiberias, situated within sight of Lake Kinneret. The contributions were used to provide *candles or oil for lighting.* (". . . housewives dropped small change into it just before kindling the Sabbath lights. . . . the box also symbolized the longing for Erez Israel. . . . In spite of the opposition on the part of both rabbis and *maskilim* [enlighteners] to the . . . boxes, the practice still continues" [*EJ* 11:1246].)

## 33. THREE GATES *TECHINNO* (VERSION 1)

1. T.C.: Little is known of Sarah *Bas Tovim*, author of the "Three Gates *Techinno.*" She was the daughter of a Rabbi Mordecai who was, in turn, the grandson of another Rabbi Mordecai. The grandfather in his time had been head of the ecclesiastic court of the Brisk (Brest-Litovsk) congregation. Brisk had been a large Jewish commercial center for generations. It was also a center for Jewish studies and one of the founding communities of the Council of Lithuania. It was no mean achievement for a rabbi to rise to prominence in the ecclesiastical court of such a community. A descendant of this rabbinical family was therefore a member of the local Jewish religious aristocracy of the time.

This family aristocracy was not destined to be continued through Sarah. It has been inferred, on the basis of a passage in the collection of *techinnot* called *Sheker ha-Chayn*, that she was childless. This is based on her statement "... may it be for a memorial after my death" (*ZHJL* 7:255). There is also evidence that she grew up in a well-to-do household, youthfully vain in her love of jewelry and finery. In old age, she was impoverished and wandered from community to community.

The name *Bas Tovim* (Daughter of Good Ones) seems to have been adopted as a *nom de plume*, to indicate her distinguished ancestry. M. Starkman (*EJ* 4:318) conjectures that *Tovim* might have been the Hebrew equivalent of the Latin *viri boni* (provincial elders, *parnassei medinah*), persons who conducted daily communal affairs of the Jewish community, well-to-do in the sense of being burghers (householders) of the Jewish community, members of what might today be called the upper middle class, persons aware of the obligation and responsibility to render services on behalf of the community.

As a member with family *yichus* (genealogical status), in addition to being a rabbi's wife, Sarah was probably literate. Her text frequently indicates that she was well versed in *Tanach* and *Midrash*, not just as these appeared in print but also via oral transmission. She lived in a premodern age that lacked such diversions and attractions as radio and television. The printed book, although hard to come by and costly in her time, probably was a primary vehicle for learning and inspiration in addition to oral transmission.

The title "Three Gates *Techinno*" is misleading. The Hebrew word for "gate" is *sha'ar* (pl. *she'orim*). The Hebrew word has many meanings, among which is found "gate" when used in the sense of a chapter, as in a book, or a division or section of one. It is used in Aramaic in the Talmud to refer to "tractate," a large section or division of an even larger unit. In his introduction to the Tractate *Nezikin* (Damages, Torts), the editor of the Soncino English translation of the Babylonian Talmud states that the fourth Order of the Talmud, *Nezikin*, was divided into and referred to as "Three Gates," The First Gate, the Middle Gate, and the Last Gate, because of the excessive length of the original single tractate. The use of "gate" in the sense that Sarah *Bas Tovim* used it has a long history—one that would not escape the notice of a Jew raised in the world of the yeshiva, or of his wife, for that matter. The plural form should have been used—*Techinnos*—because each gate contains a different *techinnah*. According to Sarah's preface:

> The First Gate is based upon the three mitzvot that we women are obligated to fulfill, the acronym of which is the three-lettered Hebrew word *Channo* [Hannah] which is the abbreviation for *challo* (Sabbath bread), *niddo*

(menstruation), and *hadlokas ner* (candlelighting for Sabbaths and festivals).

(Obligation for the fulfillment of these *mitzvos* is found in the *Mishnah, Shabbat* 2,6. "For three transgressions do women die in childbirth: for heedlessness of the laws of the menstruant, the dough-offering, and the lighting of the [Sabbath] lamp" [*The Mishnah*, trans. H. Danby, p. 102]. *Ma'aseh Alfes* commentary: The mitzvo of lighting candles before the Sabbath should be observed with two candles. This is inferred from the fact that in the two versions of the [Ten] Commandments two different verbs are used. [*Remember* the Sabbath–Ex. 20:8, and *Observe* the Sabbath–Deut. 5:12.] According to rabbinic tradition, both words were spoken simultaneously. [See Rashi in *Pentateuch and Rashi's Commentary*, Eng. trans. M. Rosenbaum and A. M. Silberman (London: Shapiro, Valentine, 1946), Ex. 20:8.] . . . . Be very serious at candle-lighting and pray that your children's eyes will be illuminated by the holy Torah [which they study]. If you keep these three mitzvos carefully and faithfully, your childbearing will be painless. The merit of the mitzvos will protect you. When the day arrives for your delivery [He will guard you from death and misfortune], you will find joy and happiness. . . .

It is worth noting that the *niddah* section doesn't really qualify as a *techinnah*, a supplicatory prayer. There is, for example, no blessing to be recited as there is over the Sabbath candles or in the taking of *challah*, nor is there a direct appeal to God for His approval, sanction or support. We have here the beginning of a discourse on the subject of *niddah* and its importance for the Jewish woman, a discourse which, in later editions, gradually expanded and evolved until it acquired the dimensions of a full-blown chapter in the 1922 Vilna edition. Only in the final paragraph is there a brief, prayerful hope that Mother Hannah's merit will protect the daughters of Israel who observe the law of *niddah*.)

The Second Gate is a *techinno* for the New Month [*Rosh Chodesh Benshen*].

(Gate One was the only one clearly indicated by large, boldface type set off from the text. Indications signifying the beginning of the second and third gates were made by the translator. The reason for their absence in the original is unclear. It may be because, while the text is continuous from page to page, pagination is confusing. Perhaps the printer [redactor?] used more than one edition. The bottom-line consideration was probably a financial one.)

The Third Gate is for the Days of Awe [*Yomim Noro'im*].

(Based on text found in the *techinnah* collection of *Seder Techinnos U-vakoshos* (Vilna: J. R. Romm, 1860), in which Sarah's collection was included with a publication year of 1859. However, *EJ* 4:318 has a photograph of the first page and, underneath it, an earlier date of 1838. The *EJ* article places Sarah in the seventeenth century. A number of other printings is known to exist. "Three Gates" was relatively popular.)

The most interesting *techinnah* is the second one. In the prayer for the New Month, Sarah's religious inspiration soars. Generally, prayers in Judaism are directed to God. There have rarely been intermediaries; in the Jewish tradition, a Jew speaks directly to his Creator, but, in this instance, Sarah addresses her ancestors among the Patriarchs and Matriarchs and urges them to rise from their graves and intercede on behalf of their descendants. She instructs them in what to say to God, what to remind Him of so that He will exercise His quality of compassion upon the living, suffering descendants. She also calls upon Moses and the King Messiah to intercede on behalf of the Children of Israel.

In Paradise there are certain rooms or chambers occupied by various personalities well known in Jewish tradition. Their function is to praise God; in addition, they must petition Him on behalf of the suffering descendants living today. Sarah hopes that in the time-to-come God and the King Messiah will lead the faithful back to Zion.

Why was this unique passage on Paradise composed in Yiddish? Most likely uppermost in Sarah's mind was to have it read and understood in vernacular Yiddish by the Jewish masses. Her purpose was at once practical and sensible.

In an entirely different context, Geoffrey H. Hartman appears to support such a line of reasoning (*Criticism in the Wilderness* [New Haven: Yale University Press, 1980], p. 144). Dante, he writes, called his poem a "Comedy" because "it was written in the vernacular and made use of low-style expressions restricted to the . . . realm of popular art. . . . In more strictly literary terms, what the divine comedy of art does is to save the **mammaloshon**" (Sic., emphasis mine, N.T.) He then finds this idea of *mammaloshon* expressed in Thoreau's chapter "Reading" in *Walden*: ". . . learned unconsciously, like the brutes, of our mothers . . . whereas the 'father' tongue is a reserved and select expression . . . which we must be born again in order to speak." This being "born again," according to Hartman, is Thoreau's introduction of theology. A similar process seems to have taken place in Yiddish prayer: significant quantities of prayers, or sections of them, found in the *Tanach* and post-*Tanach* literature, have been absorbed by the Yiddish vernacular, and those religious elements in turn were introduced into *techinnot*.

An interesting feature of this *mammaloshon* literature-liturgy is highlighted in the present translation of bracketed material, the purpose of which is to reflect the presence in the *techinnah* of a Hebrew passage, phrase, or clause. Brackets are also used to insert a clarifying word or phrase missing in the text. Whether biblical verse or theological or ethical concept, Sarah blended Hebrew into her text so naturally that one is hardly aware of two languages. This is neither unique nor original with her. Many Jews in those days, confronted with the idea that they were using Hebrew, might even have been surprised, having assumed all along it was Yiddish they were speaking and thinking. Anyone who has seen the play *Fiddler on the Roof* and heard Tevya's garbled, semiliterate meanderings will appreciate this linguistic mixing even in the English format.

Unlike Dante, with some of whose scenes Sarah's beg comparison, Sarah never questions the significance of what she envisions. Her daytime visions are simply and directly presented to pious women readers. Dante's illumination, by contrast, is a nighttime dream vision. He sees through a poet's eyes. Sarah is no Dante, much less a poet, however stimulating and inspiring her prose art may be. Dante's feeling, writes John Freccero in his introduction to Ciardi's translation of the *Inferno*, is one of "poetic inadequacy for the ultimate experience" of being in Paradise. This "poetic inadequacy" is absent from Sarah's *techinnot* because the experience of being in Paradise is not, after all, the purpose of our humble rabbi's wife. Rather than offering a tour of the place "up there," Sarah seeks only to persuade God to save and deliver His people. The sense of the medieval understanding of Paradise and the sense of an ultimate reality are absent from Sarah's prayer for the New Month. The ultimate reality for Dante was a great spiritual love that moved sun and stars, a love that saved elected individual souls and enabled them to return to their Maker. In Sarah's *techinnah* within the normative stream of traditional Judaism there is, instead, an overriding concern for the group, for *Klal Yisroel*, for all the Children of Israel, and their ultimate collective redemption. It is a moving, sensitive, yearning expressing grassroots hopes and dreams of the Jewish people collectively. Viewed thus, Sarah achieved a transtemporal significance beyond time and place.

There are some minor problems. In her prayer for the New Month, for example, Rebbetzin Sarah speaks of six women's chambers in Paradise, yet she describes only four. What happened to the other two? It seems unlikely that she would deliberately neglect to describe them. Were they lost in the many reprints the *techinnot* underwent? Could some anonymous printer or owner of a press carelessly have torn out the wrong number of pages from an earlier printing? Also, in speaking of the chambers as indescribable, Sarah notes that "no one is admitted." If so, how did she get in? How did she know what went on there? The fact is that Sarah was not the creator of this women's paradise. Professor Chava Weissler located its origin in the *Zohar*, noting perceptively that the *Zohar*'s influence "was widespread in the seventeenth and eighteenth century Yiddish literature. . . . The early part of this period . . . was a time of the popularization of Jewish mysticism, a phenomenon which made new visions of the religious life available to those outside the learned elite— women and unlearned men" ("Women in Paradise," *Tikkun* 2:2 [April– May 1987]: pp. 43ff). In a conversation with Professor Weissler, I learned that the *Zohar* passage also dealt with only four chambers. Later, I was led to another source by David Harari in his Hebrew article appearing in *Italia, "Le tracce del 'Quarto Dialogo smarrito' de Leone Ebreo negli 'Eroici Fuorici di Giordano Bruno,"* 7:1-2 (1988):143–Tractate *Derech Eretz Zuta,* end of chap. 1, p. 570; Soncino trans.: "There were nine who entered the Garden of Eden alive, viz.: Enoch the son of Yered . . . Bithiah the daughter of Pharaoh, and Serach the daughter of Asher. . . ."

The text used as a basis for this translation was found inserted in a collection of *techinnot* printed in Vilna in 1860. The inserted "Three Gates Techinno," however, has the year 1859 appended to it. The volume was located in the University of California, Los Angeles, Library Annex, un-cataloged at the time with the call number 2103928. I am indebted to Dr. Shimon Brisman, then Jewish bibliographer, for his kind help in locating the item, as well as for several illuminating comments and suggestions.

2. I have been unable to locate such a biblical passage. The only thing that comes close is Prov. 8:21–"I will fill their treasuries" as a reward to them that love God.

3. The phrase *chofeis kol chadray betten* is translated by Birnbaum (*HHPB*) as "Thou dost search all the inmost chambers of man's conscience . . ." and by Bokser (*HHDB*) as "Thou searchest out our innermost secrets. . . ." It is found in the *Machzor* in the paragraph immediately preceding what Bokser called the "Long Confession" (*Al chet*), appearing a number of times in the Yom Kippur services. The paragraph in which it is found recognizes the fact that nothing is hidden from Him.

This is a small departure from what seems to have been the basic thrust of the Proverbs verse in which the spirit or soul of man is "a Divine light illuminating all the *inward parts* . . ." (Soncino ed. of Prov., p. 137, footnote). Sarah *Bas Tovim* in her *techinnah* connected the phrase to a woman's belly or, to put it delicately, her abdomen. The metaphor is fittingly applied not only to a woman's anatomy but also to her feminine psyche in a rather down-to-earth term, the relevance of which was doubtless not lost upon Mistress Sarah's Jewish audience.

4. This is the proof text to show that a husband may not have intercourse with his menstruating wife.

5. Authority for this is found in Talmud B(avli) *Shavuot* 18b (Soncino, p. 93): "Our Rabbis taught: *Thus shall you separate the children of Israel from their uncleanness.* [The proof text is in Lev. 18:19.] R. Judah said: 'From this we deduce a warning to the children of Israel that they should separate from their wives near their periods.' And how long? Rabbah said: 'One *onah*.'" Footnote 93 defines *onah* as "a period of time (with special reference to marital duty): the whole day or the whole night. . . ."

6. "For Adam the Sabbath had a peculiar significance. When he was made to depart out of Paradise in the twilight of the Sabbath eve, the angels called after him, 'Adam did not abide in his glory overnight!' Then the Sabbath appeared before God as Adam's defender, and spoke: 'O Lord of the world! During the six working days no creature was slain. If Thou wilt begin now by slaying Adam, what will become of the sanctity and the blessing of the Sabbath?' In this was Adam rescued from the fires of hell, the meet punishment for his sins. . ." (Ginzberg, *Legends*, vol. 1, pp. 85-86).

7. "The court had the power to inflict four kinds of death-penalty: stoning, burning, [execution by] beheading, and strangling" (*Mishnah Sanhedrin* 7:1; Danby, *The Mishnah*, p. 391; B. T. *Sanhedrin*, 49b). Sarah's familiarity with the four kinds of death penalty is not based upon the *Mishnah* source but, in all probability, in the way it appears in the *Al chet* mentioned above in Bokser's "Long Confession" (footnote 10).

8. T.B. *Pesahim* 118a (Soncino trans., p. 609).

9. Sarah doesn't specify Jacob's self-sacrificing deeds, the merit of which constitute his argument in defense of his descendants. A later anonymous writer has added that this self-sacrifice consisted of Jacob's "suffering exile (from Canaan) for twenty-two years" (*Shas Techinno Rav Peninim*, p. 59).

10. The Thirteen Attributes, enumerating God's nature, originate in

Exod. 34:6-7. See Hertz, *ADPB*, pp. 477-480; Scherman, *ArtScroll Siddur*, pp. 816-819. The reader will find an interesting story on how these verses came to be. Rabbis of the Talmud had a talent for creating living scenes by which to convey their ideas. The passage from T. B., *Rosh Hashanah* 17b, is such an example: God appears to Moses in the form of a cantor to teach him the Thirteen Attributes. Today, they are chanted on festivals that occur on weekdays, at the removal of the Torah from the Ark, and on Yom Kippur. Superficial comparison of the text of the prayer reveals how skillfully Sarah *Bas Tovim* blended it into her *techinnah*.

11. These words begin the *Rosh Chodesh* prayer in the *Siddur*. See Hertz, *ADPB*, pp. 508-509, for text and footnote. From this point on, the *techinnah* abandons the Hebrew and reverts to Yiddish.

12. Serach is one of the lesser known biblical personalities. Briefly mentioned in the *Tanach* (Gen. 46:17, Num. 26:46, and 1 Chron. 7:30), it is only later, in aggadic sources, that her personality emerges. Her genealogy is found in Ginzberg's *Legends*, vol. 2, p. 39. The high esteem in which she was held by Sarah *Bas Tovim* is based on the fact that Serach was able, through her singing, to inform Jacob that Joseph was alive in Egypt. She did this gently and by degrees in order not to give her aged grandfather a fatal shock. Serach's words reawakened the prophetic spirit in Jacob, and he informed her that she would not die but enter Paradise alive (Ginzberg, *Legends*, vol. 2, pp. 115-116). This is the selfsame Serach who now, in Paradise, announces her Uncle Joseph's approach.

13. That is, at the redemption from exile.

14. There are a number of reasons in Jewish tradition for the *Shechinah*'s withdrawal—destruction of the Temple, Israel's exile, slanderers, groundless hatred, and so on—each of which evolved its own midrashic material.

Sarah is not wandering here. She has kept in mind that this *techinnah* is for *Rosh Chodesh*, on which the *Hallel* (Praise) psalms 113-118 are recited. See, for example, Hertz, *ADPB*, pp. 774-775; Scherman, *ArtScroll Siddur*, pp. 632-642.

In Psalm 118:20 we find the relevant verse that begs for midrashic interpretation: "This is the *gate* (emphasis added) of the Lord; the righteous shall enter into it." Could this be the gate from which He withdrew after the destruction? Is this the (city) gate through which He will return? Cf. *ArtScroll Siddur* p. 640, footnote: "This refers to the gate of the Temple. When the exile is over, the righteous will enter through this gate. . . ." See also the following in *The International Critical Commentary on the Book of Psalms*, vol. 2, p. 406, on verses 18-20:

18. A procession has come up to the gates of the temple, and the chorus speaks in couplets, and a priest responds in couplets.
19. Open to me the gates of *Zedek*. . . .
20. To this the priest replies: *This is the gate that belongs to Yahweh.* Only those may enter whom He permits access to His presence, and only *the righteous* people of Israel—may enter therein.

There seems to be no definite agreement on which gate is referred to and where it is located. However, in a colorful passage in *Pesikta de-Rab Kahana*, p. 480, the Sages say that Solomon expanded upon Isaiah 52:7 (How beautiful upon the mountain are the feet of the messenger of good tidings . . .) in his own verse (Songs 1:9), envisioning Israel's eventual redemption when the exiles will be gathered in: "The Presence [a Hebrew term used for God] will walk at the head of them . . . followed by the Patriarchs, the Prophets, the Ark and the Torah; then—all Israel . . . clothed in majesty, mantled in great glory. . . ."

If we bear in mind that Sarah's generation as well as preceding ones were conscious heirs to the religious tradition continuously transmitted by Israel's teachers and preachers, we see that what she says here makes sense and is relevant to the *Rosh Chodesh* theme.

15. The basis for this idea is in a well-known *piyyut* (liturgical poem) metaphor composed by Rabbi Yom Tov of York, England (12th century) found in the following stanza: "Silence the accuser and let the defender be heard. . ." (Birnbaum, *HHPB*, p. 536; see also pp. 533-534, footnote).

16. Sarah used this phrase under the influence of the literary phenomenon known as the "refrain." The refrain is frequently found in the High Holy Day liturgy, especially in medieval *piyyutim*. "Probably the very beginnings of poetry are to be found in iterated words and phrases. Refrains occur . . . in the Hebrew psalms, they blossom in the medieval ballads, Renaissance lyrics, and in the poetry of the romantic period. It may be used in such a way that its meaning varies or develops from one recurrence to the next. . ." (*Princeton Encyclopedia of Poetry and Poetics*, pp. 686-687). In the *machzor*, the example that comes to mind is found in the *piyyut* "Ha-yom te'amtzaynu" (Strengthen Us Today). Each line begins with *Ha-yom* (Today). See Birnbaum, *HHPB*, p. 405, footnote, end of Rosh Hashana *Musaf* Service; also Birnbaum, p. 875, end of the Yom Kippur *Musaf* Service. The reverberating presence of "On this day" in Sarah's *techinnah* is intentional. To emphasize the refrain, it has been set off from the text as individual lines. In the Yiddish, everything is jammed together in one large, seemingly endless paragraph.

17. "To blood is ascribed in Scripture the mysterious sacredness which belongs to life, and God reserves it to himself when allowing man the dominion over and use of the lower animals for food. Thus reserved, it acquires a . . . power: that of sacrificial atonement. . ." (*Smith's Bible Dictionary*, p. 88).

18. ". . . some parts of the suet, viz., about the stomach, the entrails, the kidneys and the tail of a sheep . . . were forbidden to be eaten in the case of animals offered to Jehovah in sacrifice" (Lev. 3:3, 9, 17; 7:3, 23) (*Smith's Bible Dictionary*, p. 189).

19. Cf. in connection with the Day of Atonement the following statement on fasting in Leviticus 16:31–"It is a Sabbath of solemn rest unto you, and you shall afflict your souls." Ignoring the nutritional needs of their bodies, Jews afflicted their souls with thoughts reminding them of their lowliness, finiteness, liability to err and, via *teshuva*, return to God's laws and ways.

20. In the mind of a traditional Jew, this metaphor easily established the connection with *Ne'ilah*, the concluding sunset service on the Day of Atonement. *Ne'ilah* means closing: the gates of heaven were closed at sunset, signifying the end of the day. This would be the last opportunity when prayers, winging heavenward, could reach God. Birnbaum (*HHPB*, p. 490) extends the metaphor poetically: "Before the closing of the gates of forgiveness which this day has opened for us. . . ."

21. The text is faulty. It could read: ". . . since then we no longer have a High Priest who can speak for us. . . ." This would be based on the Yom Kippur *Avodah* service, in which was described the elaborate Yom Kippur service held in the Temple according to the Tractate *Yoma* (see Danby, *The Mishnah,* p. 162 ff.; also Birnbaum, *HHPB*, p. 811 ff.): ". . . forgive . . . sins which thy people, the House of Israel, have committed before thee . . ." (esp. Danby, p. 169, and Birnbaum, p. 821).

### 34. THREE GATES *TECHINNO* (VERSION 2)

1. T. C.: What follows is not an alternate version of "The Three Gates *Techinno*" but, rather, an extended introduction by Dr. Alfes. The introduction by the original author Sarah *Bas Tovim* was much briefer in earlier editions. Her *techinnah* eventually became popular and was reprinted and revised many times. Somewhere along the way, her name was also dropped. The *techinnah* itself has been omitted to avoid repetition.

2. *Rishon L'tzion* commentary: The Sages say (in *Berachot* 31b) that [in 1 Sam. 1:11] Channo in her prayer to God refers to herself three times

as "handmaid" [If You will indeed look upon the affliction of Your *handmaid* . . . and will not forget Your *handmaid*, but will give Your *handmaid* a son]. The significance of the use of *handmaid* three times is: "Lord of the universe, You have given women the three *mitzvos* of *challo*, *niddo*, and *hadloko* which if, heaven forbid, they should transgress, run the risk of danger in childbirth. ['For three sins women die in childbirth: because they are not observant of (the laws of) Niddah, Hallah, and the kindling of the (Sabbath) lights'—*Shabbat* 31b, Soncino trans., p. 144.] I, however, have carefully observed these *mitzvos* as a faithful *ahmoh* [handmaid]. Have pity on me, therefore, and grant me a child."

3. In 1 Samuel 7:8—"And the Children of Israel implored Samuel, 'Do not neglect us and do not refrain from crying out to the Lord our God to save us from the hands of the Philistines'" (NJPS).

4. "The Lord God made *me* as the beginning of His way." In Proverbs, the passage really refers to *wisdom*, the subject of the entire chapter. But Jewish tradition, thinking obviously in Jewish categories, has made wisdom and Torah synonymous.

5. This is a play on the word *Wirt*, which can mean such things as count, lord and master, head of a household, and landlord.

6. *Chesed* has always been a linguistic conundrum for translators. Found in Micah 7:20, it has been variously translated. Soncino: mercy to Abraham; NJPS: loyalty to Abraham; ICC: kindness to Abraham; E. Ben Yehudah in his dictionary: grace. And these are just a few!

7. Soncino trans., *Shabbat* 32a, p. 145.

8. Dr. Alfes, not Sarah *Bas Tovim*, has ignored the last two words, which would have the House of Israel be the vineyard of the Lord, whereas here the *nations of the world* will be transformed into God's garden after being taught by the Children of Israel.

9. ". . . all the tithes of the land, whether of the seed of the land, or the fruit of the tree, is the Lord's . . ."—Leviticus 27:30. ". . . and all the tithes of the herd or the flock . . ."—Leviticus 27:32.

10. "By making their children go to the synagogue to learn Scripture and their husbands to learn Mishnah . . ."—*Berachot* 17a (Soncino trans., pp. 102-103).

11. Jedaiah Ben Abraham Bedersi (*Ha-Penini*, c. 1270-1340) was a poet and philosopher. His work, *Bechinat Olam*, was "written in florid prose and rich in imagery, combines philosophic doctrine and religious fervor. . . ." *EJ* 9:1308. According to the *EJ* article, a Yiddish translation exists.

12. Found in the Grace after Meals, it alludes to the world-to-come, to eternity. See Rabbi Menasseh Ben Israel (17th century): "The Sabbath

is a hint of life everlasting . . ."; quoted in R. Alcalay, *Words of the Wise* (Jerusalem-Ramat Gan: Massada Press, 1970), p. 425.

13. The story of Rachel's marriage to the young, poor, and illiterate shepherd Akiva is found in *Nedarim* 49b-50a (Soncino trans., pp. 155-156). A lovely and sensitive rendition of the story is found in Louis Finkelstein's biography *Akiba, Scholar, Saint and Martyr*, pp. 22ff., 49ff., 135. The 24,000 stars symbolize the 24,000 students Rabbi Akiba was reputed to have had.

14. The passage in *Shabbat* 32a continues: ". . . wherefore I commanded you concerning the lamp" (i.e., the Sabbath lights) (Soncino trans., p. 145).

## 35. TECHINNO BEFORE TAKING *CHALLO*

1. T.C.: Once upon a time, the practice of setting aside a small piece of dough prepared by the housewife for baking Sabbath loaves was universally observed in traditional Jewish homes. In my preschool childhood, I never understood why Mother set aside a portion of dough, the size of a fist, each Friday when the kneaded dough was placed in its round aluminum pan on top of the warm oven and allowed to rise. She placed the small portion in the hot coal oven to turn black and hard as a rock, unfit for eating. On one of the following weekdays it wound up in the refuse pail. Mother could not give an adequate explanation in English that my young mind could grasp, but she stuck to the routine, mumbling something under her breath that I took to be some kind of a prayer. Home-baked Sabbath loaves have generally disappeared in our modern, fast-paced age, and the taking of dough by daughters of Israel is little known, much less observed.

## 36. THE *MITZVO* OF CANDLELIGHTING (*LICHT-BENSHEN*)

1. T.C.: The following paragraphs constitute a brief list of guidelines for women to follow in connection with the lighting of candles that officially ushers in the beginning of the Sabbath. They can best be understood within a certain framework. The home, after the destruction of the Holy Temple in Jerusalem, became for exilic Jewry a miniature sanctuary of sorts; the table, upon which meals were eaten, was an altar to God upon which sacrifices were dedicated to Him. Even the custom of sprinkling salt on bread at the beginning of the meal was meant to remind one of the offerings and religious acts performed in the Holy Temple by

priests and Levites. When a man and woman married, it was more than a matter of sex and babies. There had to be purity of body as well as spirit throughout their lives. The purpose of a Jewish marriage was to build a home in which the ideals and values of Judaism found expression in specific acts, in clearly defined ways of living the sanctified life.

It is touching to see how these preparations and ablutions, in the days before electricity and indoor plumbing, were used to create the proper atmosphere with which to observe the Sabbath. At the same time, they reveal a delicate sensitivity to, and awareness of, the human condition.

*Licht benshen*: A blessing recited at candlelighting time. But where does *benshen* originate? It's not in my German-English dictionary. Could it be Slavic in origin? Fortunately, we are delivered from doubt by the *EJ* 4:518, which informs us that the term is an Ashkenazic one, "probably derived (via old French) from the Latin *benedicere*, meaning "bless" or "pronounce a benediction. . . . also used as a designation for the Prayer of the New Moon, *Rosh Chodesh benshen*, and for the benediction recited by a person who has had a perilous escape, *gomel benshen.* . . ."

2. *Sha'aray Tzion* commentary: . . . It is a *mitzvo* to rise earlier than usual on Friday to prepare for *Shabbos*. Even the richest woman who has many servants should personally attend to as much as possible in honor of *Shabbos* [*l'chovode Shabbos*]. When it is late in the day, she should help as much as possible to avoid the risk of profaning the *Shabbos* [*chilul Shabbos*], heaven forbid. We find in the holy Talmud that the richest *Tannaim*, some of whom were related to royalty, personally participated in preparations in honor of the *Shabbos* [*l'chovode Shabbos*].

In the factory, one should pay workers earlier than usual. Also, the woman who pays her domestics on Thursday night during the short winter days will be blessed.

Fill the lamps (with oil) early on Friday. One then has the opportunity to replace a wick when necessary, or a glass; also to see what needs to be emptied completely and adjusted so that it will burn brightly. Do these things early on Friday; don't discover it late in the day and run the risk of profaning the *Shabbos*, heaven forbid. See also that the clock is set correctly so that no error is made with regard to the exact time of sunset.

On Friday afternoon, check your garment to see that no needle with thread is stuck in it, that there is no money in the pocket, or any item which it is improper to carry on *Shabbos*. Tailors often had a needle with a length of thread under their coat lapel ready, as it were, to make instant repairs. Money is a reminder of the work week that one tries to keep at a distance on the Sabbath. The old maxim "Out of sight, out of mind" would seem to apply here.

One should eat a bit less on Friday afternoon in order to develop an appetite for the first *Shabbos* meal [*sehudoh*], especially from three o'clock on.

All the things for *Shabbos*, such as the wine, schnapps, *Shabbos* clothes, candles, and gas, should be prepared early and not left for the last minute.

3. Many women often had to run small businesses or shops that were economically a vital, if not the sole, source of the family income.

### 37. SABBATH CANDLE BLESSING (VERSION 1)

1. Included in a prayer that is part of the service for welcoming the Sabbath (*Kabbolas Shabbos*): "Samuel is singled out from among the multitude of prophets *who invoke His Name*, because he was the greatest prophet [after Moses] . . . Kimhi." Scherman, *Siddur Kol Yaakov*, p. 313, footnote.

2. *Niddo*—observance of the rules for menstruants.

3. *Challo*—setting aside a portion of the dough before the Sabbath bread is baked; this was the priests' share.

### 38. SABBATH CANDLE BLESSING: SPECIAL BLESSING FOR AMERICA (VERSION 2)

1. From the *Oveenu Malkaynu* (Our Father, Our King) prayer. See Hertz, *ADPB*, pp. 164-165.

2. See Hertz, ibid., *Musaf Amidah* for the three pilgrimage festivals, pp. 820-821.

3. [Judah and Israel . . . dwelt in safety, everyone under his own vine and under his own fig tree—1 Kings 5:5]. This is the classic biblical metaphor for living in peace and tranquillity.

4. Reference is to the *Sholom Alaychem* song, the greeting of the Sabbath angels. Introduced some three hundred years ago by the kabbalists, it is based on an aggadic passage in *Shabbat* 119b—"R. Jose son of R. Judah said: Two ministering angels accompany man on the eve of the Sabbath from the synagogue to his home, one a good [angel] and one an evil [angel]. And when he arrives home and finds the lamp burning, the table laid and the couch [bed] covered with a spread, the good angel exclaims, 'May it be even thus on another Sabbath [too],' and the evil angel unwillingly responds 'amen.' But if not, the evil angel exclaims, 'May it even be

thus on another Sabbath [too],' and the good angel unwillingly responds, 'Amen'" (Soncino trans.).

5. Originally found in *Berachot* 60b and incorporated into the Morning Service: "Lead us not into sin, transgression, iniquity, temptation, or disgrace. . . ." Birnbaum, *DPB*, p. 17.

6. Borrowed from the Grace after Meals—"May the Merciful One grant us a day which will be all Sabbath and rest in life everlasting"—and based on the *Mishnah Tamid* 7:4 in reference to Psalm 92, which the Levites used to sing in the Temple, explained in the Mishnah as "a Psalm, a song for the time that is to come, for the day that shall be all Sabbath and rest in the life everlasting" (Danby trans., p. 589); that is, a day entirely free of the weekday cares of work.

## 40. AFTER LIGHTING SABBATH CANDLES (VERSION 2)

1. The *mitzvo* of the first portion of the dough, or *challo*. "The portion of the dough which belongs to the priest (Num. 15:20 f.); in the Diaspora this is not given to the priest but burnt" (Soncino glossary to *Shabbat* 2:810).

2. *Niddah:* A woman in the period of her menstruation. *Shabbat* (Soncino glossary 2:811).

3. The passage concludes with "I designated you the first (Jer. 2:3); wherefore I commanded you concerning the first" (i.e., portion of the dough) (Soncino trans., *Shabbat* 32a, p. 145). At this point, it would be understandable if the English reader, inexperienced in the mental processes of the Talmud, failed to see the implication even though the word *first* has been italicized for emphasis. He would be justified in asking, "So what?" To which we respond that what we have here is an example of the *gezerah shavah,* the second of the thirteen ways by which *halachah* may be understood. The thirteen rules were formulated by Rabbi Yishmael and have been included in the traditional *Siddur.* For an extended explanation, see Scherman, *ArtScroll Siddur,* p. 98 ff. Briefly, the *gezerah shavah* is a method for finding an analogy between two laws based on identical words or phrases found in both (*ArtScroll Siddur,* p. 50).

4. ". . . held to be the smallest quantity of blood within a human being on which life can be supported" (Soncino trans., *Shabbat* 31b, p. 145, n. 1).

5. This is based on the same passage in *Shabbat* 32a (Soncino trans., p. 145): "The soul which I placed in you is called a lamp" (i.e., the Sabbath candles). Alfes, with the sure touch of a master *darshan* (interpreter), now expatiates to make it more directly applicable to the Jewish woman.

6. While Alfes apparently started out with improvement of this world by observance of the three *mitzvos*, he ends up in the world-to-come: The "day which is completely *Shabbos*" is found in Grace after Meals and is recited on the Sabbath; according to tradition, the "day which is completely *Shabbos*" alludes to the *olom ha-bo*, the world-to-come. On that wonderful Sabbath day of the future, although it is only a symbol and metaphor, it is a descriptive "footnote of Heaven as well as of immortality. . . . For the immortal life is often conceived by the Rabbis, not as inactivity, but as continual progress. . ." (*ADPB*, p. 548, footnote).

## 41. BEFORE *HAVDOLO*

1. T.C.: The *Havdalah* ceremony takes place at the end of the Sabbath. The word *Havdalah* means "separation." It recognizes the separation between the sanctity of the Sabbath and the beginning of the new week, which is a mundane time of work. According to Hertz, in the *Havdalah*

> one deliberately declares that the Sabbath is actually over and night has set in, before returning to a work-day week. . . . The idea of "separation" is not confined to that between blissful Sabbath rest and the hurly-burly of the work-a-day world, but is extended to embrace the separation between holy and profane, between light and darkness. . . . (*DPB*, p. 744)

Birnbaum, paraphrasing Maimonides, points out that

> the symbolic use of fragrant spices during the recital of the *Havdalah* is to cheer the soul which is saddened at the departure of the Sabbath. . . . It is customary to cup the hands around the candles and to gaze at the finger-nails. The reflection of the light on the finger-nails causes the shadow to appear on the palm of the hand, thus indicating the distinction "between light and darkness" mentioned in the *Havdalah*. A twisted candle of several wicks is used since the phrase [in the benediction] "lights of fire" is in the plural. (*DPB*, pp. 551-552)

I had two versions of this *techinnah* before me:

a) *Shas Techinno, Rav Peninim* (New York: Hebrew Publishing, 1916), pp. 118-120.
b) *Ahnaie Shas Techinno* (Vilna: Rochel-Esther Bas Avichayil of Jerusalem, 1930?), p. 47. JTSAL: Bm 675 74 A3.

Both versions are basically the same in content, but there is a significant stylistic difference between them; the former is smoother, more polished, whereas the latter, printed later in the 1930s, reveals an older style, crude in some respects, and replete with typos. The translation given here is an amalgam in which I tried to include the better parts of each. 2. The three things "good news, salvation, and comfort," are found in the prayer book, taken from the Grace after Meals. "The Freedom longed for by the Jew is not for vengeance, but for deliverance from unrighteousness and inhuman oppression" (Hertz, *ADPB*, p. 975, footnote).

## 42. AFTER LIGHTING *CHANUKO* CANDLES

1. Every prudent woman should clean the serpent out of her house and reintroduce the light of Torah by reading during the long winter nights such holy books as *Menoras Ha-mo'or, Ma'aseh Alfes*, and other such works of a similar cast. (*Menoras Ha-mo'or* [*Candlestick of Light*], by Rabbi Isaac Aboab [end of 14th century] was a popular work of "religious edification among the Jews in the Middle Ages." It was translated into Yiddish and published in Amsterdam in 1701 [*EJ* 2:90-92]. An English version of the work exists: *Menoras Ha-maor* [*The Light of Contentment*], by R. Yitzchok Abohav, trans. R. Yaakov Yosef Reinman [New Jersey: Chinuch Publications, 1982]. Benzion Alfes [1850-1940] was a Yiddish and Hebrew writer. His *Ma'aseh Alfes* [*Alfes' Story*] was written in reaction "to the late 19th century proliferation of secular novels . . . published serially starting in 1900." He apparently used the same title for his commentary that appears in this *techinno* collection. Many of his commentaries under this title have also been included in other liturgical works [*EJ*, 2:604].)

*Ma'aseh Alfes* commentary on card playing: The pen cannot describe the misfortunes which liquor and card playing have brought upon the world. Many a rich man has been impoverished through them and, in the end, been buried by strangers. Many have committed suicide. Others have lost their shirts and wound up wearing "sackcloth" [Yiddish acronym for *s"k*: drunkenness and cards]. The Evil Inclination [*yetzer ho-ro*] has ensnared many a decent Jew with cards. It all began on Chanuko when, so argued the duplicitous *yetzer ho-ro*, it is a *mitzvo* to play cards. We therefore wish to explain to our prudent sisters the relationship between Chanuko and cards so that they may be convinced of its error.

Antiochus passed a decree prohibiting any gathering for the purpose of Torah study upon pain of death. This was a dark and bitter time for the Jews. A Jew without Torah is like a fish out of water. What did they do? They gathered in small groups to study the Oral Torah (Talmud) which, in those days, was not written down and had to be memorized. To forestall the possibility of a surprise raid in which they would be caught unawares, they took a pack of cards and gave several to each person. These were slipped under the tablecloth and, in the event of a raid, out came the cards. The enemy was fooled into thinking the Jews had abandoned their Torah and become card players. When they left, the cards were slipped back under the tablecloth and Torah discussion resumed. Card playing indicated how precious Torah was to our ancestors and how far they were prepared to go to remain faithful to it.

Today, ignorant persons extinguish the [flame of] Torah with cards. Our ancestors' dedication to the Torah they studied night after night has been replaced by dedication to card playing, with never a word of Torah in their mouths. This is what the *yetzer ho-ro* has legitimized.

Once upon a time, two animals found a large cocoa nut in the forest. They quarreled over its possession and were about to come to blows. Mr. Fox chanced upon them and suggested a compromise. He split the nut and gave half a shell to each, taking the pith for himself as arbitrator's fee.

Card playing is like that. It shows how much our ancestors loved Torah that the *yetzer ho-ro* [took the trouble and] stole it, leaving them the shell. The shell is the card playing entire nights long before the festival begins and long after it ends.

## 43. *YOHRZEIT* (ANNIVERSARY OF PARENT'S DEATH) (VERSION 1)

1. Based on Genesis 27:15—"Rebekah then took the best clothes of her older son Esau, which were there in the house. . . ." There is a tradition based on Exodus 24:5 ("And he sent the *young* men of the Israelites and they offered burnt offerings . . .") to the effect that before the Tabernacle was set up "the [Altar] service was fulfilled by the first born" (Danby, *Mishnah*, p. 489, and Soncino, *Zebahim*, p. 554 [112b]).

Another tradition, more in keeping with the sense of this *techinnah*, that Esau honored his father Isaac, is found in the *Midrash Rabbah: Genesis* (Soncino trans., vol. 2, p. 592)—"R. Simeon b. Gamaliel said: All my lifetime I attended upon my father, yet I did not do for him a hundredth part of the service which Esau did for his father . . . when Esau attended on his father, he attended on him in royal robes, 'For,' said he, 'naught but royal robes befits my father's honour'" (See also Mirkin, *Midrash Rabbah: Genesis*, vol. 3, p. 46, Heb. trans.).

2. *Ma'aseh Alfes* commentary on parental honor: The prophet Ezekiel says [. . . nor have you acted according to the rules of the nations around you—Ezek. 5:7]. You follow what the nations of the world do in opposition to what the Torah has written. Would that you at least observed the wise practices they inherited from their ancestor Esau in honoring parents. (The Talmud's comment on this passage from Ezek. 5:7—"You did not act as the right minded, but as the corrupt amongst them," [*Sanhedrin* 39b, Soncino trans., p. 254.)

There is a story in the *Gemoro* about Sages who sought a precious stone for the *ephod* (breastplate for the high priest). They came to a heathen diamond dealer called Dama who lived in Ashkelon and had such a stone in his possession. He would have made over half a million gold ducats. His father, Natina, however, was asleep on top of the trunk containing the precious stones, and Dama was unwilling to wake him. As a result, the deal fell through.

Another incident happened to this same person. He was sitting in the Roman parliament [*sic*!] when his mentally disturbed mother came in and tore off his garment [toga?] and spat in his face. He nevertheless said nothing to shame her. Meantime, her head covering accidentally slipped off. He bent down, picked it up, and placed it on her head. (The story is at variance with the probable source from which Alfes borrowed, that is, the *Ma'aseh Book* [Eng. trans. by M. Gaster], pp. 227-228. The original sources are *Kiddushin* 31a [Soncino trans., p. 151], and *Avodah Zarah* 23b-24a [Soncino, pp. 118-119]. The story about Dama's mother is found in *Deuteronomy Rabbah*, 1:15 [Soncino trans., *Midrash Rabbah: Deuteronomy*, vol 7, p. 16].)

Our Sages, although they avoided the practices of the nations of the world, nevertheless learned something from them. The *Gemoro* tells us of the *Tanna* R. Tarfon who had an elderly mother. When she had to go to bed, he would bend down and allow his mother to use him as a footstep on which to ascend her bed. R. Joseph, hearing his mother's approach, would ask those present to rise with him out of respect since, as he explained, the Divine Presence [*Shecheeno*] accompanied her. In other words, in honoring one's mother one honors God. Which is why we honor our parents, earning the reward of length of days in this world as well as a great reward in the world-to-come.

### 44. *YOHRZEIT* (VERSION 2)

1. Included in *A New Techinno: (Ahnaie Shas Techinno) Memorial Service for the Dead.* JTSAL: BM 675 74 A3.

2. The reason for reciting this *techinnah* before the *Ashray* prayer is not readily apparent. In the *Ashray*, the first two verses are taken from Psalm 84:5 and Psalm 144:15 and are prefixed to Psalm 145. According to the Talmud (*Berachot* 4b), "Whoever recites this psalm three times a day is assured of his share in the world to come." It emphasizes the universal and eternal nature of God's kingdom and His love of those who love and revere Him. He will also guard them and they will be close to Him. These may be construed as desiderata for the righteous soul, both in this world and in the world-to-come, and, therefore, as an appropriate place to pray for the departed.

3. The title of the prayer commonly referred to as *U-vo l'tzion* makes more sense when the third word following is appended: *U-vo l'tzion go'ayl*, (a redeemer shall come to Zion). This is how the first two verses of this prayer are used here. With a finely tuned sense, those who contributed to the arrangement of the prayer inserted the last two verses from Isaiah 59:20-21 to reinforce belief in this reward from God to His faithful adherents.

Redemption alone, however important, is not the main emphasis, although it is a reward for those who recognize and declare God's *kedusha* (holiness). Man's reward for acknowledging God and keeping His Torah of truth is to have eternal life implanted in him. When the cantor chants the final words of this prayer, the congregation's mourners rise and recite the mourner's *Kaddish*, in which they glorify and sanctify His Name. The deceased is not mentioned at all. The *Kaddish* is recited not only by the mourners, but also by those observing the *Yohrzeit* of a close relative. The relationship between *Kaddish* and *kedusha* is not accidental. Both words derive from the same Hebrew verb root—*k' d' sh*, meaning some aspect of holy or holiness in a specific application. So also *Kiddush* (Sanctification of wine) and *Bays ha-mikdosh* (Holy Temple).

## 45. AN ORPHAN BRIDE'S *TECHINNO* ON HER WEDDING DAY

1. Included in *A New Techinno: Memorial Service for the Dead*, op. cit.

2. Although this is in Hebrew, there is no scriptural source for it. However, it is worth an attempt at mental reconstruction to see what has happened here. Such words or phrases, whenever appropriate, will pop into the author's mind from a wealth of sources and religious experiences. The two verbs *uree* and *heesohr'ree* must have immediately conjured up the fifth stanza in the sixteenth-century poem-song-prayer *L'cho Dodee* (Come My Beloved) by kabbalist Rabbi Shlomo Ha-Levi Alkabetz. It is still recited/sung today and is found in many prayer books in the

*Kabbalat Shabbat* service (Welcoming the Sabbath). Birnbaum, in referring to this poem, pointed out: "There is scarcely a phrase in the poem which is not borrowed from the Bible" (*DPB*, p. 244). This is also the case with the two aforementioned verb forms. While the first (*u'ree*) is found in Isaiah 52:1 and the second (*heesohr'ree*) in Isaiah 51:17, it is without doubt the constant weekly repetition and reinforcement of the poem in the *Kabbalat Shabbat* service that caused it so easily and appropriately to pop into the author's mind at this time. Besides, what could be more appropriate than this borrowing from the *Lechah dodi*, where the Sabbath is referred to in the refrain repeated after each stanza as *Shabbat Ha-malkah*, the Sabbath *queen*? In the Jewish tradition, every bride is endowed with the qualities of beauty, grace, and queenliness. This is just another of many examples in which Jews drew easily upon their religious tradition without a moment's hesitation.

### 46. A CHILDLESS WOMAN'S LAMENT

1. From *Techinno Kol B'chiyoh*, Poland-Russia, c. 1840. JNUL: S 63A 3908.
2. "I beg heaven and earth to lament on my behalf. . . ." Can anything be larger or more impressive than heaven and earth? The poor woman's fate is so devastating that only the largest and greatest mourners can bemoan this terrible fate. Such tremendous elements of nature are appropriate to the task of bemoaning the greatest misfortune that could befall a woman of this time–childlessness.
   The device of summoning great elements to witness is an old one in the literature of Israel. The first of such summonses is by Moses when he calls out in stentorian tones: "Listen, O heavens, and I shall speak; hear, O earth, the words of my mouth" (Deut. 32:1). On this verse, the incomparable Rashi poses the question: Why did Moses call upon these witnesses against the Children of Israel? He then proceeds to expand upon the six words of this laconic Deuteronomic verse and gives us a glimpse into Moses' mind. Moses' thinking goes something like this: I am merely flesh and blood and, as such, I shall eventually die. What if, some day in the future, the Israelites should deny that they ever accepted God's covenant (at Sinai)? After all, people are known to change their minds from time to time. That's human nature. If so, who would there be, if I'm no longer alive, to refute them? No one. For this reason I call upon the heavens and earth. They are witnesses destined to endure forever or, as the *Sifre* puts it, "for all eternity" (*Sifre*, R. Hammer trans., p. 303).

Only the great ones, the heavens and earth, can measure the enormity of a childless woman's misery, the author is implying, to bear witness and lament her misfortune. Observant Jews steeped in the weekly Torah portions would recognize the metaphor at once and sense the connection between the superheroic language of the poetic *Ha'azeenu* (Deut. 32:1 ff.) and the profound pain of a woman's childlessness.

3. The author had in mind the dramatic phrase of Psalm 69:2: ". . . the waters have reached my neck . . ." (NJPS) in which a "devout servant of God is undergoing cruel treatment" (Soncino trans., p. 216, footnote).

## 47. PARENTAL SUPPORT

1. In the prayer *Ahavoh raboh* (With Everlasting Love); see Weekday Morning Service in Bokser, *PB*, p. 48.

## 48. PEACE OF THE KINGDOM

1. T. C.: This curious *techinnah* is prefaced by the following passage: "Our Sages say in the *Ethics of the Fathers* (3:2) that one should pray for the welfare of the government . . . for, were it not for fear of it, men in the heat of anger would become as two-legged tigers, tearing the living flesh from one another. . . ."

In February 1917 the Russian Revolution broke out in Petrograd, and on March 15, 1917, Czar Nicholas II was forced to abdicate.

This *techinnah* for the welfare of Nicholas II appeared in the *Shas Techinno* (Vilna Edition, 1922), some years after the abdication. One wonders why the publisher-printer retained this prayer. There is a temptation to speculate on the time lag. Was it due to a deficient historical sense, or was it simply too expensive to remove the printed text and/or replace it with something else? Or does it perhaps reflect some innate conservative tendency, a hesitancy to tamper with a printed text? On the other hand, Jewish tradition does instruct: "Pray for the welfare of the government, since but for the fear thereof men would swallow each other alive" (*Ethics* 3:2). Hertz has some extended comments about loyalty to king and country in the Roman period, in Napoleon's day, and under the German kaiser and the British queen. See his *ADPB*, pp. 503-507, 647, footnotes.

2. "Nicholas II, the last Autocrat of All the Russians who ascended the throne, inaugurated the two worst decades in the bloody history of

the Jews in Russia. . . . [He] was a weak-willed superstitious puppet whose court was a refuge for fanatical pilgrims and reactionary advisors" (Sachar, *A History of the Jews*, p. 319).

## 49. ALL ISRAEL ARE BRETHREN

1. T.C.: The following is not a *techinnah*, a private devotion, in the strictly technical sense. It is thus surprising to come across it in a book of devotions. The purpose of this unique section was to emphasize and illustrate the close and devoted interrelationship of the Children of Israel to one another and to all mankind.

Alfes (?) begins by titling the passage *Chaverim kol Yisroel*—"All Israel Are Brethren"—that is, friends, comrades. The expression is found in the traditional blessing for the new month: ". . . may He redeem us soon and gather in our dispersed from the four corners of the earth, all Israel becoming comrades." The *Siddur Kol Yaakov* (*ArtScroll*) makes the interesting point in a footnote at this place that

. . . the blessing of the new month is, in effect, a prayer for the sequence of salvation. As given in this prayer, that sequence is a miraculous deliverance from oppression and an ingathering of exiles climaxed by Jewish unity, "all Israel becoming comrades."

Only through such comradeship or friendship, devotion to one another through a sensitive humanity cultivated to the highest degree—will the final redemption come about (Donin, *To Pray as a Jew*, p. 274).

The author of "All Israel Are Brethren" must have had in mind a passage in *The Fathers According to Rabbi Nathan*, in which Rabbi Joshua Ben Perahyah is quoted as saying: "Provide thyself with a teacher, and get thee a companion, and judge everyone with the scale weighted in his favor" (*Ethics* 1:6). Concerning this suggestion of Rabbi Joshua, the author of *The Fathers* asks: "How so? This teaches that a man should get a companion for himself, to eat with him, drink with him, sleep with him, and reveal to him all his secrets, the secrets of the Torah, and the secrets of worldly things" (p. 50).

With this religiocultural ethic in his historical consciousness, our author now develops the Jewish view on the subject of friendship—friendship between man and man, friendship between God and man. In the former, the method is by expounding biblical passages and showing humanity's interrelatedness; in the latter, it is accomplished by telling a story of two men and their love for one another, in which love God seeks to participate. The two types of love-friendship then coalesce in what becomes, for the author's Yiddish readers, the proper orientation to prayer in general and the object of these prayers.

2. According to Jewish tradition, the body was composed of 248 limbs and 365 veins. This numerology is study of the occult significance of numbers–*gematria* in Hebrew. The interpretation of words by the numerical value of their letters, adds up the limbs and veins and arrives at a total of 613, the traditional number of *mitzvot* the Jew is required to observe.

3. Translator's additional comments: The underlying purpose of this extraordinary segment of near-poetic prose seems to have been the desire to guide the everyday Jew into a path of living in which, knowingly or otherwise, he committed himself to actualizing the ideal of *tikkun olom*, improvement of the world. The idea of *tikkun olom* first found expression in the *Mishnah Gittin* 4,2: ". . . for the general good" (Danby trans.). Later, its meaning was expanded in the *Olaynu* prayer: *L'sahkayn olom b'malchus Shaddai* (to improve the world under the kingdom of God).

*Tikkun olom* was to be a constant reminder of the need for each person to strive each day to bring into existence the spiritual and physical improvement of mankind in this world. Joseph Klausner, late professor of Hebrew Literature at Hebrew University, once wrote that this striving was essentially the messianic idea that was first shaped by the prophets of Israel. It is this striving that the author of "All Israel Are Brethren" conveyed in another time and clime to his Yiddish-speaking -reading audience in that earthy tongue of the Jews' street in the shtetl. It was a worthy effort and a worthy goal.

## 50. DELIVERANCE FROM BAD NEIGHBORS

1. The author of this *techinnah*, quoting from memory, combined two sources: Hertz, *ADPB*, p. 24, has "*keep* us far from . . . a bad companion . . . ," whereas Hertz, *ADPB*, p. 27, has ". . . *deliver me from* a bad neighbor. . . ." The latter, Hertz points out, is a "prayer against moral hindrance," and this is what the author of this *techinnah* probably had in mind. A "bad" neighbor can be a barrier for the righteous (read: religious) person, preventing him from acting uprightly. The "bad" neighbor is the moral hindrance. Keeping oneself at a distance from such a "bad" influence enables one to act correctly more easily and without the corrupting influence, or barrier. Both prayers are recited in the Weekday Morning Service.

2. *Sha'aray Tzion* commentary: After one moves into a new building and everything is properly arranged, examine the *mezuzos* and determine whether they are kosher and properly affixed. If a *mezuzo* is needed, buy a new one and don't be too concerned with the price. Buy it from an honest, pious scribe.

A *mezuzo* is important. It's a sacred sign [that] shows that a Jew lives here and his house is holy unto God. Because of this (*mitzvo*), his children will be blessed with length of days, as we say daily (in the *Siddur*): [. . . and you shall write them upon the doorposts of your house . . .– Deut. 6:9; Hertz, *ADPB*, p. 119: "The *mezuzah* is a symbol of God's watchful care over the house and its dwellers"] [in order that your days and the days of your children be multiplied . . .–Deut. 11:21].

When the husband is not home, the wife should perform the *mitzvo* of affixing the *mezuzo* (to the doorpost) and say the blessing.

Also, if a horseshoe has been affixed to the threshold, it should be removed because it is shameful for a Jew to imitate the superstitions of heathens who regard this object as beneficial.

*Ma'aseh Alfes* commentary: The wise religious woman should see to it that the prayer said each morning (". . . deliver me from a bad neighbor . . .") does not merely remain in the *Siddur*, but she should take it to heart and use it when it comes to everyday living.

Experience has shown that when a workingman or a businessman rents a place and gives a deposit, if he later finds a competitor nearby, will leave the vicinity even if he must lose the deposit. Likewise, if a person finds a heretic living next door who profanes everything we hold dear, it's little enough to give up the deposit and reject the dwelling.

How much more so should this be the case when the enemy is admitted into one's dwelling! Many people tend to rent larger living quarters than necessary in order to sublet a portion to strangers. Before our very eyes, we see them writing on *Shabbos* and some of us tend to look upon this with indifference.

## 51. A NEW *TECHINNO* FOR *PARNOSO*

1. From *Techinno Chadosho al Parnoso* (Vilna: 1855). JNUL: S46 A 1109. *Parnoso* is used in this *techinnah* in a broad sense, connotatively, so that it signifies implications beyond the commonly recognized sense of support or livelihood: ". . . the religious materialism of the Jews springs not from disbelief, but from a superabundance of faith eager for its fulfillment not from the weakness but from the strength and energy of the

human spirit which, unafraid of being defiled by matter, purifies itself and uses it for its own ends" (William Klubach, "Israel in the Thought of Vladimer Soloviev," *Midstream* 36[8]:30).

2. A bit of the versifier has crept in. Each of the italicized words in the author's prefatory note (*composed, mind, heart, night*) indicates a pun on the word *acht*. No levity is intended. Rhythm, rhyme, or both found occasional use in the *techinnah* genre to facilitate recall. Many in the female audience did not read, but listened to the *techinnah* as it was read aloud by the rabbi's wife or another literate woman.

3. Based on the passage *malbish ahroomim*, found in the daily Morning Service (Hertz, *ADPB*, p. 22).

4. Genesis 1:11–"And God said, 'Let the earth sprout vegetation: seed-bearing plants, fruit trees of every kind on earth that bear fruit with the seed in it'" (NJPS).

5. The author probably had in mind "For He will order His angels to guard you wherever you go" (NJPS). The Yiddish *wegen und stegen* from the German is roads and paths, or ways and bypaths. Hence my translation, borrowed from Dickens, became "highways and byways," to which I added "of life." This psalm is traditionally recited in the synagogue on Sabbath morning. See Hertz, *ADPB*, pp. 71-73, footnotes, ad loc; Birnbaum, *DPB*, p. 310, footnote.

6. . . . need not rely upon "the gifts of mortals, but only etc." is paraphrased from the Grace after Meals. See *ArtScroll Siddur*, pp. 188-189, footnote.

## 52. FAR FROM HOME

1. Based on *Baba Metzia* 75b in slightly altered form.

2. Used here in two senses: associating with good friends as well as being one.

3. The idea of exile as atonement for one's sins is an old one. In *Ta'anit* 16a, Resh Lakish says: ". . . may our exile atone for us" (Soncino trans., p. 73). *Sanhedrin* 37b: "[Rabbi] Johanan said: Exile atones for everything . . ." (Soncino trans., p. 237); a few lines above, Rabbi Judah, son of Rabbi Hiyya, is credited with saying: "Exile atones for half of man's sins." The *Ma'aseh Alfes* below reduces this in his commentary to "Exile atones for sin." He eliminated the final word *mechtzo*, "half." This isn't quite kosher, but it serves his purpose.

*Ma'aseh Alfes* commentary: The holy conversations of our Sages are at first glance difficult to swallow. Isn't the Creator able to feed us where

we live so that we don't have to wander far from wife and children? This
is one of the secrets of the divine conduct [God's ways]. We must believe that everything He does is for good. . . .
Our Sages say that "Exile atones for sin" and, for a man who has to
leave his family to seek work, it is as though he's in exile. One must know
how to conduct oneself there and avoid bad company since God is test-
ing him to see whether he will be decent, observe the laws and Judaism
as much as possible. If he succeeds, this poor wanderer will remain a
father to his children. . . .
His wife should send him many letters filled with her wisdom so as
to maintain a strong contact with him and constantly remind him of home
and hearth. Since God helps them who help themselves, he will really
be found worthy of returning home happily and again be a husband to
his wife and a father to his children.

## 53. THE NEW MONTH OF SHEVOT (*ROSH CHODESH BENSHEN*)

1. T. C.: There are *techinnot* for the various months of the Jewish lunar
calendar, all of which are recited before the *Yehi rotzon* prayer preceding
the actual announcement of the new month (moon). This *techinnah* was
recited before the new month of *Shevat*, in which the New Year of the
Trees falls on the fifteenth day. Hertz (*ADPB*, pp. 508-510) furnishes a
brief historical background of the origin and development of the prayer
that states when the new month is scheduled to begin. It is recited in the
synagogue on the Sabbath preceding the actual day and date.
2. It must be remembered that the New Year of the Trees originated
in a land with a mild climate, whereas the majority of Jews were living at
the time of this *techinnah* in Eastern European lands with long, harsh,
winter months.

## 54. THE NEW MONTH OF *ODOHR*

1. T.C.: The interesting thing about this *techinnah* is that it is addressed to Moses and not to God. The fact that Moses, according to tradition, was born and died on the seventh of *Adar* does not of itself war-
rant a prayer addressed to him. However, when the Children of Israel
committed the sin of the golden calf and God wished to destroy them
(Exod. 32:10), Moses came to their defense and implored God not to
vent His anger (vv. 11 ff.). Out of this incident there developed a view of
Moses as an intercessor par excellence on behalf of the people, a *maylitz*

in Hebrew. It is thus appropriate that in this month, when Moses was born and died, he should again be implored on behalf of the Children of Israel.

2. The author of this *techinnah* chose for scriptural support a verse found in Moses' discourse on the Law. In the section on benefits accruing from observance of the Law, those blessings are enumerated that Israel will enjoy if it keeps the Law. Deuteronomy 28:12 is partially quoted by the author. The specific meaning of God's "good treasure" is, however, found in the second half of the verse: ". . . His good treasure, the heaven to give the rain of your land in its season, and to bless all your undertakings."

## 55. A PURIM *TECHINNO*

1. T.C.: According to tradition as expressed in the Talmud (*Ta'anit* 29a), "rejoicings are increased with the beginning of *Adar.*"

Jews were enjoined by Mordecai to "make them days of feasting and gladness" (Esther 9:22) as well as sending gifts to one another and to the poor on the new festival of Purim which occurs on *Adar* 14. No emphasis on celebration is reflected in this *techinnah.* The author chose rather to emphasize the importance of charity even on a festival that celebrated the Jews' salvation and deliverance from would-be executioners. The theme of righteous acts (in the case of Purim—charity) as the means for salvation for the one and the many was of overriding importance in pre-twentieth-century Judaism.

## 56. THE THREE PILGRIMAGE FESTIVALS

1. T.C.: Dr. Benzion Alfes, who claims credit for this collection of *techinnot* in the 1922 Vilna edition (see Introduction to this text), occasionally supplemented his commentary at the bottom of the *techinnah* page with reading material calculated to expand on the meaning and significance of certain occasions and/or ideas appearing in the *techinnot.* The material presented here is an example of this.

2. "Allegorical interpretation refers it to the giving of the Torah and God's speaking directly to Israel" (Soncino Bible commentary to Song of Songs, p. 1).

3. On the night of Shavuot, the *Tikkun Layl Shavuot* is read. Solomon Ha-Levi Alkabez (1505-1584), the author of the hymn *Lechah Dodee*, established that while he and Joseph Caro "were both studying the Torah

on the night of Shavu'ot, the *maggid* appeared to Caro. They therefore established the custom of staying awake on the night of Shavu'ot to study the Torah. The custom, which became widespread, is known as *Tikkun Layl Shavuot*" (*EJ* 2:635). The *maggid* is "an angel or supermundane spirit which conveys teachings to scholars worthy of such communication in mysterious ways" (*EJ*, 11:698). ". . . the holding of dusk-to-dawn vigils, which were dedicated to both ordinary and mystical study, on the nights of Pentecost, Hoshanah Rabba. . . . the liturgies and texts were referred to as *tikkunim*." (*EJ* 10:642).

4. *Akdamut Millin* is the title and the "opening words of an Aramaic poem by Rabbi Meir ben Isaac Nehorai. The poem was recited in the synagogue on Shavu'ot as an introduction to the Aramaic translation (*targum*) of Exodus 19-20 (the theophany at Mount Sinai. . . . It praises God as creator and lawgiver, expatiates on Israel's fidelity to God despite all sufferings and temptations, and ends with a description of the apocalyptic events at the end of days and the future glory of Israel. The poem is recited in the Ashkenazic rite only" (*EJ* 2:479). An excellent summation of it is found in *Siddur Sim Shalom*, p. 526.

## 57. AFTER CANDLELIGHTING—PESACH (VERSION 1)

1. *Ma'aseh Alfes* commentary: Every intelligent person will understand that the Passover *seder* is not merely a *seder* for Passover eve alone. It also teaches the Jew to live orderly and with *seder* (order) all the days and nights of the year. *Kaddesh* and *urchatz* (sanctification of the wine and washing of the hands) teach us to keep ourselves holy and removed from all base and demeaning conduct, to cleanse ourselves of all ignoble transactions. [Wash yourselves clean—Isa. 1:16, (for) your hands are stained with crime—Isa. 1:15]. For example: buying stolen goods, giving false testimony, and other such "nice" things [that] put us even deeper in the hole and give our neighbors cause to look askance at us, as though we were thieving gypsies, heaven help us!

*Karpas*. The recitation of the blessing (. . . who creates the fruit of the earth) over a bit of greens [parsley or celery] reminds us that Mother Earth [Naked came I out of my mother's womb, and naked shall I return there—Job 1:21. Rashi: "there" refers to "the earth whence I was taken"] is the great mistress who furnishes us with food, clothing, construction materials, gold, and precious stones, when the heavenly Father permits. When He does not, she is no longer the "great mistress" who provides.

Therefore, we must teach the child to give thanks to his heavenly Father, to recite a blessing for each thing he receives. This should not be merely with voice but also with thought, with understanding, that he realize [The earth is the Lord's and the fullness thereof–Ps. 24:1] the world and all therein have been furnished by Him. We pay for what we get. The Sages taught that the coin of payment is the blessing we recite. Then the child will understand that we may not simply take but also [Lift up your hands toward the sanctuary and bless the Lord–Ps. 134:2] bless and thank.

Man, however, is a strange creature. He has many strengths, both good and bad. When a great desire [ta'avo] comes upon him, he forgets everything. He becomes a wild animal, a two-legged tiger. In order to change this tiger into a civilized being, the great Teacher of the world (God) designated the middle matzo [yachatz] for division in half, to teach us that the middle one stands for the best years of one's life, when one should act and not postpone (action) until old age. The smaller piece of the yachatz matzo (representing physical needs, work, making a living) remains on the (Passover) table. The larger portion is hidden away for later consumption (at the end of the meal), that is, for spiritual needs–study of Torah and performance of good deeds

Woe unto him whose wife and children steal the afikomen from him! That which he seeks to save for later (spiritual needs) they do not allow him time in the seder of his life to study a little and achieve fulfillment [shlaymus]. They constantly demand: Give! Give us the high life, theater-going, and fancy tastes. They shut him off from all the noble impulses and he remains at the lowest level of thought. Good heavens! Where does one get the money? They force him to become a member of the society of "murderous, treacherous men" who "shall not live out half their lives" [Ps. 55:24]. They do not divide their days, half in the service of God and half for their personal needs.

Every wise woman should therefore pray at candlelighting time to God for the illumination whereby she will be able to guide her husband and children into good ways. This depends above all upon the woman of whom King Solomon says: [A capable wife is a crown for her husband–Prov. 12:4].

## 60. SABBATH OF INTERMEDIATE DAYS OF PESACH

1. On the Sabbath of the intermediate days of Passover, the prophetic portion chanted in the synagogue is Ezekiel 37:1-15 (actually, beginning with 36:37). It contains the vision of Israel's resurrection, the dramatic scene of the valley of dry bones.

## 61. MEMORIAL SERVICE FOR THE DEAD—YIZKOR (VERSION 1)

1. T.C.: This *techinnah* reflects the rabbinic view of the soul's post-mortem existence to a surprising degree. An excellent introduction to the subject of the soul in Judaism will be found in *EJ* 15:172 ff. See especially column 175 for the rabbinic view of the soul after death. The view implicit in this *techinnah* is consistent with that view. The soul's prenatal origin was beneath God's Throne of Glory, and it is that place to which it will eventually return. The body, on the other hand, is destined for the grave and decomposition (. . . dust thou art, and unto dust shalt thou return—Gen. 3:19).

The reward of one who has been completely righteous in this world is direct return of the soul after death to its place of origin and the pleasure of extreme bliss attained by proximity to God. The majority of mankind, unfortunately being fallible, creates by its sins an immovable barrier that prevents immediate spiritual repose. The result is a limbolike existence for which there can be no definite time limit. Each "sentence" is determined on a case-by-case basis. The *Yizkor* prayers in some measure can help in the redemption of these unfortunate souls, as can Torah study and almsgiving (*tzedakah*). (Recitation of *Yizkor* prayers enables the soul to rise up and gain repose among the holy souls of the righteous; ultimately, it reaches its resting place beneath God's Throne of Glory.) Devoted Torah study cannot be overemphasized. Each day, in the Morning Service, the traditional Jew recites a passage from the tractate of *Shabbat* 127a: "These are the precepts whose fruits one enjoys in this world, but its principal remains for him in the world-to-come . . . but the study of Torah is equivalent to them all." That is, the merit of the *mitzvah* of Torah study (*talmud Torah*) is equal in importance to that of all the other *mitzvot*. (Proof text: Almsgiving delivers from death—Prov. 10:2.)

Another important function of this *techinnah* is to remind God (and the reader of the *techinnah*) of the importance of the merit of good deeds and the performance of *mitzvot*. These carry much weight with God and incline Him favorably toward the deceased who has been remembered by those left behind in this world.

Of equal importance is the merit of little children. This merit lies in the study of Torah (*talmud Torah*) in all the one-room schools (*cheder, chadohrim*), which brings us full circle to the great value of Torah study in obtaining God's favorable inclination toward the souls of the deceased. Merit built up in this world can be drawn upon for the sake of the deceased in the world-to-come.

2. From *A New Techinno: Memorial Service for the Dead, Three Techinnos* (Lemberg: Hirsch Schlag Publisher & Bookseller from Lvov; V. Kubler Press, Hotel Europe, 1897). JNUL S61 A2999: 296.319.1. Below the subtitle of *Three Techinnos* on the title page, the three kinds of *techinnot* are itemized as follows:

a) Memorial Service to be said four times during the year: Yom Kippur, Shemini Atzeres, the last day of Pesach, and the last (second) day of Shovuos;

b) to be said when one has *Yohrzeit*;

c) what an orphaned woman, about to become a bride, should say on the day of her *chuppo* [lit.: wedding canopy; i.e., marriage] after the *Mincho* Service. . . .

This booklet of fourteen pages is a handbook containing the Hebrew *Yizkor* prayers, the Memorial Service for the dead, to be read on various occasions throughout the Jewish year. Inserted before, after, or between the Hebrew sections, these are either straight translations from Hebrew into Yiddish or *techinnot* that stand on their own merit.

3. Might this be a Jewish version of Limbo?

## 62. MEMORIAL SERVICE FOR THE DEAD–*YIZKOR* (VERSION 2)

1. T.C.: Following the preceding *techinnah*, which is of an introductory nature, there appears the *Yizkor* prayer for one's deceased relative(s): May God remember [*Yizkor Elohim*] the soul of my. . . .

Next comes "God full of mercy . . ." [*El molay rahchamim . . .*], recited in memory of specific individuals, of a group, and for martyrs. Texts may vary in minor details in different *siddurim*. In the present collection of *techinnot*, from which this translation has been made (Lemberg, 1897), there is an interesting feature in the *El molay rahchamim* prayer. My slightly modified translation of the opening lines is "Merciful God who dwells on high, grant perfect rest *on* the wings of the *Shecheeno*. . . ." (For a discussion of *Shecheenah*, see *EJ* 14:1349, and E. E. Urbach, *The Sages*, chap. 3). Deliberately emphasize the word *on* because, traditionally, the metaphor conveyed has been that of the Jewish soul seeking spiritual shelter and divine protection *under* the *Shecheeno*'s wing. A check of several prayer books in my collection shows that most translate as ". . . grant perfect rest *under* the wings of. . . ." Only the *ArtScroll Siddur* retains "*on* the wings." It explains why in an explanatory footnote (p. 815):

When this term is used to mean Heavenly protection from danger, we say *tachat, under* the wings, using the analogy of a bird spreading its protective wings over its young. In this prayer, where we speak of spiritual elevation, we reverse the analogy, comparing God's presence to a soaring eagle that puts its young on top of its wings and carries them aloft.

After this *El molay rahchamim* prayer comes the next *techinnah*, translated below. It is also found in the 1916 HPC edition of *Shas Techinno Rav Peninim*. The 1916 version is more polished than the 1897 Lemberg edition and lacks the earthier, grassroots feel of the earlier one that retained the quality of earlier printings. The mass crossing of the Atlantic seems to have made a noticeable difference, not necessarily for the better.

### 63. AFTER CANDLELIGHTING—*SHOVUOS*

1. *Ma'aseh Alfes* commentary: Even though the *mitzvo* of study of Torah is not incumbent upon women, the *Gemoro* says that they can merit its reward by seeing to it that their husbands and children are able to study it.

2. *Sha'aray Tzion* commentary: It is the custom to decorate the home with divers greens and flowers in remembrance of the giving of the Torah [*mattan Torah*] at Mount Sinai in the springtime when everything was in full bloom.

Shovuos is also the time when the future of all fruit-bearing trees is decided. On their behalf, we pray that they will be blessed with fruitfulness.

3. *Sha'aray Tzion* commentary: It is the custom to set in the windows a type of reed known as "rush." They are long-stemmed and grow at the edge of streams. This practice serves to remind us of the time when *Moshe Rabenu* as a child had been placed in a basket in the Nile [Exod. 2:3] and was saved [from death] because he was destined to receive the holy Torah. ("The giant reed, . . . also known as 'bulrush,' is common throughout Palestine [and] Syria, . . . [and] was used for many purposes by the ancients—for walking sticks, fishing rods, measuring rods, and musical pipes . . ." [Harold N. Moldenke and Alma L. Moldenke, eds., *Plants of the Bible*, p. 50]. For a lithograph of the Nile papyrus, see fig. 59; fig. 63 is an interesting photograph of the *cyprus papyrus* in the Huleh Swamp, which is now an historical memory. Both figures are found at the end of the Moldenke volume.)

## 64. THE SECOND DAY OF SHOVUOS (BEFORE READING PSALMS)

1. "A less observed custom is to recite the whole Book of Psalms on the second night because of the association of the festival with David" (*EJ* 14:1322). "In the synagogue, it is customary to read the Book of Ruth on Shavuot. . . . Ruth was the ancestor of David who, according to tradition, died on Shavuot . . ." (*EJ* 14:1321).

2. *Sha'aray Tzion* commentary: It is customary on Shovuos to eat dairy meals. The reason is that, concerning the Torah, the following verse is mentioned: "Honey and milk are under your tongue"—Song of Songs 4:11.

## 65. *TECHINNO* FOR *TISHO B'OV*

1. From *Techinno Imray Shefer: Six New Techinnos*, by Rabbi Israel of Ivanice, Moravia (Lemberg, 1884). JNUL S37 A 1375. The title means *A Techinno of Beautiful Sayings*. It is based on Jacob's blessing of Naftali in Gen. 49:21. Ivanice, situated in southwestern Moravia, is roughly in the middle of Czechoslovakia. It had a small Jewish community continuously in residence from the late fifteenth century on. Its Jews were deported to the death camps in 1942 (*EJ* 9:1153).

2. Cf. The Ark of the Covenant of the Lord of Hosts Enthroned on the Cherubim—1 Samuel 4:4 (NJPS); the ark of the covenant of the Lord of hosts, who sitteth upon the cherubim (OJPS).

3. According to the Talmud (*Sanhedrin* 96b, Soncino trans., p. 651), Nebuzaradan was unable to break down the gate of Jerusalem and about to give up, when a voice told him to continue "for the time has come for the Sanctuary to be destroyed and the Temple burnt." He continued and, when he reached the Temple, tried setting fire to it: ". . . it sought to rise up, but it was trodden down from Heaven. . . ." When he wanted to rejoice at what he had done, "a voice came forth from Heaven saying to him, 'Thou hast slain a dead people, thou hast burned a Temple already burned. . . .'"

4. A more detailed listing of the items is found in Jeremiah 52:17–23.

## 66. *TECHINNO* FOR THE MONTH OF *ELUL* (VERSION 1)

1. A prefatory note informs us that this collection of *techinnot* under the title of *Kol B'chiyo* [*Voice of Weeping*] was brought from the Land of

Israel. It was originally "composed in the holy tongue and translated into Yiddish by the modest, God-fearing woman Mistress Henno, daughter of Rabbi Judah, z"l [zichrono leevrocho], may his memory be for a blessing, wife of the learned Rabbi Aryeh Leyb Safro of the holy community of Brod." It was printed in "Poland-Russia," c. 1840. The title Kol B'chiyo was borrowed from Psalm 6:9—"God has heard the voice (sound) of my weeping." The month of Elul usually comes in the August-September period, a time for spiritual introspection leading up to the High Holy Days season in the month of Tishre, which generally comes in September.

2. At this point, one cannot help but recall Oscar Wilde's Picture of Dorian Gray. Two disparate cultures and, yet, how similar the idea of the morally blemished soul!

3. This could be a veiled reference to the woman's having failed to go to mikveh at the appointed times. It seems unlikely that failure to wash one's hands or face would be regarded as a major fault.

4. Israel's shefa and berocho (translated as abundance and prosperity) would be diminished by her sins. The relationship between an individual's shortcomings and the collective welfare of Israel seem tenuous at first glance. However, in an interesting footnote to one of the prayers in the counting of the Omer, Rabbi N. Scherman supplies the following insight from the Kabbalah, which comments on ". . . cleanse us from our encrustations of evil . . .":

> The Kabbalah teaches that when someone sins he creates a shell or encrustation that covers his spiritual content. . . . the evil does not change the inner essence of the Jew. As Maharal teaches, every member of Israel remains holy; evil and contamination are extraneous, like a shell or filth. Through repentance they can be washed away. (Scherman, The Prayer Book, pp. 168-169)

5. Counting the Omer is a biblical injunction in which the Jew is commanded to count forty-nine days from the second day of Passover when the Omer, the meal offering of the new barley crop, is brought to the Temple. The fiftieth day is the pilgrimage Festival of Weeks (Shovuos). See Scherman, The Prayer Book, pp. 164-165.

6. This idea of gilgul neshamot, or transmigration of souls, is Molly Bloom's now famous "met-him-pike-hoses." Since it appears several times in this confessional, a rereading of Stuart Gilbert's discussion of it in James Joyce's opus Ulysses (New York: Knopf, 1931), pp. 31-38, would be worthwhile.

7. *Shatnes* is a biblical prohibition found in Deuteronomy 22:11.

8. In the international bestiary, the raven is generally a symbol of evil or the presage of evil. However, in 1 Kings 17:4 it is the raven who will feed the prophet Elijah.

9. An echo of the *tashlich* ceremony, the casting of sins into the depths of the sea. See Scherman, *ArtScroll Siddur*, pp. 770-772, for a description of the ceremony and the prayers recited.

## 67. *TECHINNO* FOR THE ENTIRE MONTH OF *ELUL* (VERSION 2)

1. T.C.: This "*Techinno* of the Matriarchs for *Rosh Chodesh Elul*," as Zinberg translated it, contains material to be read throughout the month of *Elul*, preceding Rosh Hashana. The 1921 edition has *from* instead of *for*, which, strictly speaking, would limit it to be read only on the first two days of *Rosh Chodesh*. See *ZHJL*, vol. 7, p. 257. The problem of whether to use *for* or *from* is resolved in the title's subscript:

> This *techinno* was composed by the woman, Mistress Serel, daughter of our rabbi, Rabbi Jacob Se"gal of Dubno, wife of the rabbi, the great light, expert in wisdom, our teacher Rabbi Mordecai Ka"tz Rappaport, to be read [during] the entire month of *Elul*. . . .

The above quote is taken from *Techinno Eemohhos* (Lemberg: J. D. Suss and S. W. Menkes Publishers, F. Bednerski Press, 1891), JNUL: S51 A740: 296.319.1. (*Ka"tz* is indicated as an acronym by the double apostrophe. It stands for *Kohen tzedek*—priest of righteousness.)

Although relying primarily on the 1891 Lemberg text, I also consulted several other printings I have collected over the years. These are listed chronologically:

*a*) *Techinno Eemohhos* (Yosefov: Sh. Wachs, Printer, 1845). JNUL: R7 A966: 296.319.1. The reverse of the title page reads: "Printing permitted, subject to submission to censorship committee, the number of copies legally allowed. Kiev, Jan. 31, 1845. Censor: Novitsky." I am indebted to Ms. Bella Hess for translating the Russian.

*b*) *Techinno Eemohhos* (Zhitomir: Shapirov Brothers, 1848).

*c*) *Techinno Eemohhos* (Vilna: Widow & Brothers Romm, 1874). YIVO: 9979.

*d*) *Shas Techinno Rav Peninim* (New York: Hebrew Publishing, 1916), pp. 136-144.

*e) Shas Techinnos fun A-gantz Yohr* (Lemberg: David Balaban, Publisher 1904/1905), pp. 74-79. YIVO: 6/4658.
*f) Techinno Eemohhos*, etc. (Lemberg: n.p., 1921). JNUL: S57 A 1921.296.319.1.
*g) Techinno Kol Bo* (Brooklyn, N.Y.: Ateres, 1969), pp. 204-216.

The different biblical (and some nonbiblical) passages used, and variations in the Yiddish text, are not inconsiderable. None, however, is of major importance and a detailed treatment would only have served to becloud the subject. My translation was based on the 1891 edition for reasons I no longer remember. The day of the copyright and warning against tampering with the text had not yet descended upon the *techinnah* genre. It is written in Judges 17:6–"[Since] in those days there was no king in Israel, [every] man [editor? redactor? revisor? printer? publisher?] did that which was right in his *eyes* [and altered the text accordingly]."

Mistress Serel contributed three *techinnot* to a fifteen-page booklet, approximately 4.25" x 6". (An appreciation of the diminutive size of the booklet will help understand the difficulty of reading the text, even with a magnifying glass.) The second *techinnah* was to be read before the Thirteen Attributes were recited in the synagogue prior to taking the Torah out of the holy ark on Rosh Hashana and the third one before the blowing of the shofar. Unmentioned on the title page is the *Yizkor* (memorial) service at the end of the booklet for parents and friends, with additional passages for the three pilgrimage festivals and Yom Kippur.

The compositional method used by *techinnot* authors was not necessarily common to all *techinnot*. The author's sex, the time and place, as well as the subject of the composition, contributed various and varying factors. The use of traditional source material is truly impressive.

This type of format is generally referred to as literary patchwork. It is "formed by piecing together extracts from various works by one or several authors" (W. Thrall, A. Hibbard and C. Holman, *A Handbook to Literature* [New York: Odyssey Press, 1936; reprint, 1960], p. 342). Literary patchwork differs from pastiche in that the latter not only imitates and parodies, it also caricatures. The latter obviously doesn't apply to the *techinnah*. Literary patchwork may or may not catch something of the spirit of the original. That the *techinnah* is imitative is unimportant. What is significant is that something new and relevant to Serel's time and culture has been expressed, without her being aware of any innovation, utilizing the religious-literary tradition in which she had been culturally formed.

Familiarity with the tradition's midrashic legends, biblical figures, biblical verses and phraseology in Hebrew is always present and manifest. This *techinnah*, recited throughout the month of *Elul* before the High Holy Days season, is a prime example of Serel's familiarity with the biblical text. Professor Chava Weissler has pointed out in an essay that we may never know whether this familiarity by women authors was obtained directly from literary or oral sources (a fascinating problem in itself) (Chava Weissler, "The Traditional Piety of Ashkenazic Women," in *Jewish Spirituality*, vol. 2, ed. Arthur Green [New York: Crossroad, 1987], p. 268). Such works as the *Tze'eno u-Re'eno*, morality books, and exempla in Yiddish were available almost everywhere for the education of Jewish women. When we come to the case of women who were daughters and/or wives of rabbis, one cannot confidently say whether the familiarity with sources was direct or indirect. There simply is no documentary evidence to date, one way or the other.

The *Tze'eno u-Re'eno*, authored by Rabbi Jacob ben Isaac Ashkenazi of Janow, was composed in early seventeenth or late sixteenth century (*EJ* 16:967). It is a popular collection of *midrashim* and tales expounding selected biblical verses (*EJ* 16:801-802). Extended treatment and several samples are found in *ZHJL*, vol. 7, pp. 130-135. By way of explanation, Zinberg wrote:

> The verse was the introduction, the framework in which the preacher would spin and weave his ingenious tapestry of tender instruction, earnest words of reproof, and beautiful legends and proverbs. . . . there is very clearly discernible in the style and character of this literature the tender and womanly, the typically feminine, in which feeling and the emotive mood obtain dominance over the logically intellectual and avidly abstract. (*ZHJL* 7:131-132)

This *techinnah*, however, does reveal a remarkably intimate knowledge of biblical sources, quoted first in the Hebrew and then expanded in Yiddish. For the sake of brevity and a wish to avoid repetitiousness, Yiddish material has been omitted. Mistress Serel's use of biblical passages is brilliant; their adaptation to the spiritual needs of her day is stunning. An underlying unity and coherence cannot be denied.

The *techinnah* has been roughly divided into two unequal parts. The first and shorter of the two is a plea for God's loving-kindness, with biblical passages placed in both the author's and God's mouth, as it were. This shorter part is so brief that, when we realize it has ended after only two responses, we are somewhat disappointed. We have begun to expect more of this give and take. Instead, we find the second and larger part consisting of Serel's monologue directed at the Creator. Her rising emotions culminate in straightforward prayer. God has become the Silent Auditor. There is no response to her impassioned pleas. The divine silence, however, may be an answer of sorts with which humans must be left to wrestle. Finally, there is no prologue and no conclusion. As eavesdroppers we have witnessed a solemn, tension-laden conversation, in other words, a *techinnah*.

 2. Psalm 145:14–"The Lord upholds (supports) those who fall. . . ." Serel personalizes, as we see by the text. Instead of *upholding*, the verb *s'm'ch* is changed to first person singular. She now *relies* upon God. The slightly altered phrase nevertheless rang true for the religiously literate Jew who recited prayers each morning and afternoon. Psalm 145 is found in the familiar *Ashray* prayer. See Birnbaum, *DPB*, p. 59.

 At this point, let us consider the phenomenon of the biblical presence for the light it sheds on Serel's *techinnah*. In another literary context I dealt with this subject in my book *The Many Worlds of Gershon Shofman* (West Orange, N.J.: Behrman House, 1989), chap. 14. In commenting on the biblical presence in Shofman's work, Meir Bosak described the Bible's influence, which I summed up in the following paraphrase:

> The Tanach is a record of a people's march through history and its contact with other peoples and cultures; it is the record of thought and feeling engendered together with an awareness of the divine omnipresent Reality. The narratives, prophets, psalms, etc. constitute a national biography. (p. 226)

Shofman's work, Bosak concluded, is part of this entity. The same must be said of Mistress Serel's *techinnah*.

 In the post-*Haskalah* period of the "new" Hebrew literature, *melitzah*, as it came to be called, was regarded as "an ostentatious style using biblical verse fragments which tend to becloud the idea; use of inflated language in place of simplicity" (Even-Shoshan, *Ha-millon he-chadash*, vol. 2, p. 806). Serel's method did not descend to this level. First, she was composing sacred, religious literature, whereas the concern of the *maskilim* (enlighteners) was the "rebirth" of the Hebrew language as a means of ultimately bringing about the "rebirth" of the Jewish people and their desacralization in order to free both from a stultifying medieval atmosphere, to enable them to enter the secular mainstream of modern ninteenth-century Europe. This would never have occurred to Serel. She was a child of the medieval period, the Renaissance having come and gone without affecting her intellectual and spiritual outlook. Second, the excessive and debased use of biblicisms in a quixotic attempt by *maskilim* to modernize the language led to extremes, exaggerations, follies, and amusing, sometimes pathetic, results. All this in a premodern, pre-Zionist period before the language and its traditional land were reunited in a "normal" relationship. None of this was a matter of concern in Serel's pristine era. It simply did not exist as a subject for discussion or action in her generation, notwithstanding the religious yearning for a mass return to the homeland in the Messiah's time.

3. Isaiah 65:24–Before they call, I shall answer. In this text, God responds to Serel: Before *you* call. . . .

4. Psalm 119:124–Deal with *Your* servant. . . . Here: Deal with *me*. . . .

5. Exodus 34:7–He keeps mercy to the thousandth generation, forgives iniquity, transgression, and sin; He does not remit all punishment, but visits the iniquity of parents upon children and children's children. . . . Here: I shall deal mercifully and remember the merit of the fathers upon the children. . . . In the Exodus passage, God is described as keeping mercy. Here, God speaks: I shall, and so on. In Exodus, parental sins are visited upon three generations. Here, God says that He will remember the fathers' merit for the benefit of successive generations.

6. Psalm 119:76–No change.

7. Psalm 86:17–Minor change from first person singular in the original to first person plural here.

8. Isaiah 61:1–God has sent the prophet to bind up. Here: God will personally do the binding. (The textual quote is defective in Serel.)

9. Psalm 119:91–They stand this day to [carry out] Your rulings. The verse makes no sense here. Serel's quote is defective. Verb should be in first person plural: *We* shall stand. . . .

10. Psalm 103:13–As a father *has compassion* for his children, so the Lord *has compassion*. . . .

Psalm 8:3–Out of the mouths of *babes and sucklings*. . . . Here: Serel combines the emphasized elements of both verses into one descriptive statement of those qualities she finds in God, with which she hopes her spiritual Father will act toward His children who are entirely dependent upon Him.

11. *a)* Lam. 3:8–Though I cry and call for help, He shuts out my prayer.

*b*) Ps. 39:13–Hear my prayer, Lord, give ear to my cry, be not silent in response to my tears.

*c*) *Berachot* 32b (Soncino trans., p. 199)–... though the gates of prayer are closed, the gates of weeping are not closed. (The gates of prayer were closed from the day on which the Temple was destroyed.)

*d*) Tears shed by Jews at the destruction (of the Holy Temple) and because of their exilic sufferings will be placed in a (skin) bottle, which, when filled, will herald the coming Redemption. See *node* in Even-Shoshan, *Ha-millon he-chadash*, vol. 2, p. 817.

*e*) In the Yiddish, Serel asks that God accept her shed tears and store them in a bottle so that with them He will wash away "our sins." The psalmist (56:9) begs God to put His tears in a (skin) bottle and save them. These tears were shed in suffering and, since all sufferings were recorded in God's Book of Remembrance, they will be a testimony and reminder that in the future He will deliver the petitioner from death (56:14) and enable him to walk before God "in the light of the living" (Soncino trans., pp. 178-179).

12. Cf. "What can we say, what can we speak, or how can we justify ourselves?" See the sixth of the seven elegies comprising the long *Vehu rachum* in Hertz, *ADPB*, p. 176.

13. The verb form "I shall give thanks to You" appears in two places:

*a*) Psalm 118:21–I shall give thanks to You, for You have answered me. See Hallel Service in Hertz, *ADPB*, p. 770.

*b*) Psalm 138:1–I shall give thanks to You with all my heart. This is not, to the best of my knowledge, found in the prayer book. In a *Tillim Yid*, a Jew who frequently recited psalms, it would reverberate with familiar tones.

14. Psalm 6:2–Lord, *do not rebuke me* (*ahl tocheechaynee*) in Your anger, and *do not chastise me* (*ahl tyahsraynee*) in Your wrath. The negative imperatives in each half of the verse are interchangeable, as is often the case in parallelism. The nouns *anger* (*ahpcho*) and *wrath* (*chamoscho*) could also be interchanged. This is what the author, writing from memory, has done.

15. The Hebrew text is defective. The particle *mem* is missing from the word *deeds*. It should be "from deeds." Also, there should be no definite article on the adjective *good*. Finally, there is no scriptural source for the Hebrew although, the verb *r'-h'-q"* is used in the sense of "*far from*" in the following:

*a*) Exodus 23:7–keep *far from* a false charge.
*b*) Psalm 71:12–God, be not *far from* me.
*c*) Proverbs 22:5– . . . who values his life will keep *far from* them.

16. Psalm 119:38–Fulfill Your promise to Your servant. Serel substituted "maidservant" for "manservant" and "loving-kindness" for "promise."

17. Based on a passage in *Berachot* 60b and later incorporated into the *Siddur*. See Birnbaum, *DPB*, pp. 17-19: ". . . and cause us to cling to the Good Inclination and to good deeds . . ." in the *yehhe rohtzone* prayer. Serel singularized the plurals.

18. Esther 6:1– . . . and he ordered the Book of Records . . . to be brought. . . .

19. *Chesed*, (God's) mercy, loving-kindness, is not only ubiquitous in the *Tanach*; its presence so many times in the *Siddur* immediately conjures up the basic and outstanding quality of God. Here are just a few examples (The italicized translations show how differently the term may be understood):

*a*) Exodus 20:6–[He shows] *kindness* to the thousandth generation, the Thirteen Attributes, recited on festivals falling on weekdays. See Birnbaum, *DPB*, p. 363.

*b*) Ruth 1:8–May the Lord deal *kindly* with you.

*c*) Psalm 5:8–But I in (through) Your abundant *love*, enter Your house. . . . See the *Mah tovu* prayer in Birnbaum, *DPB*, p. 3.

*d*) Psalm 36:8–How precious is Your *faithful care*, O God! Said after wrapping one's self in the *tallit*, the prayer shawl (Birnbaum, *DPB*, p. 5).

*e*) Psalm 118:29–His *steadfast love* is eternal, found in the Hallel Service, Birnbaum, (*DPB*, p. 571).

Although the line by Serel has no direct biblical source, the many connotations for the concept of God's *chesed* were deeply embedded in the Jewish collective religious memory.

20. *Maytzar lee* echoes Psalm 118:5–*min ha-maytzar*: From [or out of] distress I called. . . . However, in the psalm, *maytzar* is used as a noun, whereas here it is a verb.

21. Psalm 103:13–As a father has compassion upon his children. . . . Hertz, *ADPB*, p. 1054 uses the entire psalm in "Prayer in Sickness."

22. Psalm 103:13. The loose translation here is based on the Yiddish immediately following the Hebrew in the *techinnah*.

23. Cf. Birnbaum, *HHPB*, pp. 547-548: "Turning away from thy good precepts and love . . . ," where first person plural is used, while here it has been singularized to make it more personal for the reader of the *techinnah*.

24. Based on Psalm 145:19–He will hear their cry and save them.

25. Psalm 145:18–The Lord is near unto all who call upon Him.

One final comment here concerning Serel's use of biblical sources: There were some twenty source selections from Psalms, of which four are not found in the *Siddur*. Next, in order of frequency, came Isaiah and the Talmud with four each, followed by Exodus with three, Jeremiah with two, and Esther with one. Conclusion: We still have a *Tillim Yid*, a psalms-reading Jew primarily, but not exclusively, in Mistress Serel. No mean achievement for a woman of her time!

## 68. A *TECHINNO* FOR THE COURTYARD OF DEATH

1. From *Ahnaie Shas Techinno* (Vilna: Rochel-Esther Bas Avi-chayil of Jerusalem, 1930?), pp. 209-210. JTSAL: BM 675 74 A3.

In Genesis 10:26 the compound "Courtyard of Death" appears as a single word. It is found in the collection of post-Flood genealogical listings to which N. Sarna refers as The Table of Nations (vv. 1-32). In his commentary, Sarna points out that "this well-known kingdom mentioned in South Arabic inscriptions is the present-day Hadramaut on the southern coast east of Yemen" (*The JPS Torah Commentary: Genesis*, p. 79).

Rashi ad loc: "He was so-called (Court of Death) after his city." Rashi also mentions the *aggadah* in *Genesis Rabbah* in which, according to R. Huna, "It refers to a place called Hezar Maweth, whose people eat leeks, wear garments of papyrus, and hope only for death" (Friedman, *Midrash Rabbah: Genesis*, vol. 1, p. 300). Friedman adds in footnote 3, p. 300, that "it is a place of extreme poverty and misery." He quotes (Julius) Th(eodor) that "the reference is probably not to a place of that name in Southern Arabia, which was rich and fertile." On Theodor (1849-1923), see *EJ* 15:1100.

The author of our *techinnah* used *Hazar Mavet* as a synonym for "cemetery," the "House of Eternal Life," unaware of the term's academic peregrinations.

2. "It is the custom to go about the graves (i.e., around, from one to another) to recite *techinnos* and contribute charity (money) to the poor people (seeking alms at the cemetery)" (Rabbi M. Isserles in *Shulchan Aruch, Orach Chayim*, 581, 4). The reason for this custom, according to

the *B'er Heiteiv* commentary, is that "the cemetery is a place of eternal rest for the deceased righteous, and therefore a pure and sacred place, [where] one's prayers are more readily acceptable on [at] the graves of the righteous . . . to seek [God's] compassion for the sake of the merit of the righteous ones resting there . . . giving charity (*tzedoko*) before reciting the *techinnos*. . . ."

3. *Cheeboot ha-kever:* literally, "beating in the grave." This is a belief in which the dead are punished for their sins in this life by "being struck with a fiery chain immediately after death by the Angel of Death. . . . Only those who die in *Eretz Yisrael* or, if outside, who are buried on Friday afternoon before sunset, are exempted from this punishment" (*EJ* 8:464).

## 69. A *TECHINNO* FOR THE ANGELIC ADVOCATE OF JUSTICE

1. From *Ahnaie Shas Techinno* (Vilna: Rochel-Esther Bas Avi-chayil of Jerusalem, 1930?), p. 210. JTSAL: BM 675 74 A3.

## 70. TO THE RIGHTEOUS DEAD

1. From *Ahnaie Shas Techinno* (Vilna: Rochel-Esther Bas Avi-chayil of Jerusalem, 1930?), pp. 210-211. JTSAL: BM 675 74 A3.

2. The custom of visiting the cemetery during the month of *Elul* before Rosh Ha-shanah was generally observed by families living within reasonable proximity to the cemetery. The graves visited were usually confined to those of close relatives.

This custom is recorded in the *Shulchan Aruch*. Rabbi M. Isserles writes: "It is the custom to visit the graves, recite many *techinnos* [sic] and give alms to the poor."

On the word *graves*, the *B'er Heiteiv* commentary states:

The cemetery is the resting place of the righteous (*tzaddikim*) and, because of that, is a holy and pure place. Prayer is therefore more readily acceptable (by God) there. One who prays at the graves of the righteous should not direct his prayers to them, but to the Name, may He be blessed, so that He will take pity on him because of the merit (*z'chus*) of the righteous ones who lie here. He should go around the graves and give alms before praying (before reading the *techinnos*).

An abbreviated English version is found in *Code of Jewish Law: Shulchan Aruch*, by Rabbi Solomon Ganzfried, trans. H. E. Goldin, vol. 3, p. 73, par. 13.

## 71. BEFORE, DURING, AND AFTER ROSH HA-SHONO

1. *Freger Techinno* (Lemberg, 1897).

2. "Visiting cemeteries on public fast days to offer prayers at the graves of the departed 'in order that they may intercede in behalf of the living' was a widespread custom throughout the ages, especially on the Ninth of Av and in the month of Elul. . . ." *EJ* 5:272.

## 72. *SELICHOS TECHINNOS* (VERSION 1)

1. From *Techinno Imray Shefer: Six New Techinnos*, by Rabbi Israel of Ivanice, Moravia (Lemberg, 1884). JNUL: S37 A 1375. This is a series of *techinnot*, some of which have been shortened to avoid the literary sin of repetition and its bedfellow, boredom.

2. One even slightly familiar with the *Siddur* will catch this echo of the *Adon olam* hymn found usually at the beginning of the Weekday Morning Service and often sung at the end of the Sabbath Morning Service as an alternate choice to the *Ayn kaylohaynu* hymn. It has been attributed to the eleventh-century Spanish Hebrew poet Solomon Ibn Gabirol, a rhymed English translation of which is found in Harlow, *Siddur Sim Shalom*, p. 7. It emphasizes God's timelessness, His unlimited dominion and goodness, His redemptive quality, and the placing in His hand (His care) the spirit with which man has been blessed. These ideas are also reflected in the opening section of this *techinnah*.

3. The actual translation makes no sense: "Also, the nighttime sacrifices atoned for transgressions committed during the day." As far as is known, sacrifices were offered only in the daytime. There seems to be a corrupted text at this point.

4. The reference is to the Mount Carmel incident, when Elijah mocked the false prophets of Baal: Cry aloud; for he is a god; either he is musing or he is gone aside, or he is on a journey, or peradventure he sleepeth and must be awaked—1 Kings 18:27 (OJPS).

5. The verse continues: . . . Your people Israel, a unique nation on earth, whom God went and redeemed as His people. . . . This is a fine example of the author's blending of a rich liturgical tradition with the petitioner's words. The passage from 2 Samuel was inserted by the framers of the *Siddur* into the Sabbath Afternoon Service (Scherman, *ArtScroll Siddur*, p. 517, footnote: "Israel is unique because it alone accepted the Torah and dedicated itself to God's service"). The appropriateness of the *techinnah* passage at this point is that, since Israel is God's selected and

beloved people, it stands to reason that He should continue His love for and beneficence to them in the coming year. This is a methodology of telescopy: ideas from various traditional source texts are brought to bear in the petitioner's prayers and condensed in these prayers, less as proof texts and more as condensations or concentrates that save space on the printed page and take advantage of the Jew's traditional knowledge for brevity's sake.

6. Since our author does not quote the Hebrew source as other authors sometimes do, but relies on paraphrases, I surmise that reference is to Isaiah 7:14—Therefore the Lord Himself shall give you a sign. . . . Whether it is "for good" in the Isaiah passage is difficult to say, given the biblical and political perplexities of the time. For our author here, there is no doubt that the hope is for a good sign for the coming year.

7. In the burnt offering the sacrificial animal was completely burned upon the altar, generally in the morning. The purpose of this ritual seems to have been to render homage to God, where "homage" is used in the medieval sense of an individual acknowledging himself in service to God.

8. To this verse, the Soncino edition, in a footnote on p. 164, adds the words "the sacrifices of God," which are acceptable to Him. On "a broken spirit" Soncino adds that the "Midrash . . . points out that a fractured limb disqualified an animal as a sacrifice, whereas a *broken spirit* in man was approved by God." While our author was of course unacquainted with the twentieth-century Soncino edition, he was obviously on intimate terms with the Midrash, the spirit of which he successfully transferred into his *techinnah*.

9. Rabbi Israel probably had Psalm 145:9 in mind, a part of the *Ashray* prayer frequently recited in the synagogue—The Lord is good to all and *His tender mercies are over all His works* (i.e., all His creations).

10. Based on the narrative in 1 Sam. 1:9-20.

11. Up to this point, the passage is based on Psalm 71:9—Do not cast me off in old age; when my strength fails, do not forsake me. At this point, the Soncino footnote on p. 224 explains that "with the advancing years his physical strength declines, making him more exposed to the attack of the wicked. . . ." (The editor-rabbis of the High Holy Days *Machzor* changed the verse from the singular to the plural when they inserted it in the *Shema kolenu* prayer, to have it express the wishes of *klal Yisroel*. See, for example, Birnbaum, *HHPB*, pp. 847-848.) The gist of this request is that the person seeks help to ward off evil at a time in his life when he is physically weak and may be overcome by satanic forces.

This, however, is not the thrust of Rabbi Israel's *techinnah*. His point is that the petitioner prays that when he or she is old and helpless, he or she will be able to rely entirely upon God's help and not upon the charitable feelings of humans, which may not always be forthcoming. It is a powerful *cri de coeur* no matter how softly spoken.

### 73. *SELICHOS*: A *TECHINNO* OF *TESHUVO, TEFILLO,* AND *TZEDOKO* (VERSION 2)

1. *Techinno Teshuvo, Tefillo u-tzedoko* (Vilna: Romm, 1862). JNUL: R0 85A 534.

2. The *Book of the Pious* was a "major work in the field of ethics, produced by the Jews of medieval Germany" (*EJ* 7:1388-1390). It apparently originated among the members of the Kalonymide family in the thirteenth century and provides "deep insight into the real life of a Jewish community in all its aspects" (G. Scholem, *Major Trends in Jewish Mysticism*, pp. 82-83).

3. The author of this prayer is unidentified. However, in a collection of the same title (no title page available), the author is identified as "Mistress *Mem'el* (?), daughter of the famous and faithful Rabbi Hirsch, wife of the illustrious Rabbi Isaac of blessed memory, head of the holy congregation of *Bl'ez* (Belz?)." The *techinnah* is similar to this one but not identical. An editor's or writer's hand has been at work on this expanded text.

My colleague Professor Eliezer Slomovic has made an interesting suggestion for the name *Mem'el*, based on information found in a little book entitled *Qav ve-nagi*, by David, son of Yehuda-Loeb Lo-wot (reprint, Brooklyn, 1951), p. 22b. The book contains lists of male and female names, together with their variations. These were apparently referred to in the course of preparation of *gittin*, bills of divorcement.

On the final page of the booklet we learn from a Russian declaration that this *Seder Techinnos* was passed by the Censor Kookolnik and permission was granted for printing the work on January 17, 1859. Place of publication: Vilna. The printers, once again, were the well-known Romm family. JNUL: S51 A 800. 296.319.1.

### 74. *SELICHOS* (VERSION 3)

1. T.C.: The word *selichot* (plural form) derives from the triliteral root s' l' ch'—forgive. *Selicha* in the singular means "forgiveness." The *selichot* are prayers cast in the form of *piyyutim*, religious poems, the purpose of

which is to enable the Jew to pray for forgiveness (*kaporo*) of sins. There is a vast literature of these penitential prayers or *selichot* for a variety of occasions such as special fast days (nonstatutory), on the Monday, Thursday and Monday following Passover and Sukkot, by members of the burial society (*chevrah kaddisha*) at their annual service.

This group of *techinnot*, however, was recited in the month of *Elul*, from the Sunday preceding Rosh Hashanah until Rosh Hashanah in conjunction with the *selichot*—those penitential prayers, or prayers for forgiveness, being recited usually at midnight in the synagogue. If Rosh Hashanah fell on Monday or Tuesday, the *selichot* were recited during the entire preceding week.

> The mystics found good reason of an esoteric nature in support of the predawn penitential services: God's attribute of mercy is preeminent during the still hours before sunrise. The pious would therefore rise before dawn and betake themselves to the synagogue for the *Selichot* service. Ordinary Jews, however, could not subject themselves to such a rigorous regimen. They were satisfied with one *Selichot* service, the one that usually takes place on the Saturday night preceding Rosh Hashannah. For the convenience of the multitude, this *Selichot* service is held at midnight instead of the pre-dawn hours. (Millgram, *Jewish Worship*, p. 288)

The threefold subheading (#72, #73, and #74) is actually the title in the original text. However, since the primary subject of this group of *techinnot* is *selichot*, the *teshuvo*, *tefillo*, and *tzedoko* were relegated to a subheading. The terms are nevertheless keys to understanding the nature of the penitential season: through them the Jew may achieve forgiveness, *kaporo*, for transgressions committed against God and/or man during the preceding year.

*Teshuvo* involves the idea of return for the Jew to the way of God as laid down in the Torah, the Book that teaches him how to live according to God's dictates via the fulfillment of the *mitzvos*—specific acts that have a variety of purposes, the main one being to bring him back to God's way on the road of life (*ohrach chayim*). *Tefillo* is prayer directed to God on a variety of occasions and times. *Tzedoko*, often misunderstood as "charity," involves acts of loving-kindness toward one's fellowman.

These three words constitute part of a classic liturgical passage found in the *U-nessaneh Tokef* prayer, said to have been composed by Kalonymos ben Meshullam of Mayence around 1100 C.E. The first, *teshuvo*, is often mistranslated as "repentance." More correctly, as Max Arzt has pointed out, it constitutes a "break with evil and a *return* to God." *Tefillo*, prayer,

rightly understood, means "reestablishment of our relationship with God."
*Tzedoko* involves "tangible acts of love and concern for our fellow men"
(Arzt, *Justice and Mercy*, pp. 166-167). These, says the author of the
*U-nessaneh Tokef*, are what can "annul the severity of the [divine] judgment." We find here the tone that has been set for the following selection
of *techinnot* recited in conjunction with the *selichot* before the High Holy
Days.
   2. Opening words of prayer found in the Memorial Service. See Birnbaum, *HHPB*, p. 731.
   3. Cf. Psalm 145:16. The rough restatement is nevertheless recognizable. Why verses from this psalm appear in the *techinnot* is understandable in light of the footnote in the Bokser *Machzor* (*HHPB*), p. 6: "This
psalm is especially appropriate for *Selichot*. It affirms God's concern for
all His creatures, and it declares that He hears all who call upon Him in
truth."
   4. Cf. the beginning of the prayer, "My God, guard my tongue from
evil and my lips from speaking falsehood . . . ," is generally found at the
end of the *Amidah*, the Eighteen Benedictions.
   5. This is a personalized version of "Do not cast us off in our old
age; when our strength fails, forsake us not." See Birnbaum, *HHPB*,
p. 546, and elsewhere.

## 75. *TECHINNO* FOR FORGIVENESS (VERSION 1)

   1. From *Techinno Kol B'chiyo* (Poland-Russia, c. 1840). JNUL: S63 A
3908.
   2. The point is that general welfare is proportionately diminished
by each individual's sins. There is collective responsibility and benefit,
as well as individual responsibility and benefit. Society and its members
exist in a constant, dynamic interrelatedness.
   3. The source for this practice is found in the *Shulchan Aruch, Orach
Chayim* 611:1. See abbreviated English version, *Code of Jewish Law*, vol. 3,
ch. 133, 8, p. 88. B. Z. Bokser explains as follows:

Rabbi Moses Isserles (1520-1573), the great medieval codifier of Jewish law,
explained the practice of not wearing leather shoes on Yom Kippur as an
expression of concern for animal welfare. On the holiest day of the year we
are to shed the symbol of our predatory nature, the shoes which were made
from the skin of a living creature. Wearing shoes is generally permitted, but
this permission is a tragic yielding to necessity, and on the holiest day of the
year, according to Isserles, we ought to reach out for a higher moral standard than is expected of us on other days. (Bokser, *Judaism*, p. 170)

4. This is odd: just as King Manasseh was forgiven? The story of Manasseh's reign is narrated in 2 Kings 21:1 ff. He committed many abominations of the nations—idol-worshiping, the offering of child sacrifices, shedding of innocent blood, and so on. A similar biography of him is found in 2 Chronicles 33:1 ff. with a slight variance: he is brought to Babylon in chains and tortured. Ultimately, he prays to God and is delivered, eventually returned to his throne in Jerusalem. This is hardly the portrait of a saint.

The rabbis must have found it difficult to swallow the fact that this man's prayer was heard by God. Echoes of their theological concern are found in the two Talmuds. An eloquent rendition of this incident and resolution of the rabbis' dilemma concerning the wicked king is found in the English translation of the *Pesikta de-Rab Kahana* by W. G. Braude and I. J. Kapstein (Piska 24, pp. 375-376) where we learn that God accepts any and all repentance, even Manasseh's.

While being tortured, Manasseh applied to all the idols of the world— but to no avail. Suddenly, he remembered his father teaching him a particular passage in Deuteronomy 4:30-31—. . . when you are in distress because all these things have befallen you and, in the end, return to the Lord your God and obey Him. . . . For the Lord your God is a compassionate God: He will not fail you nor will He let you perish . . . [NJPS]. Manasseh calls upon God for deliverance. The angels, in reaction, begin shutting the windows of heaven so that the wretch's prayer will be unable to get through to God. The angels ask God how such a man, who once set up an idol in the Temple, can be accepted in repentance.

> The Holy One replied: If I do not receive him in his repentance, I shall be barring the door to all who would repent. What did the Holy One proceed to do for Manasseh? He contrived an opening for his sake under His very own throne of glory [where the angels could not interfere with] His having Manasseh's supplication.

Similar versions are found in the Soncino translation of *Midrash Rabbah: Deuteronomy*, 2:20, pp. 48-49 and Soncino, *Midrash Rabbah: Ruth*, 5:6, pp. 63-64.

5. Found in the Grace after Meals. See Bokser, *PB*, p. 360.

## 76. *TECHINNO* FOR FORGIVENESS (VERSION 2)

1. From *Techinno Kol B'chiyo* (Poland-Russia, c. 1840). JNUL: S63 A 3908.

2. On this verse, A. Cohen, in *The Soncino Chumash*, quotes Abraham Ibn Ezra in a footnote on p. 339: "God gave them this title because their ancestors were the first to acknowledge Him." See also Rashi ad loc: The term expresses the idea of dignity. Moses is reputed as meaning that, if God thinks so much of Israel, He should forgive them their all-too-human failings and frailties.

3. The author combined Moses' prayer and God's reply from two separate sources to make the point that God will forgive His petitioners on Yom Kippur. One never ceases to be amazed at this at-homeness in the *Tanach* and the ability to create new meanings.

4. The origin of the term *bochayn levohvos*, "probes hearts," is probably Psalm 7:10. However, while the word there is *leebos* and not *levohvos*, the meaning is unchanged. In the *hakafot* (Circuits) for Simchat Torah, we find the term used as it was familiar to most pre-twentieth-century observant Jews (*levohvos*) who sang it annually. See, however, Scherman, *ArtScroll Siddur*, pp. 780-781, where it is translated as "Tester of Hearts." (A verb may also be used as a noun in Hebrew.)

5. One is tempted to translate "may You in Your mercy *straighten me out*," but this would be taking a bit too much liberty with the text. The source of the phrase is probably Isa. 40:4, the chapter beginning with the words "Comfort ye, comfort ye My people." Israel, having suffered double for all her sins, is going to be delivered. This prophetic portion is chanted in the synagogue annually on the Sabbath after the ninth of *Av*, which commemorates the destruction of both Temples in Jerusalem. This *Shabbat*, called *Shabbat Nachamu* (the Sabbath of Consolation), was calculated to serve as a consolation to the people and a reminder of God's deliverance.

*V'hoyo hehokove l'meeshor* in verse 4 translates as "and the rugged shall be [made] level." That is, the people returning to Zion from exile will find their return easy going. There will be no obstacles in their way of return. The author, dredging up the phrase from a collective literary heritage dormant in the people's subconscious, has legitimately given the phrase new meaning and relevance for his time and place. This is true literary forging in the smithy of the Jewish national soul.

6. Reference is to Isaiah 65:24, but it is not all that simple. Two things should be noted. First, the author does not cite the original Hebrew passage in parentheses. This was a common enough practice among other authors. Second, the Yiddish is not a translation; it is, rather, an adaptation of the original source to the need of the petitioner's current situation.

Thus, where Isaiah speaks to God's loyal servants in God's Name (so that it is, as it were, God speaking) and says: "I shall answer them even before they call on Me; while they are still speaking to Me, I shall hear (and respond)," our author has placed the words in the petitioner's mouth: "I have so much faith in You, God, that I know You will. . . ." In the original passage, God speaks; here, it is the petitioner quoting an adapted version of what God said. An interesting turn, to say the least.

## 77. A *TECHINNO* FOR THE TEN DAYS OF REPENTANCE

1. T. C.: The term "Ten Days of Repentance" refers to the period between Rosh Ha-shanah and Yom Kippur, a time when acts of penitence are performed. These days are regarded as an integral part of the High Holy Days season. In addition to sounding the *shofar* after morning services in the synagogue (to remind the Jew of the need to repent of his misdeeds), there were a number of changes in the regular service. During this period, Jews were encouraged to read this *techinno* each day.

2. The author had Genesis 3:19 in mind: "By the sweat of your brow will you eat bread until you return to the ground. . . ." The Hebrew does not seem to be a direct quote.

3. This idea has its origin in a discussion between the schools of Shammai and Hillel, Beth Shammai "asserting that it were better for man not to have been created, and the latter maintaining that it is better to have been created than not to have been created. They finally took a vote and decided that it were far better not to have been created, but now that he has been created, let him investigate his past deeds or, as others say, let him examine his future actions" (*Erubin* 13b, Soncino trans., pp. 86-87).

4. The "day of sorrow and wrath" echoes Zephaniah 1:15. The seventh-century B.C.E. prophet was speaking of a day when God's anger manifested itself.

5. This idea is found in the *Yizkor* (Memorial) Service.

6. All these words signal the source that the author expropriated as a basis for his idea: *Ethics of the Fathers* (*Pirkay Ovos*) 3:1. Slightly different translations of the *Ethics* are found in the Hertz, Bokser, and Birnbaum prayer books. The following is Bokser's: "*Whence you came*—from a putrid drop; *whither you are going*—to a place of dust, worms, and maggots; and *before whom you are destined to give an accounting*—before the King of kings. . . ."

7. Originating in *Yoma* 87b, these rhetorical questions were inserted

into the *Neilah* (Closing or Concluding) Service for Yom Kippur (Birnbaum, *Machzor*, p. 971) and into the weekday Morning Service (Birnbaum, *DPB*, p. 23).

8. This idea, frequently expressed in the *techinnot*, was well known to the observant Jew(ess) who recited his/her Grace after Meals [*Birkat ha-mozon*]. In the prayer *Rachaym*, we find: "Our God, our Father, tend us, nourish us, sustain us, support us, and relieve us. . . ." "The *Etz Yosef* explains each of the apparently redundant phrases. *Tend us* means provide us with the absolute necessities of life, i.e., bread and water; *nourish us* is a request for additional food such as fruits and vegetables—foods that are important but not indispensable; *sustain us* with clothing and shelter, *support us* by providing our needs steadily and securely rather than sporadically . . . *relieve us* of the need to scrimp and budget by providing our needs generously and abundantly" (Scherman, *ArtScroll Siddur*, p. 188).

## 78. PRAYER BY THE WRITER NOAM ELIMELECH

1. From *Shas Techinnos: Techinnos for the Entire Year* (Lemberg: D. Balaban, 1904/1905). YIVO: 6/4658.

T.C.: The "Writer Noam Elimelech" in the title of this *techinnah* is misleading. If, in the Yiddish on the title page, there had been inserted the preposition *of* between the first and second words, a clearer meaning would have emerged. There is no author by the name of Noam Elimelech. Noam Elimelech is the name of a book. The emended title should read thus: ". . . by the Writer [ie., Author] of [a work entitled] *Noam Elimelech*." The author of this work was the third-generation *tzaddik* Elimelech of Lyzhansk (1717-1787), one of the founders of Galician hasidism (*EJ* 6:661-663). Failure to have recognized the book is perhaps excusable since we are so far removed not only in time and place but also from the spiritual world of eighteenth-century hasidism. The reader interested in a taste of *Noam Elimelech* in English will find a selection in the anthology *Hasidic Thought*, ed. and trans. Louis Jacobs (New York: Behrman House, 1976), pp. 100-107. The first edition of *Noam Elimelech* appeared in Lemberg in 1788.

Life in the eighteenth and nineteenth centuries for Jews in eastern Europe could never be construed as easy. Too many things were wrong with this temporary "vale of tears" in which Jews found themselves before it came time to enter the world-to-come. Recognition of the presence of evil was not enough. As flesh-and-blood human beings subject to the temptations of the flesh and material things of this world, which could reduce one to abandoning such primary values as the study of Torah (a necessary instrument wherewith to gain entrance into life eternal), the Jews realized the omnipresent power of the *yetzer ho-ro*, the Evil Inclination, and its ability to deflect them from the true course in life. The *yetzer ho-ro* had to be fought constantly, night and day, by means of Torah study (*talmud Torah*) and right action (*mitzvos*), by recognizing and acknowledging one's errant behavior and returning (*teshuvo*) to the one right way, God's way (*derech ha-Shem*).

In addition to developing the themes of *teshuvo* and *tefillo* as a means for being united with God in truth and love, Rabbi Elimelech places his final emphasis on love of one's fellow man as the way to give God pleasure. This is basic to the idea of *tikkun olom*, the restoration of the world order, its perfection. (Chaos is evil's realm.)

One of the central beliefs of hasidism is not stressed, namely, the importance of the *tzaddik* (later known as the *rebbe*) and his obligation to uplift his religious community to higher spiritual planes. Given that neither a first edition of this *techinnah* nor its manuscript is available, one is tempted to speculate on whether the original text was tampered with in order to make it more acceptable to a nonhasidic Jewish world. We shall probably never know.

2. In translating this section, I am reminded of a passage in "Of Bygone Days," a nostalgic piece of autobiographical fiction by Mendele Mocher Seforim (Sh. Y. Abramovitch) in which eleven-year-old Shloymele is seduced by his Evil Impulse (Inclination) to discover the beauties of nature and thereby become alienated, as it were, from the Jewish world of learning in the mid-nineteenth century Pale of Settlement in eastern Europe. "Of Bygone Days" was originally composed by Mendele in Yiddish and later translated into Hebrew. Shloymele is approached by the Evil Impulse "deviously." He is encouraged to lift up his eyes "and admire the miracle of God's creation—the starry sky, the rainbow, drops of dew sparkling on the grass in the garden. . . . And Shloymele gave in, interrupted his study to look at everything, exclaiming, 'How lovely the world is!'" (Mendele Mocher Seforim, "Of Bygone Days," in *A Shtetl and other Yiddish Novellas*, ed. Ruth R. Wisse, trans. David G. Roskies, p. 231).

This attitude of the Jewish folk-mind toward nature was grounded in the *Sayings of the Fathers*, in which Rabbi Jacob said: "He who is walking by the way and rehearses what he has learnt, and breaks off from his rehearsing and says, How fine is that tree, how fine is that field, him the Scripture regards as if he were guilty against himself" (Hertz, *ADPB*,

p. 653). In his footnote to Rabbi Jacob, Rabbi Hertz writes: "The Rabbis were . . . not indifferent to the beauty of Nature, as they prescribed various Benedictions on beholding beautiful persons and things." On the phrase "breaks off," Hertz writes: "What is deprecated here is a wilful distraction of the mind from Torah-meditation by the surrounding scenery." Finally, on "Scripture regards," Hertz remarks pointedly: "No text is, or could well be, quoted in support of the statement." The rabbinic world in the talmudic period, which could regard nature favorably, was separated by more than just centuries from the mid-nineteenth-century eastern European diasporic mind-set.

3. Ezekiel 36:25—I will sprinkle clean water upon you, and you shall be clean (NJPS). The Hebrew text uses the term *mahyim t'horim*, literally, pure water (as distinguished from that which is ritually unclean).

4. Psalm 111:10—"The beginning of wisdom is the fear of the Lord; all who practice it gain sound understanding" (NJPS). "By *fear* is to be understood the feeling of *awe*. . . . That feeling must be the starting point of a life which is to be lived on a higher plane than animal existence" (*Psalms*, Soncino trans., p. 375, footnote).

5. Deuteronomy 6:7—And thou shalt teach them diligently unto thy children, and shalt talk of them when thou sittest in thy house, and when thou walkest by the way, and when thou liest down, and when thou risest up (OJPS) (*Chumash*, Soncino trans., p. 1022).

6. Sins of my youth—"Inadvertent errors . . . due to youthful indiscretion" (*Psalms*, Soncino trans., 25:7, p. 72, footnote).

7. Transgressions—"Acts of rebellion against God's will in mature age" (*Psalms*, Soncino trans., 25:7, p. 72, footnote).

## 79. A BLESSING FOR CHILDREN BEFORE YOM KIPPUR

1. This is the reverse of the custom practiced before Sabbaths and festivals when parents blessed children either at the conclusion of the synagogue service or at home. See notes in Hertz, *ADPB*, pp. 402-403; Scherman, *ArtScroll Siddur*, p. 354. The blessing is based on Jacob's blessing of Joseph's two sons in Gen 48:20.

## 80. *TECHINNO* FOR THE *OLAYNU* PRAYER

1. T.C.: An anonymous editor has written: "This *techinno* originates in Frankfurt-am-Main. It was composed by a great *gaon* (literally, genius or excellence; an honorary title for one very learned). Women should

say it on Rosh Hashono and Yom Kippur when the cantor begins to say in the *Olaynu* ['. . . bend the knee and bow . . .'], to prostrate himself; at that time, say the following."

In the *techinno* collection of Sarah *bas Tovim* (daughter of Rabbi Mordecai), the preface merely states: "On Rosh Hashono and Yom Kippur, when we prostrate ourselves, we say this." The collection entitled *Techinno Shlosho Sheorim* by Sarah *bas Tovim* was published in Vilna in 1859. The two versions differ slightly in language. This translation is based on the *Siddur Bays Yisroel* text. (Estimated publication date is 1939 or prior to that year, based on calendars appearing in the book on pp. 242–243.) Typeface and language are of a more recent vintage and simplified the translator's task. While the bracketed English represents the Hebrew quotation from the original Hebrew, it is interesting to note that some of the Hebrew is not found in the original *Olaynu* prayer.

2.  Found in the Evening Service, Birnbaum *DPB*, p. 529, and the *Neilo* Service for Yom Kippur, Birnbaum, *HHPB*, p. 989.

3.  The idea of the prosecutor and defense attorney, accuser, and pleader arguing the Jew's guilt or innocence is found in the *Omnom kayn piyyut*, composed by Rabbi Yom Tov of York. See Birnbaum *HHPB*, p. 533, footnote, for historical background. The accuser–pleader motif is found in T.B., *Rosh Hashanah* 27a.

4.  The *Avodah* was the service of the High Priest in the Temple on the Day of Atonement. The *Mishnah*, Tractate *Yoma*, has preserved a detailed description of the priest's activities. (See Danby trans. of the *Mishnah*, pp. 162–172.) A good description in twentieth-century English of the *Avodah* is found in L. Barish, *High Holiday Liturgy*, pp. 144–151. Standard American *machzorim*, such as Birnbaum (p. 811 ff.), Bokser (p. 417 ff.), and Silverman (p. 368 ff.), have brief introductions and paraphrase the *Amitz koach piyyut* by Rabbi Meshullam ben Kalonymus (eleventh century), a brief description of the *Avodo* in verse. The *Olaynu* is not in the *Avodah* Service, but precedes it.

5.  The connection between this and Isa. 1:18 (Be your sins like crimson,/ They can turn snow-white . . .") was not lost on the Yiddish readers and their listeners. In *Yoma* (Danby trans., p. 172), Rabbi Ishmael relates that "a thread of crimson wool was tied to the door of the Sanctuary and when the he-goat reached the wilderness the thread turned white; for it is written, *Though your sins be as scarlet they shall be as white as snow.*"

6.  Familiar to traditional Jews from two sources: (1) as part of the *Ashray*, recited mornings and afternoons; (2) in the Grace after Meals, last section.

7. Found in the Sabbath Morning Service; Birnbaum, *DPB*, p. 305.
8. While not a direct quote, it seems to echo the fourth benediction in the *Amidah*.
9. "You keep mercy unto the thousandth generation . . ."–Exodus 34:6. The author has changed *notzer* (keep, guard, preserve) to *oseh* (do). *Lo'alofim* remains the same, but a subtle change in meaning has taken place, from "the thousandth generation" to "thousands" that is, countless people.

## 81. A *TECHINNO* BEFORE *NEILO*

1. From *Ahnaie Shas Techinno* (Vilna: Rochel-Esther Bas Avi-chayil of Jerusalem, 1939?), p. 184. (JTSAL: BM 675 74 A3.) The *Neilah* (Closing Service) has its origins in the ritual of the Second Temple.

The full name of the service is *Ne'ilat She'arim* ("Closing of the Gates"), referring to the daily closing of the Temple gates. On the Day of Atonement this literal closing (*ne'ilat sha'arei heikhal*) was associated with the symbolic closing of the heavenly gates, which remained open to prayer until sunset (*ne'ilat sha'arei shamayim*). (*EJ* 12:943-944)

A more poetic and dramatic explanation is rendered by Millgram:

The liturgy of the Neilah service is quite exceptional. The uniqueness derives from the concept that the gates of prayer close at the end of the Day of Atonement. . . . The congregation feels that now is the last chance to pour out one's heart before the divine throne of mercy. . . . the Yom Kippur service reaches a tense climax during the closing service. Even those who have retired from the synagogue because of weakness induced by the fast usually return to participate in the Neilah service. A tangible feeling of mysticism and holiness envelops the congregation. The sun is setting, the shadows are lengthening, and the worshipers make their supreme effort to reach the divine throne and to move the merciful One to grant atonement to His penitent children. (*Jewish Worship*, pp. 259-260)

## 82. AFTER CANDLELIGHTING–SUCCOS

1. *Ma'aseh Alfes* commentary: Candlelighting should be in the *succo* only when the family will eat in the *succo*. When it is too cold to do so or there are other extenuating circumstances and the family must eat in the house, the woman should light the candles in the house. The pur-

pose of candlelighting is to illuminate the place where one eats. Besides, a woman should not leave the candle holders in the *succo* because there is an ever-present danger of theft. Thieves are always lurking in the shadows beyond the *succo* and, heaven forbid, it would be a shame to darken the *yom tov*.

2. In that day will I *raise up David's fallen Succo*—Amos 9:11. The emphasized section was incorporated into the Grace after Meals (*Birkas Hamozon*) as a special additional prayer to be recited on Succos. A Soncino footnote is of particular interest here because it relates to the religious-national aspiration of the Jew: "There will be a return to national splendour under the re-established dynasty of David" (p. 112). More specifically, in the *techinnah*, it is the hope for the restoration of the Holy Temple.

## 83. THE FOUR SPECIES

1. T. C.: This is not, strictly speaking, a *techinnah* and, as its contents will show, is not directed solely at the Jewish woman. On the other hand, it behooved every Jewish woman to be aware of the need to encourage her husband. The daily struggle for survival, food, and raiment in a harsh exilic environment could easily have enabled a Jew to overlook the *mitzvo* of study and the *mitzvo* of religious practice. Reinforcement by a willing and understanding wife was of utmost importance. By virtue of her husband's positive actions, she shared in the spiritual reward and the blessing of a good life not only for herself but also for her children.

Our author realized the value of heightened awareness in the Jewish woman in this respect and attempted to convey it here. Jewish males who were not learned also read *techinnah* collections for educational and inspirational purposes. The nature of Jewish education (*lernen*) was by extension ideally universal. These qualities and mental sets, which we shall discover while reading the text, were embedded in a hortatory approach. In some respects, this approach is also an exemplary one in the general history of education.

2. Found in the Sabbath Morning Service prayer *Nishmat*. See Birnbaum, *DPB*, pp. 333-334.

3. Found in the Sabbath Afternoon Service. See Birnbaum, *DPB*, p. 469.

4. The term is found in both *Tanach* and Talmud. It seems to be used loosely to cover a spectrum of mental conditions: depression, gloom, despondency, and so on.

5. In translating Rashi ad loc., Soncino *Chumash* explains in a foot-note: "The singular form of the verb [*va-yechan*] (whereas the other verbs are in the plural) teaches that unlike their other encampments, this was marked by the complete unanimity of the whole people."

6. The passage makes sense only if *vault* (Hebrew: *agudo*) is changed to *group*. The *darshan* in our author has made a legitimate transition from text to application: A scholar doing God's work will bind his students together for the study of Torah into a bundle (*agudo*), a cohesive group.

## 84. *TECHINNO* FOR *HOSHANO RABBO* BEFORE *HALLEL*

1. T.C.: The seventh and last day of the Sukkot festival is called *Hoshano Rabbo*, the great *hoshano*. The day's origins date back at least to Temple times when seven circuits or processions were made around the altar. The name of the day derives from the many *hoshanos* (*hosannas* in English), special prayers for help and salvation, that are recited. There is a curious custom of beating willows on the ground or on the synagogue benches on this day, which dates back at least to the Mishnaic period.

While this custom was familiar to me from my boyhood synagogue attendance, I must have wondered about the reason for the practice, since it was never explained. We did it because that's the way it was. As I grew older, I became aware that it was not a generally observed festival by the Jews of my New England boyhood. Was this due to the esoteric nature of a rite that did not attract the mundane Jewry of the period?

Later, with the accumulation of some Jewish knowledge, came the beginning of understanding:

> In Temple times, the people formed a procession around the altar on each of the first six days of *Sukkoth* while chanting: "We implore thee, O Lord, save us" (Psalm 118:25). On the seventh day of *Sukkoth* they formed seven such processions, following which they would beat willow-sprigs against the ground, symbolically casting off sins as the leaves were beaten off. (Birnbaum, *Encyclopedia of Jewish Concepts*, p. 159)

In the course of time,

> Sukkot came to be regarded as the extension of the period of repentance. The period of judgment which began with Rosh Ha-Shanah was extended to include Sukkot. . . . The talmudic sages expressed the belief that the world is judged at four different periods of the year: "On Passover, for grain;

on Shavuot for the fruit of the trees; on the New Year all the inhabitants of the world pass before Him, like flocks of sheep. . . . and on the Festival [Sukkot] they are judged for water."

As the judgment period for water, Sukkot became the most appropriate time to concentrate on prayers for water. . . . the period of rain in Israel begins at just about the time of Sukkot and there was widespread concern for an adequate rainfall. (Donin, *Sukkot*, p. 20)

Although the traditional view was that "on Rosh Hashanah it (God's judgment) is written and on Yom Kippur it is sealed, *Hoshana Rabba* came to be viewed as the day when the decrees that were sealed on Yom Kippur were confirmed." Thus, with prayer on *Hoshana Rabba*, it was still possible to avert an evil decree and the day was gradually transformed into a "day of judgment, first for water, then also of men . . ." (Donin, *Sukkot*, p. 21). Hence, the serious petitionary nature of this *techinnah* for *Hoshana Rabba*.

An interesting feature about this *techinnah* is the section in which each passage begins with *Ribono shel olom* (Lord of the universe). It immediately stirs echoes of the *Ohveenu Malkaynu* prayer (Our Father, our King), recited a number of times during the High Holy Days. The *Ohveenu Malkaynu* is as somber as it is petitionary in tone, and, with the passage of centuries, there have been added to it elements reflecting the Jews' accumulation of disasters and persecutions. These *Ribono shel olom* petitions are of a doleful nature, hardly in keeping with the happy, celebratory nature surrounding the festival of Sukkot as generally observed today, for example, in Israel. Life in the State of Israel since its establishment has not been a totally happy experience, but, if this is so with regard to Jews living in their homeland, how much more so must it have been for Jews living in the hostile Diasporas of the past.

There are many parallels to be found in the *Ribono shel olom* prayers and those in the *Ohveenu Malkaynu* group, but those chosen for translation here are not found in the latter. There are some surprising innovations introduced by the anonymous author, not for the sake of innovation, but to reflect the harsh exilic environment in which Jews found themselves, particularly from the seventeenth century on, the period during which the production of *techinnot* flourished. Regrettably, the original date of composition is unknown. This is *Techinno* #4 in *Techinno Shesho Sedorim* (Russia-Poland, c. 1840). JNUL: R 70 A 4382.

2. Cf. Ps. 30:10–"What is to be gained from my death,/from my descent into the Pit?/Can dust praise You?/Can it declare Your faithful-

ness?" (NJPS). The entire psalm is traditionally recited during Weekday and Sabbath Morning Services.

## 85. *TECHINNO* FOR *SIMCHAS TORAH* (VERSION 1)

1. T.C.: Simhat Torah, rejoicing with the Torah, falls on the ninth day of the festival Sukkot, the festival of the Booths. It is an autumnal celebration of the completion of the annual cycle of weekly Torah readings in the synagogue on Sabbaths.

It is a happy time of prayers, of dancing with the Torah, around the Torah, in circles, and so on. In my boyhood, youngsters crawled under benches and tied the prayer shawl fringes of the men together. The men took it good-naturedly, with feigned anger and with what sounded like scoldings in Yiddish, while everyone laughed or smiled. We enjoyed sweet raisin wine and mounds of sponge cake after the service while the elders toasted one another and the Torah with a *schnaapsel.*

Many years later, reading Samuel Pepys' diary (seventeenth century), I came across his entry regarding a visit to a London "Jewish church" wherein he described a scene that, to him, seemed like bedlam, a total absence of decorum.

By contrast, we find in these *techinnot* (the first one read during the Simchat Torah synagogue service and the second one read when the woman is about to leave the synagogue and return home) that the mood is serious. Both *techinnot* reveal the woman's sobriety as she first addresses the personalized Torah and then the Creator Himself.

More interesting material about Sukkot is found in Millgram, *Jewish Worship,* pp. 222-224, and *EJ,* 14:1571-1574.

This selection is from *Ahnaie Shas Techinno* (Vilna: Rochel-Esther Bas Avi-chayil of Jerusalem, 1930?), p. 201. JTSAL: BM 675 74 A3.

## 86. *TECHINNO* FOR SIMCHAS TORAH (VERSION 2)

1. From *Ahnaie Shas Techinno* (Vilna: Rochel-Esther Bas Avi-chayil of Jerusalem, 1930?), p. 201. JTSAL: BM 675 74 A3.

## 87. *TECHINNO* FOR SIMCHAS TORAH (VERSION 3)

1. From *Techinno Shesho Sedorim* (Russia-Poland, c. 1840). JNUL: R 70 A 4382.

2. Traditionally, Song of Songs is read after the Passover *Seder,* with

scriptural substantiation for this practice based on 2:9–I have compared you, my love, to a steed in Pharaoh's chariotry. Soncino footnote points out that "the beauty of the Egyptian horse suggested a comparison which is strange to the western mind but frequent in Arabic poetry" (p. 3). Likewise, the Middle Eastern mind would doubtless be puzzled by Robert Burns's love that "is like a red, red rose."

The custom of reading Song of Songs Friday evenings was based on the metaphoric love by Israel of the Sabbath Queen. Every new bride has traditionally been likened to a queen. Now, if the Sabbath is like a queen and the relationship between Israel and its Sabbath is a love affair, there is no more appropriate act for Israel to perform than to read the Song of Songs at that time to strengthen and enhance this special love relationship between the Sabbath Queen (*Shabbat ha-malkah*) and its lover, Israel.

In this *techinnah*, the instruction to recite Song of Songs 1:2 seems out of place unless we bear in mind this love relationship between Israel and the Torah. Viewed in this light, reciting the verse not once but three times, according to the author's instructions, will have even more of an emotional impact.

## 88. FLEE, MY BELOVED

1. From *Ahnaie Shas Techinno* (Vilna: Rochel-Esther Bas Avi-chayil of Jerusalem, 1930?), p. 211. JTSAL: BM 675 74 A3.

Flee, my beloved–Songs of Songs 8:14 (NJPS): Hurry, my beloved. . . . Thus begins the final verse of Song of Songs. The lovers will reunite upon mountains of spices. Soncino quotes Midrash as reading a prayer into this verse: "Mayest Thou hasten the advent of the redemption and cause Thy *Schechinah* to dwell on the mountain of spices (i.e., Moriah, as though derived from *mor*, 'myrrh') and rebuild the Temple speedily in our days" (Soncino trans., *The Five Megilloth*, p. 32).

Since the *techinnah* deals with the prayer and hope that Jews who have suffered persecutions, pogroms, and so on, in the lands of their dispersion will ultimately be redeemed, the title "Flee, My Beloved" (and not "*Hurry*, My Beloved") is appropriate to the theme. The number 70,000 is apparently an estimate.

2. Moroccan Jews suffered during periods of internal and external strife throughout the nineteenth century. In the Spanish-Moroccan War of 1860 many fled to Gibraltar for refuge, and in Tetuan they were pogrom victims, to cite but two examples. During the second half of the nineteenth century, thousands of impoverished Jews were also driven

off the land and subsequently swelled large urban populations, adding to the general misery, with little aid from abroad (*EJ* 12:339-340).

Romania was known for its violent anti-Semitism, especially during the nineteenth-century rise of nationalistic elements on both the left and right. Despite visits by Cremieux and Montefiore, little could be done to stop the persecutions (*EJ* 14:388 ff.).

## 89. RACHEL WEEPING FOR HER CHILDREN

1. T.C.: This title reverberates with the despair of Mother Rachel bemoaning her children's exile. Based on verse 14 of chapter 31 in Jeremiah, it is but a short interlude (not in human time!) to a glorious hope for the future a mere two verses later, in verse 16, with the eventual return of the children to their homeland as they collectively leave behind them the long night of exile. On this optimistic hope the *techinnah*, indeed this entire booklet of *techinnot*, comes to an end.

From *Ahnaie Shas Techinno* (Vilna: Rochel-Esther Bas Avi-chayil of Jerusalem, 1930?), p. 224. JTSAL: BM 675 74 A3.

A cry is heard in Ramah—wailing, bitter weeping—Rachel weeping for her children, who are gone—Jeremiah 31:14 (NJPS).

2. The subject of angelology in Judaism is vast and complex, from Ezekiel's vision in his first chapter to the modern period. We recommend the excellent article in *EJ* 2:956-977. The phraseology encountered here, *serofim, ofanim,* and so on, was familiar to Jews from the last line of the Sabbath hymn (*piyyut*) *El adon* (God, Lord of all . . .), still sung on Sabbath mornings in synagogues.

3. The appropriateness of this text is better understood in the wider context of the next section of the verse: "Your people shall all of them be righteous, they shall inhabit the land forever. . . ." It is found in a chapter that speaks of a brighter future. The use of the feminine in the word *ahmaych* (your people) is even more appropriate: whereas Isaiah's message is directed at Jerusalem (cities are feminine in Hebrew), God's speech in the *techinnah* is directed at Mother Rachel.

4. A more dramatic case could have been made by the author if he had also quoted the first half of the verse: "There is hope for your future." To this, the Soncino edition has added a trenchant footnote encapsulating the eternal dream: "That has been the sustaining thought in the long night of Jewish dispersion: hope, amounting to conviction, of a restoration to Zion."

## 90. EMBARKING ON AN OCEAN VOYAGE

1. T.C.: With the great westward migrations of Jews to the New World at the end of the nineteenth and beginning of the twentieth century, it seems appropriate to end this book with a *techinnah* reflecting those momentous times.

2. Included in the Friday Evening *Kabbalat Shabbat* Service and the *Shabbat* Morning Service during the return of the Torah scrolls to the Holy Ark.

3. Another example of quoting from memory: the author changed *for* to *and*.

# SELECT GLOSSARY

This list is short because most Jewish terms (Hebrew and Yiddish) in this book were used in such a way as to be understood contextually, were briefly explained or translated in brackets immediately after their appearance in the text. This tactic was chosen so that the English reader would not be slowed down in his reading. The reader seeking extended explanation should turn to that remarkable work mentioned in the Bibliography, the *Encyclopaedia Judaica*. A less daunting reference work, however, would be the one-volume *Encyclopedia of Jewish Concepts* by Philip Birnbaum (New York: Hebrew Publishing-Sanhedrin Press, 1979). Although arranged according to the Hebrew alphabet with English translations or transliterations of terms, there is an extensive English alphabetized index at the end of the book.

**Aggadah**          Nonlegal aspects of talmudic literature: legends, proverbs, ethics, morals, and so on.

| | |
|---|---|
| **Amora, amoraim** | Sages who explained or interpreted the *Mishnah* after its redaction by Rabbi Judah the Prince (c. 210 C.E.) to the end of the sixth century C.E. |
| **Chumash** | Pentateuch. |
| **Gaon, geonim** | Originally referred to spiritual heads of two major Babylonian academies in Sura and Pumbeditha; term later used to refer to any outstanding Talmud scholar, such as the *Vilner Gaon* (Rabbi Elijah Gaon of Vilna). |
| **Gemoro, gemara** | That portion of the Talmud, generally in Aramaic, that discusses and seeks to explain material found in the *Mishnah*. |
| **Halachah** | Talmudic law, as opposed to the *aggadah*. |
| **Midrash, midrashim** | A literary genre that interpreted biblical text, often homiletic in nature and containing aggadic material. |
| **Mishnah** | Text containing Jewish law compiled and edited by Rabbi Judah the Prince in a classic Hebrew style. |
| **Talmud** | An inclusive term referring to both the *Mishnah* and *Gemara*. |
| **Tanach** | Acronym for Torah, *Nevi'im* and *Ketubim*, the three major collections of the Hebrew Bible: Pentateuch, Prophets, Writings. |
| **Tanna, tannaim** | Sages active during the Mishnaic period. |

# BIBLIOGRAPHY

Abohav, Y. *Menoras Ha-Maor* (The Light of Contentment). Trans. Y. Y. Reinman. New Jersey: Chinuch, 1982.

*Ahnaie Shas Techinno*. Vilna: Rochel-Esther Bas Avi-chayil of Jerusalem, 1930?. JTSAL: BM 675 74 A3.

*A New Tehinno: Memorial Service for the Dead, Three Tehinnos*. Lemberg: Hirsch Schlag Publisher and Bookseller from Lvov, V. Kubler Press, Hotel Europa, 1897. JNUL: S61 A 2999: 296.319.1.

Arzt, M. *Justice and Mercy: Commentary on the Liturgy of the New Year and the Day of Atonement*. New York: Holt, Rinehart and Winston, 1963.

Ben Yehudah, E. *A Complete Dictionary of Ancient and Modern Hebrew*, 8 vols. New York: Thomas Yoseloff, 1960.

Biguenet, J., and Schulte, R., eds. *The Craft of Translation*. Chicago: University of Chicago Press, 1989.

Birnbaum, P. *Daily Prayer Book*. New York: Hebrew Publishing, 1949.

———. *Encyclopedia of Jewish Concepts*. New York: Sanhedrin Press, 1979.

———. *High Holyday Prayer Book*. New York: Hebrew Publishing, 1951.

Bokser, B. Z. *Judaism: Profile of a Faith*. New York: Knopf, 1963.

———, trans. *The Prayer Book: Weekday, Sabbath and Festival*. Reprint, New York: Hebrew Publishing, 1961.

*Chumash.* Trans. A. Cohen. London: Soncino Press, 1956.

*Code of Jewish Law: Shulchan Oruch, Orach Chayim.* Ed. S. Ganzfried. Trans. H. Goldin. New York: Hebrew Publishing, 1927.

Cohen, A., ed. *The Five Megilloth.* London: Soncino Press, 1952.

Donin, H. H. *To Pray as a Jew.* New York: Basic Books, 1980.

———, ed. *Sukkot,* Jerusalem: Keter, 1974.

*Encyclopaedia Judaica,* 16 vols. Jerusalem: Keter, 1973.

Even-Shoshan, A. *Ha-millan he-chadash.* Jerusalem: Kiryat Sepher, 1972.

*The Fathers According to Rabbi Nathan.* Trans. J. Goldin. New Haven: Yale University Press, 1955.

Finkelstein, L. *Akiba: Scholar, Saint and Martyr.* Northvale, NJ: Jason Aronson, 1990.

Freehof, S. "Devotional Literature in the Vernacular," *Central Conference of American Rabbis* 33 (1923): 375-423.

*Freger Techinno.* Lemberg: Israel David Suss, Publisher, 1897. JNUL: S 62A 948: 296.319.1.

Garfiel, E. *The Service of the Heart.* Reprint, Northvale NJ: Jason Aronson, 1989.

Ginzberg, L. *Legends of the Jews.* Reprint, Philadelphia: Jewish Publication Society of America, 1954.

Goldsmith, E. S. "Yiddishism and Judaism." *Judaism: A Quarterly Journal* (Fall 1989).

Harari, D. "*Le tracce del'Quarto Dialogo smarrito' de Leone Ebreo negli 'Eroici Fuorici di Giordano Bruno,*" (in Hebrew) in *Italia,* 7:1-2 (1988).

Hartman, G. H., and Budick, S., eds. *Midrash and Literature.* New Haven: Yale University Press, 1986.

Hertz, J. H. *The Authorised Daily Prayer Book.* New York: Bloch, 1948.

———. *Sayings of the Fathers (Pirke Aboth).* New York: Behrman House, 1945.

Holtz, B. W., ed. *Back to the Sources.* New York: Summit Books, 1984.

*International Critical Commentary: Micah.* Ed. J. M. P. Smith. Edinburgh: Clark, reprint, 1959.

*International Critical Commentary: Psalms,* vol. 2. Ed. C. A. Briggs and E. G. Briggs. Edinburgh: Clark, reprint, 1951.

*The JPS Torah Commentary: Genesis.* Trans. N. N. Sarna. Philadelphia: Jewish Publication Society of America, 1989.

Klubach, W. "Israel in the Thought of Vladimir Soloviev." *Midstream* 36: 8 (December, 1990).

Mark, Y. "Yiddish Literature." In *The Jews: Their History, Culture and Religion.* Ed. L. Finkelstein. Philadelphia: Jewish Publication Society of America, 1949.

*Ma'aseh Book.* Trans. M. Gaster. Reprint, Philadelphia: Jewish Publication Society of America, 1981.

Mendele Mocher Seforim. "Of Bygone Days," in *A Shtetl and Other Yiddish Novellas*. Ed. Ruth R. Wisse, trans. David G. Roskies. New York: Behrman House, 1973.

*Midrash on Proverbs*. Trans. B. Visotsky. New Haven: Yale University Press, 1982.

*Midrash Rabbah: Deuteronomy*. Trans. J. Rabinowitz. London: Soncino Press, 1951.

*Midrash Rabbah: Esther*. Ed. H. Friedman. Trans. M. Simon. London: Soncino Press, 1956.

*Midrash Rabbah: Genesis* (Hebrew). Ed. A. Mirkin. Tel-Aviv: Yavneh, 1958.

*Midrash Rabbah: Genesis*. Ed. and trans. H. Friedman. Reprint, London: Soncino Press, 1951.

*Midrash Rabbah: Ruth*. Trans. L. Rabinowitz. London: Soncino Press, 1939.

*Midrash Tanhuma*, Vol. 1. Ed. F. Rosen. Warsaw: Piment, 1887.

Millgram, A. E. *Jewish Worship*. Philadelphia: Jewish Publication Society of America, 1971.

*The Mishnah*. Trans. H. Danby. London: Oxford University Press, 1933.

Moldenke, H. N., and Moldenke, A. L., eds. *Plants of the Bible*. New York: Ronald Press, 1952.

*Pentateuch with Targum Onkelos and Rashi*, 2 vols. Trans. M. Rosenbaum and A. M. Silberman. London: Shapiro, Valentine & Co., 1946.

*Pesikta de-Rab Kahana*. Trans. W. G. Braude and I. J. Kapstein. Philadelphia: Jewish Publication Society of America, 1975.

*Princeton Encyclopedia of Poetry and Poetics*. Ed. A. Preminger. Princeton, NJ: Princeton University Press, 1974.

Sachar, A. L. *A History of the Jews*. New York: Knopf, 1955.

Scherman, N., trans. *The Complete ArtScroll Siddur*. Brooklyn, NY: Menorah Publications, 1984.

——, trans. *The Prayer Book: A New Translation with Halachic Instruction and Commentary Anthologized from Classical Rabbinic Sources*. Brooklyn, NY: Menorah Publications, 1981.

Scholem, G. *Major Trends in Jewish Mysticism*. New York: Schocken Books, 1946.

*Seder Techinnos: Teshuvo, Tefillo, and Tsedoko*. Vilna: Widow and Brothers Romm, 1862. JNUL: RO 85A 534. Second card: S51 A 800. 296.319.1.

Seltzer, R. M. *Jewish People, Jewish Thought*. New York: Macmillan, 1980.

*Shas Techinno fun A-gantz Yohr*. Lemberg: David Balaban Publisher, 1904/5. YIVO 6/4658.

*Shas Techinno Rav Peninim*. New York: Hebrew Publishing, 1916.

*Shas Techinno Rav Peninim.* Piotrokowie (Pyotrokov): M. Zederboim Publisher, 1923. JTSAL: BM 675 74 A3.

*Siddur Bays Yisroel.* New York: Hebrew Publishing, 1939 (?).

*Siddur Sim Shalom: A Prayerbook for Shabbat, Festivals, and Weekdays.* Ed. and trans. J. Harlow. New York: Rabbinical Assembly-United Synagogue of America, 1985.

*Sifre.* Trans. R. Hammer. New Haven: Yale University Press, 1986.

Smith, W. *Smith's Bible Dictionary.* New York: Pillar Books, 1976.

*Talmud, Babylonian,* Eng. trans., 35 vols. London: Soncino Press.

Tarnor, N. *The Many Worlds of Gershon Shofman.* West Orange, NJ: Behrman House, 1989.

*Techinno Chadosho al Parnoso.* Vilna, 1855. JNUL: S46 A 1109.

*Techinno Eemoh-hos.* Yosefov: Sh. Wachs Printer, 1845. JNUL: R7 A 966: 296.

*Techinno Eemoh-hos.* Vilna: Widow and Brothers Romm, 1874. YIVO: 9979.

*Techinno Eemoh-hos.* Lemberg: J. D. Suss and S. W. Menhes Publishers, F. Bednarski Press, 1891.

*Techinno Eemoh-hos.* Lemberg, 1921. JNUL: S57 A1921. 296.319.1.

*Techinno Imray Shefer: Six New Techinnos,* by Rabbi Israel of Ivanice, Moravia, Lemberg: 1884. JNUL: S37 A 1375.

*Techinno Kol B'chivo,* by Mistress Henno, Poland-Russia, c. 1840. JNUL: S63 A 3908.

*Techinno Kol Bo.* Brooklyn, NY: Ateres Publishers, 1969.

*Techinno Sheesho Sedorim.* Russia-Poland, c. 1840. JNUL: R70 A 4382.

"Three Gates Techinno: A Seventeenth Century Yiddish Prayer." *Judaism* 40:2 (Summer, 1991): 334-367.

Urbach, E. E. *The Sages: Their Concepts and Beliefs.* Trans. I. I. Abrahams. Cambridge, MA: Harvard University Press, 1987.

Waxman, M. *A History of Jewish Literature.* New York: Bloch, 1943.

Weissler, Ch. "Prayers in Yiddish and the Religious World of Ashkenazic Women." In *Jewish Women in Historical Perspective.* Ed. J. R. Baskin. Detroit: Wayne State University Press, 1991.

———. "The Traditional Piety of Ashkenazic Women." In *Jewish Spirituality,* vol. 2. Ed. A. Green. New York: Crossroad, 1987.

———. "Women in Paradise." *Tikkun* 2:2 April-May, 1987).

Zinberg, I. *A History of Jewish Literature.* Trans. B. Martin. Vols. 1-3, Cleveland: Case Western Reserve University Press, 1972-1973; vols 4-12. New York: KTAV, 1974-1978.

## About the Author

Norman Tarnor, a native Bostonian, is a graduate of Boston University's College of Liberal Arts and the Boston Hebrew College. He studied at the Hebrew University Graduate School in Jerusalem and was ordained and earned his doctorate in modern Hebrew literature at the Jewish Theological Seminary of America in New York. He is professor emeritus of Hebrew at the University of Judaism in Los Angeles and has taught at universities and colleges in southern California. The author of numerous articles in Hebrew and English, he has translated from Hebrew and written short stories and poems in English. He is author of *The Many Worlds of Gershon Shofman*, the first book-length study in English of the distinguished Hebrew writer. In collaboration with his wife, Pearl, he also publishes popular Hebrew texts for children.